Frommer's®

PORTABLE

San Diego

by Stephanie Avnet Yates

Macmillan • USA

ABOUT THE AUTHOR

A native of Los Angeles and an avid traveler, antique hound, and pop-history enthusiast, **Stephanie Avnet Yates** believes that California is best seen from behind the wheel of a little red convertible. Prior to becoming a travel writer, she worked in the music business, but now prefers to hit the road exploring the Golden State. Stephanie authors *Frommer's Los Angeles* and *Frommer's Wonderful Weekends from Los Angeles,* in addition to cowriting *Frommer's California* and *Frommer's California from $60 a Day.* She confesses to a special fondness for San Diego, having attended the University of California at San Diego (UCSD) in La Jolla.

MACMILLAN TRAVEL

Macmillan General Reference USA, Inc.
1633 Broadway
New York, NY 10019

Find us online at **www.frommers.com**

ISBN 0-02-863110-2
ISSN 1047-787X

Production Editor: Scott Barnes
Photo Editor: Richard Fox
Design by Michele Laseau
Staff Cartographers: John Decamillis, Roberta Stockwell
Page Creation by Natalie Evans, Kendra Span and John Bitter

SPECIAL SALES

Bulk purchases (10+ copies) of Frommer's and selected Macmillan travel guides are available to corporations, organizations, mail-order catalogs, institutions, and charities at special discounts, and can be customized to suit individual needs. For more information, write to Special Sales, Macmillan General Reference, 1633 Broadway, New York, NY 10019.

Manufactured in the United States of America
5 4 3 2 1

Contents

List of Maps v

1   The Best of San Diego 1

1 Frommer's Favorite San Diego Experiences 1

2 Best Hotel Bets 3

3 Best Restaurant Bets 4

2   Planning a Trip to San Diego 6

1 Visitor Information 6

2 When to Go 7

   San Diego Calendar of Events 8

3 Tips for Travelers with Special Needs 12

4 Getting There 14

3   Getting to Know San Diego 16

1 Orientation 16

   San Diego Neighborhoods in Brief 19

2 Getting Around 21

   Fast Facts: San Diego 29

4   Accommodations 34

1 Downtown 35

2 Hillcrest/Uptown 45

3 Old Town & Mission Valley 48

4 Mission Bay & the Beaches 51

5 La Jolla 58

6 Coronado 66

7 Near the Airport 71

5   Dining 73

1 Restaurants by Cuisine 74

2 Downtown 77

3 Hillcrest/Uptown   83

4 Old Town   89

5 Mission Bay & the Beaches   92

6 La Jolla   95

7 Coronado   101

8 Only in San Diego   105

6   What to See & Do   108

1 The Three Major Animal Parks   108

2 San Diego's Beaches   113

3 Attractions in Balboa Park   117

4 More Attractions   124

5 Free of Charge & Full of Fun   132

6 Especially for Kids   134

7 Organized Tours   135

8 Outdoor Pursuits   139

9 Spectator Sports   147

7   Shopping   150

1 The Shopping Scene   150

2 Shopping Neighborhoods   151

3 Shopping A to Z   155

8   San Diego After Dark   162

1 The Performing Arts   162

2 The Club & Music Scene   165

3 The Bar & Coffeehouse Scene   167

4 The Gay & Lesbian Nightlife Scene   169

5 Lights, Camera . . . Movies!   170

6 Only in San Diego   170

Index   172

General Index   172

Accommodations   184

Restaurants   185

List of Maps

San Diego Area at a
  Glance   17

Downtown San Diego
  Accommodations
  & Dining   37

Accommodations & Dining
  in Mission Bay & the
  Beaches   53

La Jolla Accommodations
  & Dining   61

Coronado Accommodations
  & Dining   67

San Diego Area
  Attractions   109

San Diego Beaches   115

Balboa Park   119

AN INVITATION TO THE READER

In researching this book, we discovered many wonderful places—hotels, restaurants, shops, and more. We're sure you'll find others. Please tell us about them, so we can share the information with your fellow travelers in upcoming editions. If you were disappointed with a recommendation, we'd love to know that, too. Please write to:

Frommer's Portable San Diego
c/o Macmillan Travel
1633 Broadway
New York, NY 10019

AN ADDITIONAL NOTE

Please be advised that travel information is subject to change at any time—and this is especially true of prices. We therefore suggest that you write or call ahead for confirmation when making your travel plans. The authors, editors, and publisher cannot be held responsible for the experiences of readers while traveling. Your safety is important to us, however, so we encourage you to stay alert and be aware of your surroundings. Keep a close eye on cameras, purses, and wallets, all favorite targets of thieves and pickpockets.

WHAT THE SYMBOLS MEAN
✪ Frommer's Favorites

Our favorite places and experiences—outstanding for quality, value, or both.

The following abbreviations are used for credit cards:

AE	American Express	EU	Eurocard
CB	Carte Blanche	JCB	Japan Credit Bank
DC	Diners Club	MC	MasterCard
DISC	Discover	V	Visa
ER	enRoute		

FIND FROMMER'S ONLINE

Arthur Frommer's Budget Travel Online (www.frommers.com) offers more than 6,000 pages of up-to-the-minute travel information—including the latest bargains and candid, personal articles updated daily by Arthur Frommer himself. No other Web site offers such comprehensive and timely coverage of the world of travel.

1

The Best of San Diego

*I*f you've never been to San Diego or your last visit was more than a few years ago, this relaxed and scenic city will hold some surprises for you. It's grown up. San Diego is no longer just a laid-back navy town—avant-garde architecture, sophisticated dining options, and a booming tourist industry all point to its coming-of-age.

San Diego has always had great weather and beaches, but now it has a lot more to offer than just surf and sun. This change has resulted in part from the influx of high-tech (especially biotech) industry. The new arrivals contribute to the growth of the performing arts and support sophisticated dining, nightlife, and shopping.

The escalating success of San Diego's Convention Center has made a tremendous difference. The center attracts several hundred meetings, conventions, exhibits, and trade shows each year. Its proximity to the Gaslamp Quarter initiated the Quarter's rebirth. Wandering among the chic restaurants and hot nightspots along Fourth and Fifth avenues, it's hard to remember how run-down this area used to be.

Some things about San Diego, however, haven't changed. The residents still love to get out and enjoy their beautiful surroundings. San Diegans are often busy in-line skating, cycling, sailing, and surfing; and it's no coincidence the most activity-oriented parts of town —near Balboa Park, Mission Bay, and La Jolla's shore—are the most desirable in which to live.

Approximately 1.2 million people live in San Diego, making it the seventh-largest city in the United States (after New York, Los Angeles, Chicago, Houston, Philadelphia, and Phoenix). Although the city's population keeps increasing, you'll find that San Diego hasn't lost its small-town ambiance, and it retains a strong connection with its Hispanic heritage and culture.

1 Frommer's Favorite San Diego Experiences

- **Strolling Through the Gaslamp Quarter.** Victorian commercial buildings that fill a 16½-block area will make you think you've stepped back in time. The beautifully restored buildings, in the heart of downtown, house some of the city's most popular shops, restaurants, and nightspots.

- **Renting Bikes, Skates, or Kayaks in Mission Bay.** Landscaped shores, calm waters, paved paths, and friendly neighbors make Mission Bay an aquatic playground like no other. Explore on land or water, depending on your energy level, then grab a bite at funky Mission Cafe.

- **Listening to Free Sunday Organ Recitals in Balboa Park.** Even if you usually don't like organ music, you might enjoy these outdoor concerts and the crowds they draw—San Diegans with their parents, their children, their dogs. The music, enhanced by the organist's commentary, runs the gamut from classical to contemporary. Concerts start at 2pm.

- **Taking the Ferry to Coronado.** The 15-minute ride gets you out onto San Diego Harbor and provides some of the best views of the city. The ferry runs every hour from the Broadway Pier, so you can tour Coronado on foot, by bike, or by trolley and return whenever you please.

- **Driving Over the Bridge to Coronado.** The first time or the fiftieth, there's always an adrenaline rush as you follow this engineering marvel's dramatic curves and catch a glimpse of the panoramic view to either side. Driving west, you can easily pick out the distinctive Hotel Del in the distance long before you reach the "island."

- **Riding on the San Diego Trolley to Mexico.** The trip from downtown costs a mere $2 and takes only 40 minutes, and the clean, quick trolleys are fun in their own right. Once in Tijuana, load up on colorful souvenirs and authentic Mexican food.

- **Listening to Jazz at Croce's.** Ideally located in the center of downtown in a historic Gaslamp Quarter building, Croce's celebrates the life of musician Jim Croce and showcases the city's jazz musicians.

- **Watching the Sun Set Over the Ocean.** It's a free and memorable experience. Excellent sunset-watching spots include the Mission Beach and Pacific Beach boardwalks, as well as the beach in Coronado in front of the Hotel del Coronado. At La Jolla's Windansea Beach, wandering down to the water at dusk, wineglass in hand, is a nightly neighborhood event.

- **Drinking Coffee at a La Jolla Sidewalk Cafe.** San Diego offers a plethora of places to enjoy lattes, espressos, and cappuccinos, but the coffeehouses in La Jolla serve them up with special panache.

- **Walking Along the Water.** The city offers walkers several great places to stroll. One of my favorites, along the waterfront from the Convention Center to the Maritime Museum, affords views of aircraft carriers, tuna seiners, and sailboats.
- **Applauding the Performing Sea Lions at Sea World.** San Diego's famous aquatic theme park earns its reputation as one of California's favorite attractions, and the exuberantly clever performing seals, sea lions, whales, and their caring trainers are always a must-see.
- **Going to the Movies Before the Mast.** Imagine sitting on the deck of the world's oldest merchant ship afloat, watching a film projected on the "screen-sail," or floating on a raft in a huge indoor pool while a movie is shown on the wall. Only in San Diego!
- **Picnicking in a Park.** San Diego's nearly perfect climate invites casual outdoor dining. Favorite spots include Balboa Park (seek out the lawn next to the reflecting pool), Embarcadero Marina Park (near Seaport Village), and Ellen Browning Scripps Park, overlooking the ocean in La Jolla.

2 Best Hotel Bets

- **Best Historic Hotel:** The **Hotel del Coronado,** 1500 Orange Ave. (☎ **800/HOTEL-DEL** or 619/435-8000), positively reeks of history. Opened in 1888, this Victorian masterpiece had some of the earliest electric lights in existence, and legend has it that the course of history was changed when the Prince of Wales met Wallis Simpson here at a ball. Planned restoration will only enhance this glorious landmark, whose early days are well chronicled in displays throughout the hotel.
- **Best for Families:** The **Hilton San Diego Resort,** 1775 E. Mission Bay Dr. (☎ **800/962-6307** or 619/276-4010), offers enough activities to keep family members of all ages happy. In addition to a virtual Disneyland of on-site options, the aquatic playground of Mission Bay lies outside the back door.
- **Best Moderately Priced Hotel:** The **Sommerset Suites Hotel,** 606 Washington St. (☎ **800/962-9665** or 619/692-5200), feels like a home away from home and puts you within easy walking distance of Hillcrest's hot spots.
- **Best Budget Hotel:** In San Diego's Little Italy, **La Pensione Hotel,** 606 W. Date St. (☎ **800/232-4683** or 619/236-8000), feels like a small European hotel and offers tidy lodgings at

bargain prices. There's an abundance of great dining in the surrounding blocks, and you'll be perfectly situated to explore the rest of town by car.

- **Best Unusual Lodgings:** Fulfill the fantasies of your inner yachtsman with the **San Diego Yacht & Breakfast Company,** 1880 Harbor Island Dr., G-Dock (☎ **800/YACHT-DO** or 619/297-9484). It provides powerboats, sailboats, and houseboats docked in a Harbor Island marina. You can sleep on board, lulled by the gentle rocking of the hull, then have breakfast nearby.

- **Best for Bringing Your Pooch:** Check in with your dog at the **U.S. Grant Hotel,** 326 Broadway (☎ **800/237-5029** outside California, **800/334-6957** or 619/232-3121 in California,), and your pet might just be treated better than you. Pampering starts with gourmet dinners, chewy bones, sleeping pillows, and a nightly "turn-down biscuit." Walking service and special dog-walk maps (guide to local hydrants?) are available, and you'll be welcomed in all the hotel's public spaces. The best part? There's no extra charge.

- **Best Place to Stay on the Beach:** At **The La Jolla Beach & Tennis Club,** 2000 Spindrift Dr. (☎ **800/624-CLUB** or 858/454-7126), you can walk right onto the wide beach and frolic in the great waves. Lifeguards and the lack of undertow make this a popular choice for families. Though the rooms are plain, the country-club staff will cater to your every whim.

- **Best for Travelers with Disabilities:** While many of San Diego's hotels make minimal concessions to wheelchair accessibility code, downtown's **Hyatt Regency,** 1 Market Place (☎ **800/233-1234** or 619/232-1234), goes the distance. There are 23 rooms with roll-in showers, and lowered closet racks and peepholes. Ramps are an integral part of all the public spaces, rather than an afterthought. The hotel's Braille labeling is also thorough.

3 Best Restaurant Bets

- **Best View:** Many restaurants overlook the ocean, but only from **Brockton Villa,** 1235 Coast Blvd., La Jolla (☎ **858/454-7393**), can you see the La Jolla Cove. Diners with a window seat will feel as if they're looking out on a gigantic picture postcard.

- **Best Value:** The word *huge* barely begins to describe the portions at **Filippi's Pizza Grotto,** 1747 India St. (☎ **619/232-5095**), where a salad for one is enough for three and an order of lasagne must weigh a pound. There's a kids' menu, and Filippi's has locations all over: in Pacific Beach, Mission Valley, and Escondido, among others.

- **Best Italian Cuisine: Fio's,** 801 Fifth Ave., in the Gaslamp Quarter (☎ **619/234-3467**), offers fine northern Italian food in chic surroundings.

- **Best Seafood:** Not only does **The Fish Market/Top of the Market,** 750 N. Harbor Dr. (☎ **619/232-FISH** or 619/234-4TOP), offer the city's best fish, it also offers a memorable view across San Diego Bay.

- **Best Mexican Cuisine:** Rather than the "combination #1" fare that's common on this side of the border, **Palenque,** 1653 Garnet Ave., Pacific Beach (☎ **619/272-7816**), offers a delightful array of freshly prepared, generations-old recipes from Veracruz, Chapas, Puebla, and Mexico City.

- **Best Desserts:** You'll forget your diet at **Extraordinary Desserts,** 2929 Fifth Ave., Hillcrest (☎ **619/294-7001**)—heck, it's so good you might forget your name! Proprietor Karen Krasne has a *Certificate de Patisserie* from Le Cordon Bleu in Paris, and she makes everything fresh on the premises daily.

- **Best Fast Food:** Fish tacos from **Rubio's,** 4504 E. Mission Bay Dr. (☎ **619/272-2801**) and other locations, are legendary in San Diego. Taste one and you'll know why.

- **Best Picnic Fare:** Pack a humongous sandwich from the **Cheese Shop,** 401 G St. (☎ **619/232-2303**), for a picnic lunch and you won't be hungry for dinner. In La Jolla, head to **Girard Gourmet,** 7837 Girard Ave. (☎ **858/454-3321**), for sandwiches, prepared salads, imported cheeses, and baked goodies.

2

Planning a Trip to San Diego

*T*his chapter contains all the practical information and logistical advice you need to make your travel arrangements a snap, from deciding when to go to getting up-to-the-minute local information.

1 Visitor Information

You can do your homework by contacting the **International Visitor Information Center,** 11 Horton Plaza, San Diego, CA 92101 (☎ **619/236-1212;** fax 619/232-1707; www.sandiego.org; e-mail: sdinfo@sandiego.org). Ask for the *San Diego Official Visitors Guide,* which includes information on accommodations, activities, and attractions, and has excellent maps. Also request the *Super Savings Coupon Book,* which is full of discount coupons. The center is open Monday through Saturday from 8:30am to 5pm year-round and Sunday from 11am to 5pm June through August.

Additional visitor information is available from the **Balboa Park Visitors Center,** 1549 El Prado, San Diego, CA 92101 (☎ **619/239-0512**).

The **Coronado Visitors Bureau,** 1047 B Ave., Coronado, CA 92118-3418 (☎ **800/622-8300** or 619/437-8788; fax 619/437-6006; www.coronado.ca.us) is a must for anyone visiting the "island." The bureau staff has maps of the area, information-packed brochures and newsletters, and enthusiasm that just won't quit.

Another good source of information is the San Diego North County Convention and Visitors Bureau. Call ☎ **800/848-3336** to request its *Visitors Guide.* You can also find lots of information on San Diego at the following Web sites:

- **gocalif.ca.gov/guidebook/SD** has helpful information on San Diego County, including maps that can be downloaded.
- **www.infosandiego.com** is the Web site for the San Diego Visitor Center.

- **www.sandiego.org** is maintained by the San Diego Convention & Visitors Bureau and provides, among other things, up-to-date weather data.
- **www.sandiego-online.com,** the *San Diego* magazine Web site, features abbreviated stories from the current month's issue, plus dining and events listings.
- **www.sannet.gov** is San Diego's home page, maintained by the city.
- **www.sdreader.com,** the site of the free weekly *Reader,* is a great source for club and show listings, plus edgy topical journalism.
- **travel.to/san.diego** is "The Local Guy's Guide to San Diego." It gives lots of information on things to do and local history and facts, plus some good links to other regional sites.
- **www.gaslamp.com** is the online home of the Gaslamp Quarter Historical Foundation.
- **www.iaco.com/features/lajolla/homepage.htm** features information about what's happening in La Jolla.

2 When to Go

San Diego is blessed with a mild climate, low humidity, good air quality, and welcoming blue skies. In fact, *Pleasant Weather Rankings,* published by Consumer Travel, ranked San Diego's weather number two in the world (behind Las Palmas, in the Canary Islands). Oceanside, the northernmost town in San Diego County, was number five.

Although the temperature can change 20°F to 30°F between day and evening, it doesn't usually reach a point of extreme heat. San Diego receives very little precipitation (9½ inches of rainfall in an average year); what rain does fall comes primarily between late December and mid-April.

San Diego is most crowded between Memorial Day and Labor Day. The kids are out of school and *everyone* wants to be by the seashore; so if you visit in summer, you can expect fully booked hotels, crowded family attractions, and full parking lots at the beach. San Diego's popularity as a convention destination and its year-round pleasant weather keep the tourism business steady the rest of the year, too. The only "slow" season is from Thanksgiving through mid-February. Hotels are less full, and the beaches are peaceful and uncrowded; the big family attractions are still busy, though, with residents taking advantage of holiday breaks.

Average Monthly Temperature & Rainfall (inches)

	Jan	Feb	Mar	Apr	May	June	July	Aug	Sept	Oct	Nov	Dec
High(°F)	65	66	66	68	70	71	75	77	76	74	70	66
(°C)	18	19	19	20	21	21	24	25	25	23	21	19
Low(°F)	46	47	50	54	57	60	64	66	63	58	52	47
(°C)	7	9	10	12	14	15	17	19	17	15	10	8
Rainfall	1.88	1.48	1.55	0.81	0.15	0.05	0.01	0.07	0.13	0.34	1.25	1.73

SAN DIEGO CALENDAR OF EVENTS

January

✪ **Whale Watching.** Mid-December to mid-March is the eagerly anticipated whale-watching season. Scores of graceful yet gargantuan California gray whales make their annual migration to warm breeding lagoons in Baja, then return with their calves to springtime feeding grounds in Alaska. For information on vantage points and excursions that bring you closer to the largest mammals, see "Whale Watching," in chapter 6.

February

✪ **Buick Invitational,** Torrey Pines Golf Course, La Jolla. This PGA Tour men's tournament, an annual event since 1952, draws more than 100,000 spectators each year. It features 150 of the finest professionals in the world. For information, call ☎ **800/888-BUICK** or 619/281-4653, fax 619/281-7947, or write Buick Invitational, 3333 Camino Del Rio S., Suite 100, San Diego, CA 92108. Early to mid-February.

March

• **Ocean Beach Kite Festival.** The late-winter skies over the Ocean Beach Recreational Center get a brilliant shot of color. Not only can you learn to make and decorate a kite of your own, but there's an all-ages flying contest and lots of food and entertainment, culminating in a parade down to the beach. For more information, call ☎ **619/224-0189.** First weekend of March.

• **Flower Fields in Bloom at Carlsbad Ranch.** One of the most spectacular sights in North County is the yearly blossoming of a gigantic sea of bright ranunculus during March and April, creating a striped blanket that's visible from the freeway. Visitors are welcome to view and tour the fields, which are off Interstate 5 at the Palomar Airport Road exit. For more information, call ☎ **760/431-0352.**

April

- **Del Mar National Horse Show,** Del Mar Fairgrounds. The first event in the Del Mar racing season takes place from late April into early May at famous Del Mar Fairgrounds. The field at this show includes Olympic-caliber and national championship horse-and-rider teams; there are also Western fashion boutiques and artist displays and demonstrations. For more information, call ☎ 858/792-4288 or 755-1161.

- **Temecula Valley Balloon & Wine Festival.** Colorful hot-air balloons dominate the sky over Lake Skinner during the 3-day festival, which also features wine tastings, good food, jazz music, and other entertainment. General admission is $15 ($12 in advance), and reservations for balloon rides ($100 and up) should be made in advance. The lake is about 10 miles northeast of Temecula and 70 miles north of San Diego. To find out about this year's festival or purchase advance tickets, call the event organizers (☎ 909/676-6713). Late April.

May

- **Cinco de Mayo Celebration,** Old Town. Uniformed troops march and guns blast to mark the 1862 triumph of Mexican soldiers over the French. Festivities include a battle re-enactment with costumed actors, mariachi music, and margaritas galore. Free admission. For further details, call ☎ 619/296-3161. Weekend closest to May 5.

June

- **Del Mar Fair.** This is the *other* event at the Del Mar Fairgrounds. All of San Diego County participates in this annual fair. Livestock competitions, thrill-a-minute rides, food and craft booths, carnival games, and home arts exhibits dominate the event, and concerts by top-name performers are free with admission. The fair usually lasts three weeks, from mid-June to early July. For details, call ☎ 858/793-5555.

- **Twilight in the Park Concerts,** Spreckels Organ Pavilion, Balboa Park. These free concerts have been held since 1979 and run from late June through late August. For information, call ☎ 619/226-0819.

July

- ✪ **World Championship Over-the-Line Tournament,** Mission Bay. This tournament is a San Diego original; the beach softball event dates from 1953 and is renowned for boisterous, anything-goes behavior—it's a heap of fun for the open-minded, but might be a bit much for small kids. It takes place on two consecutive weekends in July, on Fiesta Island in Mission Bay, and the public is invited. Admission is free. For more details, call ☎ **619/688-0817.**

- **Annual San Diego Lesbian and Gay Pride Parade, Rally, and Festival.** This parade is one of San Diego's biggest draws. It begins at noon on Saturday, followed by a massive festival into the night. The festival continues Sunday afternoon and evening. The parade route is along University Avenue from Normal Street to Sixth Avenue. For more information, call ☎ **619/297-7683.** Third or fourth weekend of the month.

- **Thoroughbred Racing Season.** The "turf meets the surf" in Del Mar from July to September during the Thoroughbred racing season at the Del Mar Race Track. Post time is 2pm (4pm on the first four Fridays only), and the track is dark on Tuesday. Hollywood stars continue to flock here, in the grand tradition begun by Bing Crosby, Betty Grable, and Jimmy Durante. For this year's schedule of events, call ☎ **858/792-4242** or 755-1141.

August

- **U.S. Open Sandcastle Competition,** Imperial Beach Pier. I consider this the quintessential beach event. There's a parade and children's sandcastle contest on Saturday, followed by the main competition Sunday. Past years have seen creations of astounding complexity, and (weather permitting) the castles remain on view for a while after the event. For further details, call ☎ **619/424-6663.**

- **Sunset Cinema Film Festival.** If you're visiting in August, try to catch a flick during the weeklong film festival, one of the city's more unusual events. The audience sits on the beach (B.Y.O. chair or blanket) and views movies projected onto offshore floating barges. Classic and current films are featured, as well as cartoons. The free event takes place at various locations; for a schedule, call ☎ **619/454-7373.**

September

- **Street Scene, Gaslamp Quarter.** This 3-day extravaganza fills the historic streets of downtown's Gaslamp Quarter with music, food, dance, and international character. Twelve separate stages are erected to showcase jazz, blues, reggae, rock, and soul music all weekend. Saturday is usually all-ages day—attendees must be 21 or over the other two days. For ticket and show information, call ☎ 619/557-8487. Weekend after Labor Day.

✪ **La Jolla Rough-Water Swim,** La Jolla Cove. The country's largest rough-water swimming competition began in 1916 and features masters men's and women's swims, a junior swim, and an amateur swim. All are 1-mile events except the junior swim and gatorman 3-mile championship. Spectators don't need tickets. To register or receive more information, call ☎ 858/456-2100. For an entry form, send a self-addressed stamped envelope to Entries Chairman, La Jolla Rough-Water Swim, P.O. Box 46, La Jolla, CA 92038. Sunday after Labor Day.

October

- **Concours d'Elegance,** Torrey Pines Golf Course, La Jolla. Classic car buffs won't want to pass this up. And we're not talking hot rods and jalopies here; the show features antique cars of the highest caliber, such as classic Jaguars, Rolls Royces, and Aston Martins. One year featured a salute to Ferrari, another to Alfa Romeo. For more information, call ☎ 619/283-4221. Mid-October.

- **Underwater Pumpkin Carving Contest,** La Jolla. The event might never make it to the Olympics, but plenty of divers have turned out each year since 1981. The rules are relaxed, the panel of judges is serendipitous (one year it was the staff of a local dive shop, the next year five kids off the beach), and it's always a fun party. Spectators can hang out and wait for triumphant artists to break the surface with their creations. For details, call ☎ 858/565-6054. Weekend before Halloween.

November

- **Carlsbad Village Faire.** Billed as the largest 1-day street fair in the United States, this festival features more than 800 vendors on 24 city blocks. Items for sale include ceramics, jewelry, clothing, glassware, and plants. Mexican, Italian, Japanese, Korean, Indonesian, and other edible fare is sold at booths along the way. Ground zero is the intersection of Grand Avenue and Jefferson Street. Call ☎ 760/931-8400 for dates.

December

- **Dr. Seuss Christmas Readings.** The late Theodor Geisel's adopted home honors the author by celebrating the holidays with his best-loved characters. Beginning the weekend after Thanksgiving, the lobby of **Loews Coronado Bay Resort** is transformed into "Who-ville," where the Cat in the Hat assembles an eager young (and not-so-young) audience for regular readings of *How the Grinch Stole Christmas*. Punch and cookies are served, and carolers perform following each reading. The free event runs through Christmas Eve, with readings Saturday afternoons and Sunday through Tuesday evenings. For more information, call ☎ **619/ 424-4000.**

- **Christmas on the Prado,** Balboa Park. Lovely Balboa Park is decked out in holiday splendor for a magical weekend of evening events. A candlelight procession, traditional caroling, and baroque music ensembles are just part of the entertainment. There are craft displays, ethnic food, traditional hot cider, and a grand Christmas tree and nativity scene in Spreckels Pavilion. The event is free and lasts from 5 to 9pm both days; the park's museums are free during those hours. For more information, call ☎ **619/239-0512.** Early December.

3 Tips for Travelers with Special Needs

FOR TRAVELERS WITH DISABILITIES

The Accessible San Diego Hot Line (☎ **619/279-0704;** fax 619/ 279-5118; www.accessandiego.com) helps travelers with disabilities find accessible hotels, tours, attractions, and transportation. If you call long distance and get the answering machine, leave a message and the staff will call you back collect. Ask for the annual *Access in San Diego* pamphlet, a city-wide guide with specifics on which establishments are accessible for those with visual, mobility, or hearing disabilities.

In the **San Diego Convention & Visitors Bureau's Dining and Accommodations** guide, a wheelchair symbol designates places that are accessible to persons with disabilities.

On buses and trolleys, riders with disabilities pay a fixed fare of 75¢. Many MTS buses and all trolleys are equipped with wheelchair lifts; priority seating is available on buses and trolleys. Stops served by accessible buses are marked with a wheelchair symbol. People with visual impairments benefit from the white reflecting ring that circles the bottom of the trolley door to increase its visibility.

FOR GAY & LESBIAN TRAVELERS

Gay and lesbian visitors might already know about Hillcrest, the stylish part of town near Balboa Park that's the city's most prominent gay community. Many gay-owned restaurants, boutiques, and nightspots cater to a gay and straight clientele, and the scene is lively and colorful most nights of the week.

The **Lesbian and Gay Men's Community Center** is at 3916 Normal St. (☎ **619/692-2077**). It's open Monday through Friday from 9am to 10pm and Saturday from 9am to 7pm. Community outreach and counseling are offered.

The **Annual San Diego Lesbian and Gay Pride Parade, Rally, and Festival** is held the third or fourth weekend in July. The parade begins at noon on Saturday at University Avenue and Normal Street, and proceeds west on University to Sixth Avenue. A festival follows on Saturday from 2 to 10pm and Sunday from noon to 10pm. For more information, call ☎ **619/297-7683.**

The free *San Diego Gay and Lesbian Times,* published every Thursday, is often available at Obelisk bookstore, 1029 University Ave., Hillcrest (☎ **619/297-4171**).

FOR SENIORS

Nearly every attraction in San Diego offers a senior discount; age requirements vary, and prices are discussed in chapter 6. Public transportation and movie theaters also have reduced rates. Don't be shy about asking for discounts, but always carry identification, such as a driver's license, that shows your date of birth. Also, mention the fact that you're a senior citizen when you first make your travel reservations. For example, both **Amtrak** (☎ **800/USA-RAIL;** www.amtrak.com) and **Greyhound** (☎ **800/752-4841;** www. greyhound.com) offer discounts to persons over 62.

A delightful way to meet older San Diegans, many of whom are retired, is to join a free Saturday-morning stroll with **Downtown Sam,** a footloose retiree and guide with **Walkabout International** (see "Organized Tours," in chapter 6).

San Diego's special senior citizens referral and information line is ☎ **619/560-2500.**

FOR FAMILIES

Several books offer tips on traveling with kids. **Family Travel** (Lanier Publishing International) and **How to Take Great Trips with Your Kids** (The Harvard Common Press) are full of good general advice.

Family Travel Times is published six times a year by Travel with Your Children, or TWYCH (☎ **888/822-4388** or 212/477-5524), and includes a weekly call-in service for subscribers. Subscriptions are $40 a year. A free publication list and a sample issue are available by calling or sending a request to the above address.

Families Welcome!, 92 N. Main, Ashland, OR 97520 (☎ **800/ 326-0724** or 541/482-6121), is a travel company specializing in worry-free vacations for families.

The "Especially for Kids" section in chapter 6 offers tips about which San Diego sights and attractions have the most appeal for the little ones.

4   Getting There

BY PLANE

Flights arrive at San Diego International Airport/Lindbergh Field (named after aviation hero Charles Lindbergh), served by many national and regional air carriers as well as Aeromexico and British Airways.

Terminal 1 airlines include: **Aeromexico** (☎ 800/237-6639), **Alaska Airlines** (☎ 800/426-0333; www.alaskaair.com), **Southwest Airlines** (☎ 800/435-9792; www.iflyswa.com), **Trans World Airlines** (☎ 800/221-2000; www.twa.com), **United Airlines** (☎ 800/241-6522; www.ual.com), and **US Airways** (☎ 800/ 428-4322; www.usair.com).

Terminal 2 airlines include: **American Airlines** (☎ 800/433-7300; www.aa.com), **British Airways** (☎ 800/247-9297; www.britishairways.com), **Canadian Airlines** (☎ 800/426-7000; www.

Packing Tips

Bring a **sweater or light jacket,** even in summer. Because the ocean is close by, cold, damp breezes are common after the sun sets. But leave behind your heavy coats and cold-weather gear, no matter when you're coming. Pack **casual clothes.** Shorts, jeans, and T-shirts are common at all tourist attractions and many restaurants. Men who plan to try one of San Diego's nicer restaurants may want to bring a sports jacket, but this is really an informal town. Bring **good, comfortable walking shoes;** you can cover a lot of ground in this pleasant, outdoorsy city.

Don't forget **sunglasses,** an essential accessory (especially if you'll be on or near the water, which reflects and amplifies the sun's rays). Regardless of the time of year, it's wise to pack a **bathing suit.** Most hotels have heated pools and whirlpools, and you might be surprised by a day warm enough for the beach.

cdnair.com), **Midwest Express** (☎ 800/452-2022), **Northwest Airlines** (☎ 800/225-2525; www.nwa.com), and **Reno Air** (☎ 800/RENO-AIR; www.renoair.com).

The airlines in the Terminal 2 expansion are **America West** (☎ 800/235-9292; www.americawest.com), **Continental Airlines** (☎ 800/525-0280; www.flycontinental.com), and **Delta Airlines** (☎ 800/221-1212; www.delta-air.com).

You may be able to find a good deal on airfare by calling a consolidator. Try calling 800/FLYCHEAP (www.1800flycheap. com), **Cheap Seats** (☎ 800/451-7200; www.cheapseatstravel. com), or **Cheap Tickets** (☎ 800/377-1000; www.cheaptickets. com). Another strategy is to surf the Web for bargains. **Microsoft Expedia** (www.expedia.com), **Travelocity** (www.travelocity.com), the **Internet Travel Network** (www.itn.com), and **Yahoo** (www.yahoo.com) are all good places to start.

BY CAR

Visitors driving to San Diego from Los Angeles and points north do so via coastal route I-5. From points northeast, take I-15 (link up with I-8 West and Highway 163 South or Highway 94 West); from the east, use I-8 (link up with Highway 163 South). Entering the downtown area, Highway 163 turns into 10th Avenue, and Highway 94 turns into F Street. Try to avoid arriving during weekday rush hours, between 7 and 9am and 3 and 6pm. If you are heading to Coronado, take the Coronado Bridge from I-5. If you have a passenger, stay in the far-right lanes to avoid paying the toll. Maximum speed in the San Diego area is 65 miles (105km) per hour, and many areas are limited to 55.

San Diego is 130 miles and 2 hours from **Los Angeles;** 149 miles from **Palm Springs,** a 2¹/₂-hour trip; and 532 miles, or 8 hours, from **San Francisco.**

3

Getting to Know San Diego

*S*an Diego is laid out in an easy-to-decipher manner, so learning the lay of the land is neither confusing nor daunting. Most San Diegans welcome visitors and are eager to answer questions and provide assistance; you'll feel like a local before you know it.

1 Orientation

ARRIVING
BY PLANE

San Diego International Airport/Lindbergh Field lies just north of downtown. The landing approach is right over the central business district, creating the familiar sight of planes threading through high-rise buildings on their way to the airport. A curfew (11:30pm to 6:30am) cuts down on noise in the surrounding residential areas.

General **information desks** with visitor materials, maps, and other services are in **Terminal 1,** near the United Airlines ticket counter, and in **Terminal 2** in the baggage-claim area and near the American Airlines ticket counter. **Hotel reservation phones** and **car-rental courtesy phones** are in the baggage-claim areas of Terminals 1 and 2.

Getting into Town from the Airport

BY BUS   The new **Metropolitan Transit System (MTS) Route 992** provides service between the airport (there are stops at each terminal) and downtown San Diego. Buses run every 10 minutes on weekdays, every 15 minutes on weekends. The one-way fare is $2. Downtown, Route 992 stops on Broadway. The trip from the airport to downtown should take about 15 minutes.

BY TAXI   Taxis line up outside both terminals and charge $7 to $10 for the trip to a downtown location, usually a 5- to 10-minute ride.

BY SHUTTLE   Several airport shuttles run regularly from the airport to downtown hotels; you'll see designated areas outside each terminal. The fare is $5 to $9 per person. Companies that serve the

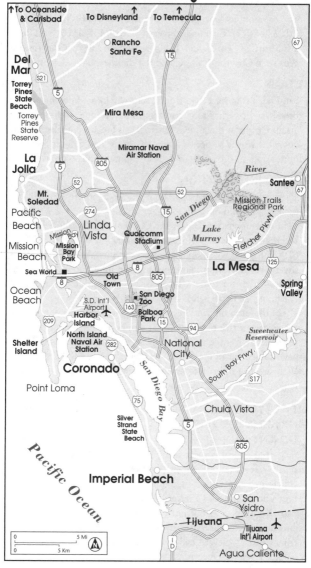

whole county include **Cloud 9 Shuttle** (☎ **800/9-SHUTTLE** or 619/278-8877), **Coronado Livery** (☎ **619/435-6310**), and **Peerless Shuttle** (☎ **619/554-1700**). Coronado Livery is the least expensive to Coronado, and Cloud 9 is the cheapest to downtown.

BY TRAIN

San Diego's **Santa Fe Station** is centrally located downtown, on Broadway between Front Street and First Avenue, within walking distance of most downtown hotels. Taxis line up outside the main door, the trolley station is across the street, and a dozen local bus routes stop on Broadway or Pacific Highway, one block away.

VISITOR INFORMATION

There are staffed information booths at both airport terminals, the train station, and the cruise-ship terminal.

In downtown San Diego, the Convention & Visitors Bureau's **International Visitor Information Center** (☎ **619/236-1212;** fax 619/230-7084; www.sandiego.org) is on First Avenue at F Street, street level at Horton Plaza. For detailed information on this and other area visitor centers, see "Visitor Information" in chapter 2, "Planning a Trip to San Diego".

For the latest on San Diego nightlife and entertainment, pick up the *Reader,* a free newspaper that comes out on Thursday and is available all over the city. Also check "Night and Day," the Thursday supplement in the *San Diego Union-Tribune.* For addresses of Web sites with plenty of up-to-the-minute information, see chapter 2.

CITY LAYOUT
MAIN ARTERIES & STREETS

DOWNTOWN   The primary thoroughfares are Broadway (a major bus artery), Fourth and Fifth avenues (which run south and north, respectively), C Street (the trolley line), and Harbor Drive, which hugs the waterfront and passes the Maritime Museum, Seaport Village, and the Convention Center. Balboa Park, home of the San Diego Zoo, lies northeast of downtown San Diego. The park and zoo are easily reached by way of Twelfth Avenue, which becomes Park Boulevard and leads to the parking lots; an alternative is Fifth Avenue, which runs along the western edge of the park up toward Hillcrest.

HILLCREST   In this area near Balboa Park, the main streets are University Avenue and Washington Street, both two-way running east and west, and Fourth and Fifth avenues. Park Boulevard bisects Balboa Park itself, south to north, and continues into the community of University Heights.

PACIFIC BEACH   Mission Boulevard is the main drag, and perpendicular to it are Grand and Garnet Avenues and Pacific Beach Drive. East and West Mission Bay Drives and Ingraham Street enable you to zip around the periphery of the bay or bisect it.

LA JOLLA   The main avenues are Prospect and Girard, which are perpendicular to each other.

CORONADO   The main streets are Orange Avenue, where most of the hotels and restaurants are clustered, and Ocean Drive, which follows Coronado Beach.

SAN DIEGO NEIGHBORHOODS IN BRIEF

In this guide, San Diego is divided into six areas, each with its own accommodations and dining listings (see chapters 4 and 5).

Downtown   The business, shopping, dining, and entertainment heart of the city, the downtown area encompasses Horton Plaza, the Gaslamp Quarter, the Embarcadero (waterfront), and the Convention Center. The Maritime Museum, the downtown branch of the Museum of Contemporary Art, and the Children's Museum are also here. Visitors with business in the city center would be wise to stay downtown. This is also the best area for those attending meetings at the Convention Center. The **Gaslamp Quarter** is the center of a massive redevelopment kicked off in the mid-1980s with the opening of Horton Plaza; now, the once-seedy area is filled with trendy boutiques, restaurants, and nightspots. **Little Italy,** a small neighborhood along India Street between Cedar and Fir at the northern edge of downtown, is the best place to find gelato, espresso, pizza, and pasta.

Hillcrest/Uptown   At the turn of the century, the neighborhoods north of downtown were home to San Diego's white-collar elite (hence such sobriquets as Bankers Hill and Pill Hill, named for the area's many doctors). Hillcrest was the city's first self-contained suburb in the 1920s. Despite the cachet of being next to Balboa Park (home to the San Diego Zoo and numerous museums, including the Museum of Art, the Museum of Photographic Arts, and the Reuben H. Fleet Science Center) the area fell into neglect in the '60s and '70s. However, as the turn of the century looms once more, legions of preservation-minded residents—including an active and fashionable gay community—have restored Hillcrest's charms. I'd say Hillcrest is the local equivalent of L.A.'s West Hollywood or New York's SoHo. Centrally located and packed with the latest in stylish restaurants and avant-garde boutiques, Hillcrest also offers less expensive and more personalized accommodations than any other area in the city. Other uptown neighborhoods of interest are **North Park** and **Kensington.**

Old Town & Mission Valley   This area encompasses the Old Town State Historic Park, Presidio Park, Heritage Park, and numerous museums that recall the turn of the century and the city's beginnings. There's shopping and dining here, too—all aimed at tourists. Not far from Old Town lies the vast suburban sprawl of Mission Valley, home to San Diego's gigantic shopping centers. Between them is Hotel Circle, adjacent to I-8, where a string of moderately priced and budget hotels offer an alternative to the ritzier neighborhoods.

Mission Bay & the Beaches   Here's where they took the picture on the postcard you'll send home. Mission Bay is a watery playground perfect for waterskiing, sailing, and windsurfing. The adjacent communities of Ocean Beach, Mission Beach, and Pacific Beach are known for their wide stretches of sand, active nightlife, and casual dining. Many San Diego singles live here, and once you've visited you'll understand why. The boardwalk, which runs from South Mission Beach through North Mission Beach to Pacific Beach, is a popular place for in-line skating, bike riding, and watching sunsets. This is the place to stay if you are traveling with beach-loving children or want to walk barefoot on the beach.

La Jolla   With an atmosphere that's a cross between Rodeo Drive and a Mediterranean village, this seaside community is home to an inordinate number of wealthy folks who could live anywhere. They choose La Jolla, surrounded by the beach, the University of California, San Diego, outstanding restaurants, pricey and traditional shops, and some of the world's best medical facilities. The wise tourist beds down here, taking advantage of the community's attributes without having to buy its high-priced real estate. The name is a compromise between Spanish and American Indian, as is the pronunciation (la-*hoy*-ya); it has come to mean "the jewel."

Coronado   You may be tempted to think of Coronado as an island. It does have an isolated, resort ambiance and is accessible only by ferry or bridge, but the city of Coronado is actually on a bulbous peninsula connected to the mainland by a narrow sand spit, the Silver Strand. The northern portion of the peninsula is home to the massive U.S. Naval Air Station. The southern sector has a rich history as an elite playground and a reputation as a charming community of suburbs. Quaint shops line the main street, Orange Avenue, and you'll find plenty of ritzy hotels and resorts, including the landmark **Hotel del Coronado.** Coronado has a lovely duned beach (one of the area's most popular), fine restaurants, and a downtown area that's reminiscent of a small Midwest town; it's also home to more retired admirals than any other community in the country.

2 Getting Around

San Diego has many walkable neighborhoods, from the historic downtown area, to Hillcrest and nearby Balboa Park, to the Embarcadero, to Mission Bay Park. You get there by car, bus, or trolley, and your feet do the rest. Always remember to cross the street at corners or in crosswalks; there's a $54 fine for jaywalking.

BY CAR

San Diegans complain of increasing traffic, but the city is still easy to navigate by car. Most downtown streets run one way, which may frustrate you until you learn your way around. Finding a parking space can be tricky, but some reasonably priced lots are fairly centrally located.

RENTALS

If you don't drive to San Diego with your own car, you'll want to rent one. While it's possible to get around by public transportation, having your own wheels is a big advantage.

All the major firms have offices at the airport and in the larger hotels, including **Avis** (☎ 800/331-1212; www.avis.com); **Budget** (☎ 800/527-0700; www.budgetrentacar.com); **Dollar** (☎ 800/800-4000; www.dollarcar.com); **Hertz** (☎ 800/654-3131; www.hertz.com); and **National Car Rental** (☎ 800/CAR-RENT; www.nationalcar.com).

Saving Money on a Rental Car

Car rental rates vary even more than airline fares. Prices depend on the size of the car, where and when you pick it up and drop it off, the length of the rental period, where and how far you drive it, whether you buy insurance, and a host of other factors. A few key questions could save you hundreds of dollars.

- Are weekend rates lower than weekday rates? Ask if the rate is the same for pickup Friday morning, for instance, as it is for Thursday night. Reservations agents won't volunteer this information, so don't be shy about asking lots of questions.
- Does the agency assess a drop-off charge if you don't return the car to the same location where you picked it up?
- Are special promotional rates available? If you see an advertised price in your local newspaper, be sure to ask for that specific rate; otherwise you may be charged the standard cost. Terms change constantly.
- Are discounts available for members of AARP, AAA, frequent-flyer programs, or trade unions? If you belong to any of these organizations, you may be entitled to discounts of up to 30%.
- How much tax will be added to the rental bill? Local tax? State use tax?
- How much does the rental company charge to refill your gas tank if you return with the tank less than full? Though most rental companies claim these prices are "competitive," fuel is almost always cheaper in town. Try to allow enough time to refuel the car yourself before returning it.

Some companies offer "refueling packages," in which you pay for an entire tank of gas up front. The cost is usually fairly competitive with local prices, but you don't get credit for any gas remaining in the tank. If a stop at a gas station on the way to the airport will make you miss your plane, then by all means take advantage of the fuel-purchase option. Otherwise, skip it.

Kemwel Holiday Auto (KHA) (☎ **800/678-0678**), a rental-car wholesaler, will search for the lowest price offered by the major agencies.

Demystifying Renter's Insurance

Before you drive off in a rental car, be sure you're insured. Hasty assumptions about your personal auto insurance or a rental agency's additional coverage could end up costing you tens of thousands of dollars, even if you are involved in an accident that was clearly the fault of another driver.

If you already hold a **private auto insurance** policy, you are most likely covered in the United States for loss of or damage to a rental car, and liability in case of injury to any other party involved in an accident. Be sure to find out whether you are covered in the area you are visiting, whether your policy extends to everyone who will be driving the car, how much liability is covered in case an outside party is injured in an accident, and whether the type of vehicle you are renting is included under your contract. (Rental trucks, sport utility vehicles, and luxury vehicles or sports cars may not be covered.)

Most **major credit cards** provide some degree of coverage as well, provided they're used to pay for the rental. Terms vary widely, however, so be sure to call your credit card company directly before you rent.

If you are **uninsured,** your credit card provides primary coverage as long as you decline the rental agency's insurance. This means that the credit card will cover damage or theft of a rental car for the full cost of the vehicle. (In a few states, however, theft is not covered; ask specifically about state law where you will be renting and driving.) If you already have insurance, your credit card will provide secondary coverage, which basically covers your deductible.

Note: Though they may cover damage to your rental car, ***credit cards will not cover liability,*** or the cost of injury to an outside party, damage to an outside party's vehicle, or both. If you do not hold an insurance policy, you may seriously want to consider purchasing additional liability insurance from your rental company. Be sure to check the terms, however. Some rental agencies cover liability only if the renter is not at fault; even then, the rental company's obligation varies from state to state.

The basic insurance coverage offered by most car rental companies, known as the **Loss/Damage Waiver (LDW)** or **Collision Damage Waiver (CDW),** can cost as much as $20 a day. It usually covers the full value of the vehicle with no deductible if an outside party causes an accident or other damage to the rental car. In all states but California, you will probably be covered in case of theft as well. Liability coverage varies according to the company policy and state law, but the minimum is usually at least $15,000. If you are at fault in an accident, you will be covered for the full replacement value of the car, but not for liability. Some states allow you to buy additional liability coverage for such cases. Most rental companies will require a police report to process any claims you file, but your private insurer will not be notified of the accident.

Package Deals

Many packages are available that include airfare, accommodations, and a rental car with unlimited mileage. Compare these prices with the cost of booking airline tickets and renting a car separately to see if these offers are good deals.

PARKING

The **garage at Horton Plaza,** at G Street and Fourth Avenue, is free to shoppers for the first 3 hours. (The parking ticket must be validated by a merchant, or you must show your cinema or theater stub from Horton Plaza.) After the first 3 hours, it's $1 per half hour. A quick way to zip into Horton Plaza and avoid the ever-upward spiral is to enter the back way, off Third Avenue. The fenced-in lot adjacent to the Embarcadero, **Allright Parking,** 900 Broadway, at Harbor Drive (☎ **619/298-6944**), charges $3 to park between 5:30am and midnight. More convenient to downtown shopping and the Children's Museum is the open-air **lot on Market Street** between Front and First streets, where you can park all day on weekdays for $3, and weekends for $2.

Parking meters are plentiful in most areas: downtown and the Gaslamp Quarter, Hillcrest, and the beach communities. Posted signs indicate operating hours—generally 8am to 6pm, even on weekends. Be prepared with several dollars in quarters—most meters take no other coin, and 25¢ rarely buys more than 15 minutes, even on a 2-hour meter. Most unmetered areas have signs restricting street parking to 1 or 2 hours; count on vigilant chalking and ticketing during the regulated hours. Three-hour meters line Harbor Drive opposite the ticket offices for harbor tours; even on weekends, you have to feed them.

DRIVING RULES

California has a seatbelt law for both drivers and passengers, so buckle up before you venture out. You may turn right at a red light after stopping unless a sign says otherwise. Likewise, you can turn left on a red light from a one-way street onto another one-way street after coming to a full stop. Keep in mind when driving in San Diego that pedestrians have the right of way at all times, so stop for pedestrians who have stepped off the curb.

BY PUBLIC TRANSPORTATION
BY BUS

San Diego has an adequate bus system that will get you to where you're going—eventually. Most drivers are friendly and helpful. The system encompasses more than 100 routes in the greater San Diego area. The **Transit Store,** 102 Broadway, at First Avenue (☎ **619/233-3004,** TTY/TDD 619/234-5005), dispenses passes, tokens, timetables, maps, brochures, and lost-and-found information. It issues ID cards for seniors 60 and older, and for travelers with disabilities, all of whom pay 75¢ per ride. Request a copy of the useful brochure *Your Open Door to San Diego,* which details the city's most popular tourist attractions and the buses that will take you to them. You may also call the number above and say where you are and where you want to go; the Transit Store staff will tell you the nearest bus stop and what time the next couple of buses will pass by. The office is open Monday through Friday from 8:30am to 5:30pm, Saturday and Sunday noon to 4pm. If you know your route and just need schedule information, call ☎ **619/685-4900** from any touch-tone phone. You can call between 5:30am and 8:30pm daily except Thanksgiving and Christmas. The line is often busy; the best times to call are from noon to 3pm and on weekends.

Bus stops are marked by rectangular blue signs every other block or so on local routes, farther apart on express routes. More than 20 bus routes pass through the downtown area. Most **bus fares** range from $1.75 to $2.25, depending on distance and type of service (local or express). Buses accept dollar bills, but the driver can't give change.

You can request a free transfer as long as you continue on a bus or trolley with an equal or lower fare (if it's higher, you pay the difference). Transfers must be used within 2 hours, and you can return to where you started.

Some of the most popular tourist attractions served by bus and rail routes are Balboa Park (Routes 1, 3, 7, 7A, 7B, and 25); the San Diego Zoo (Routes 7, 7A, and 7B); the Children's Museum, Convention Center, and Gaslamp Quarter (San Diego Trolley Orange Line); Coronado (Route 901); Horton Plaza (most downtown bus routes and the San Diego Trolley's Blue and Orange Lines); Old Town (San Diego Trolley's Blue Line); Cabrillo National Monument (Route 26 from Old Town Transit Center); Seaport Village (Route 7 and the San Diego Trolley's Orange Line); Sea World (Route 9 from the Old Town Transit Center); Qualcomm Stadium (San Diego Trolley Blue Line); and Tijuana (San Diego Trolley Blue Line to San Ysidro).

The **Coronado Shuttle,** bus Route 904, runs between the Coronado Island Marriott Hotel and the Old Ferry Landing and then continues along Orange Avenue to the Hotel del Coronado, Glorietta Bay, Loews, and back again. It costs 50¢ per person. Route 901 goes all the way to Coronado from San Diego and costs $1.75 for adults and 75¢ for seniors and children. Call ☎ **619/233-3004** for more information about this and other bus routes.

Money-Saving Tip

The **Day Tripper pass** allows unlimited rides on MTS (bus) and trolley routes. Passes are good for 1, 2, 3, and 4 consecutive days, and cost $5, $8, $10, and $12, respectively. Day Trippers are for sale at the Transit Store and all Trolley Station automatic ticket vending machines.

When planning your route, note that schedules vary and most buses do not run all night. Some stop at 6pm, while other lines continue to 9pm, midnight, and 2am—ask your bus driver for more specific information. On Saturdays some routes run all night.

BY TROLLEY

The San Diego Trolley routes serve downtown, the Mexican border (a 40-minute trip from downtown), Old Town, and the city of Santee, to the east. The recently completed Mission Valley extension carries sports fans to Qualcomm Stadium, major hotels, and shopping centers. Downtown, trolleys run along C Street (one block north of Broadway) and stop at Broadway and Kettner (America Plaza), Third Avenue (Civic Center), Fifth Avenue, and 12th Avenue (City College). Trolleys also circle around downtown's Bayside (parallel to Harbor Drive), with stops serving the Gaslamp Quarter, the Convention Center, Seaport Village, and the Santa Fe Depot.

Trolleys operate on a self-service fare-collection system; riders buy tickets from machines in stations before boarding. The machines list fares for each destination and dispense change. Tickets are valid for 3 hours from the time of purchase, in any direction. Fare inspectors board trains at random to check tickets. The bright-red trains run every 15 minutes during the day (every 10 minutes on the Blue Line, between Old Town and the border, during weekday rush hours) and every 30 minutes at night. Trolleys stop at each station for only 30 seconds. To open the door for boarding, push the lighted green button; to open the door to exit the trolley, push the lighted white button.

Trolley travel within the downtown area costs $1; the fare to the Mexican border from downtown is $2. Children under 5 ride free; seniors and riders with disabilities pay 75¢. For recorded transit information, call ☎ **619/685-4900.** To speak with a customer service representative, call ☎ **619/233-3004** (TTY/TDD 619/234-5005) daily from 5:30am to 8:30pm. The trolley generally operates daily from 5am to about 12:30am; the Blue Line, which goes to the border, runs 24 hours on Saturday.

Privately owned **Old Town Trolley Tours** (☎ 619/298-TOUR) offers an alternative way to tour the city by trolley. If you'd like to hit the tourist high points in a short visit, without having to drive, it is a worthwhile option. The narrated tours cover a 30-mile route, including the highlights of areas such as Old Town, Downtown, Coronado, and Balboa Park. You can board and reboard the trolley at over a dozen stops every half hour. The fare is $24 for adults, $12 children 4 to 12, free for children under 4 (who must sit on an adult's lap).

BY TAXI

Half a dozen taxi companies serve the San Diego area. They do not charge standard rates, except from the airport into downtown, which costs about $8.50 with tip. Taxis don't cruise the streets as they do in other cities, so you have to call ahead for quick pickup. If you are at a hotel or restaurant, the front-desk attendant or maître d' will call for you. Among the local companies are **Orange Cab** (☎ 619/291-3333), **San Diego Cab** (☎ 619/226-TAXI), and **Yellow Cab** (☎ 619/234-6161). The **Coronado Cab Company** (☎ 619/435-6211) serves Coronado. In La Jolla, use **La Jolla Cab** (☎ 858/453-4222).

BY TRAIN

San Diego's express rail commuter service, the **Coaster,** travels between the downtown Santa Fe Depot station and the Oceanside Transit Center, with stops at Old Town, Sorrento Valley, Solana Beach, Encinitas, and Carlsbad. Fares range from $2.75 to $3.50 each way, depending on how far you go. Eligible seniors and riders with disabilities pay half price. The trip between Oceanside and downtown San Diego takes just under an hour. Trains run Monday through Saturday; call ☎ 800/COASTER for the current schedule.

Amtrak (☎ 800/USA-RAIL) trains run daily between San Diego and Los Angeles. Trains to L.A. depart from the Santa Fe Depot and stop at Solana Beach and Oceanside. Some trains stop at San Juan Capistrano. A round-trip ticket to Solana Beach is $10, to Oceanside $15, to San Juan Capistrano $24, and to Los Angeles $40.

BY FERRY, WATER TAXI, OR BOAT

BY FERRY   There's regularly scheduled ferry service between San Diego and Coronado (☎ 619/234-4111 for information). Ferries leave from the Broadway Pier on the hour from 9am to 9pm Sunday through Thursday and from 9am to 10pm Friday and Saturday. They return from the Old Ferry Landing in Coronado to the Broadway Pier every hour on the 42-minute mark from 9:42am to 9:42pm Sunday through Thursday and from 9:42am to 10:42pm Friday and Saturday. The ride takes 15 minutes. Ferries also run from the Fifth Avenue Landing near the Convention Center to the Old Ferry Landing every hour on the half hour from 9:30am to 9:30pm Sunday through Thursday and from 9:30am to 10:30pm Friday and Saturday. The trip from Coronado to the Fifth Avenue Landing is every hour at the 18-minute mark from 9:18am to 9:18pm Sunday through Thursday and from 9:18am to 10:18pm Friday and Saturday. The fare is $2 for each leg of the journey (50¢ extra if you bring your bike). You can buy tickets in advance at the Harbor Excursion kiosk on Broadway Pier, the Fifth Avenue Landing in San Diego, or the Old Ferry Landing in Coronado.

BY WATER TAXI   Water taxis (☎ 619/235-TAXI) will take you around most of San Diego Bay for $5. If you want to go to the southern part of the bay (to Loews Coronado Bay Resort, for example), the flat fee is $25.

You can call a taxi to pick you up from any landing in the bay, or go to the Harbor Excursion Dock at the foot of Broadway Pier, where taxis wait for passengers.

BY BOAT   Boat tours provide a great way to explore San Diego from one of its many bays, including Mission Bay and San Diego Bay. **Bahia Belle** (☎ 619/539-7779), **Hornblower Invader Cruises** (☎ 619/234-8687), and **San Diego Harbor Excursions** (☎ 619/234-4111) offer narrated cruises of the local bays and drop off and pick up passengers at hotels along the way. Mission Bay cruises cost $6 per person; San Diego Harbor cruises run $12 for a 1-hour trip, $17 for 2 hours, half-price for children.

BY BICYCLE

San Diego is flat enough for easy exploration by bicycle, and many roads have designated bike lanes. The San Diego Ridelink publishes a comprehensive map of the county detailing bike *paths* (separate rights-of-way for bicyclists), bike *lanes* (alongside motor vehicle ways), and bike *routes* (shared ways designated only by bike-symbol signs). The **San Diego Region Bike Map** is available at visitor centers; to receive a copy in advance, call ☎ **619/231-BIKE.**

Bikes are available for rent in most areas; see "Biking" in chapter 6 for suggestions. If you want to take your two-wheeler on a city bus, look for bike-route signs at the bus stop. The signs mean that the buses that stop here have bike racks. Let the driver know you want to stow your bike on the back of the bus, then board and pay the regular fare. With this service, you can bus the bike to an area you'd like to explore, do your biking there, then return by bus. Not all routes are served by buses with bike racks; call ☎ **619/233-3004** for information.

The San Diego Trolley has a **Bike-N-Ride** program that lets you bring your bike on the trolley for free. You'll need a bike permit before you board. Permits for bikers 16 and older cost $4 and are issued through the **Transit Store,** 102 Broadway, at First Avenue (☎ **619/234-1060**). Bikers must board at the back of the trolley car, where the bike-storage area is located; cars carry two bikes except during weekday rush hours, when the limit is one bike per car. Several trolley stops connect with routes for buses with bike racks. For more information, call the **Transit Information Line** (☎ **619/ 233-3004**).

Bikes are permitted on the ferry connecting San Diego and Coronado, which has 15 miles of dedicated bike paths.

Fast Facts: San Diego

Airport   See "Arriving," in section 1 of this chapter.

American Express   A full-service office is downtown at 258 Broadway (☎ **619/234-4455**).

Area Codes   Dial **619** to call most of San Diego, except for La Jolla, Del Mar, Rancho Sante Fe, and Ranco Bernado, which received the new area code **858** during 1999. Use **760** to reach the remainder of San Diego County, including Encinitas, Carlsbad, Oceanside, Escondido, Ramona, Julian, and Anza–Borrego. Toward the end of 2000, the 619 area code will split further, with Coronado and the southern portion of San Diego County getting a new area code—**935.** Don't worry, though, this change doesn't go into effect until December 8, 2000, and the rest of the city of San Diego will remain in the 619 area code.

Baby-sitters   A number of hotels will secure a bonded sitter for guests, or you can call **Marion's Child** (☎ **619/582-5029**), whose sitters are bonded.

Business Hours   Banks are open weekdays from 9am to 4pm or later, and sometimes Saturday morning. Shops in shopping malls tend to stay open until about 9pm weekdays and until 6pm weekends.

Camera Repair   Both **George's Camera & Video,** 3827 30th St. (☎ **619/297-3544**), and **Professional Photographic Repair,** 7910 Raytheon Rd. (☎ **619/277-3700**), provide cameras and repair services. In La Jolla, try **Bob Davis' Camera Shop,** 7720 Fay St. (☎ **619/459-7355**). Other good choices are **Nelson Photo Supply,** 1909 India St., at Fir Street (☎ **619/234-6621;** fax 619/232-6153) and **Point Loma Camera Store,** 1310 Rosecrans St. (☎ **619/224-2719**).

Car Rentals   See "Getting Around," earlier in this chapter.

Climate   See "When to Go" in chapter 2.

Dentists   For dental referrals, contact the San Diego County Dental Society at ☎ **800/201-0244,** or call 800/DENTIST.

Doctors   Hotel Docs (☎ **800/468-3537** or 619/275-2663) is a 24-hour network of physicians, dentists, and chiropractors who claim they'll come to your hotel room within 35 minutes of your call. They accept credit cards, and their services are covered by most insurance policies. In a life-threatening situation, dial ☎ **911.**

Driving Rules   See "Getting Around," earlier in this chapter.

Drugstores   See "Pharmacies," below.

Emergencies   Call ☎ **911** for fire, police, and ambulance. The main police station is at 1401 Broadway, at 14th Street (☎ **619/ 531-2065** or 619/531-2000 for the hearing impaired).

Eyeglass Repair   Optometric Expressions, 55 Horton Plaza (☎ **619/544-9000**), is at street level near the Westin Hotel; it's open Monday, Wednesday, and Friday from 8am to 6pm and Tuesday, Thursday, and Saturday from 9:30am to 6pm. **Optometry on the Plaza,** 287 Horton Plaza (☎ **619/239-1716**), is open daily from 10am to 6pm (later during the summer). Both can fill eyeglass prescriptions, repair glasses, and replace contact lenses.

Hospitals   In Hillcrest, near downtown San Diego, **UCSD Medical Center–Hillcrest,** 200 W. Arbor Dr. (☎ **619/543-6400**), has the most convenient emergency room. In La Jolla, **Thornton Hospital,** 9300 Campus Point Dr. (☎ **858/657-7600**), has a good emergency room, and you'll find another in Coronado, at **Coronado Hospital,** 250 Prospect Place, opposite the Marriott Resort (☎ **619/435-6251**).

Hot Lines   HIV Hot Line: ☎ **800/922-2437** (English) or 800/922-7432 (multilingual). Alcoholics Anonymous: ☎ **619/265-8762.** Debtors Anonymous: ☎ **619/525-3065.** Mental Health Crisis Line: ☎ **619/236-3339.** Overeaters Anonymous: ☎ **619/563-4606.** Traveler's Aid Society: ☎ **619/231-7361.**

Information   See "Visitor Information," earlier in this chapter and in chapter 2. For telephone directory assistance, dial ☎ **411.**

Liquor Laws   The drinking age in California is 21. Beer, wine, and hard liquor are sold daily from 6am to 2am and are available in grocery stores.

Newspapers/Magazines   The *San Diego Union-Tribune* is published daily, and its informative entertainment section, "Night & Day," is in the Thursday edition. The free alternative *Reader,* published weekly (on Thursday), is available at many shops, restaurants, theaters, and public hot spots; it's the best source for up-to-the-minute club and show listings. *San Diego* magazine is filled with entertainment and dining listings for an elite audience (that explains all the ads for face-lifts and tummy tucks). *San Diego Home-Garden Lifestyles* magazine highlights the city's homes and gardens, and includes a monthly calendar of events and some savvy articles about the restaurant scene. Both magazines are published monthly and sold at newsstands.

Pharmacies   Long's, Rite-Aid, and Sav-On sell pharmaceuticals and non-prescription products. Look in the phone book to find the one nearest you. If you need a pharmacy after normal business hours, the following branches are open 24 hours: **Sav-On Drugs,** 8831 Villa La Jolla Dr., La Jolla (☎ 858/457-4390), and 3151 University Ave., North Park; **Rite-Aid,** 535 Robinson Ave., Hillcrest (☎ **619/291-3703**); and **Long's Drug Store,** 5685 Balboa Ave., Clairemont (☎ **619/279-2753**). Local hospitals also sell prescription drugs.

Police   The downtown police station is at 1401 Broadway (☎ **619/531-2000**). Call ☎ **911** in an emergency.

Post Office   The downtown branch of the post office, 815 E St., between Eighth and Ninth Avenues, is open Monday through Friday from 8:30am to 5pm, Saturday from 8:30am to noon. The more centrally located branch at 51 Horton Plaza, beside the Westin Hotel, is open Monday through Friday from 8am to 6pm and Saturday 9am to 5pm. For post office information, call ☎ **800/ 275-8777.**

Rest Rooms Horton Plaza and Seaport Village downtown, Balboa Park, Old Town State Historic Park in Old Town, and the Ferry Landing Marketplace in Coronado all have well-marked public rest rooms. In general, you won't have a problem finding one.

Safety Avoid deserted areas, especially at night, and don't go into public parks at night unless there's a concert or similar occasion that will attract a crowd. In **Balboa Park,** stay on designated walkways and away from secluded areas, day and night. In the **Gaslamp Quarter,** don't walk east of Fifth Avenue.

Always try to park in well-lit and well-traveled areas. Never leave any packages or valuables in sight. If someone attempts to rob you or steal your car, don't try to resist the thief or carjacker. Report the incident to the police department immediately by calling ☎ **911.** This is a free call, even from pay phones.

Smoking Smoking is prohibited in nearly all indoor public places, including theaters, hotel lobbies, and enclosed shopping malls. In 1998, California enacted legislation prohibiting smoking in all restaurants and bars, except those with outdoor seating. Opponents immediately began preparing to appeal the law, so things may have changed by the time you visit; be sure to inquire before you light up, or if you're determined to avoid those who do.

Taxes Sales tax in restaurants and shops is 7.75%. Hotel tax is 10.5%.

Taxis See "Getting Around," earlier in this chapter.

Television The main stations in San Diego are 6 (Fox), 8 (CBS), 10 (ABC), 7 or 39 (NBC), and 15 (PBS). Independent stations include channels 51 and 69. Channels 12, 19, and 52 offer programming in Spanish. Many hotels have cable TV.

Time Zone San Diego, like the rest of the West Coast, is in the Pacific standard time zone, which is 8 hours behind Greenwich mean time. Daylight saving time is observed. To check the time, call ☎ **619/853-1212.**

Transit Information Call ☎ **619/233-3004** (TTY/TDD 619/234-5005). If you know your route and just need schedule information, call ☎ **619/685-4900.**

Useful Telephone Numbers   For the latest San Diego arts and entertainment information, call ☎ **619/238-0700;** for half-price day-of-performance tickets, call ☎ **619/497-5000;** for a beach and surf report, call ☎ **619/221-8884.**

Weather   Call ☎ **619/289-1212.**

4

Accommodations

W here would you prefer to sleep? Over the water? On the beach? In historic surroundings? Facing the bay? With ocean views? Whatever you fancy, San Diego offers a variety of places to stay that range from pricey high-rise hostelries to inexpensive low-rise motels and some out-of-the-ordinary B&Bs.

A note on air-conditioning: Unless you have a particular sensitivity to even mild heat, A/C is more a convenience than a necessity. In San Diego's temperate climate, ocean breezes cool the air year-round.

TIPS FOR SAVING ON YOUR HOTEL ROOM

A hotel's rack rate is the official published rate—we list these prices to help readers make a fair comparison. The truth is, hardly anybody pays these prices, and you can nearly always do better.

- **Don't be afraid to bargain.** Get in the habit of asking for a lower price than the first one quoted. Always ask politely whether a less expensive room is available, or whether any special rates apply to you. You may qualify for corporate, student, military, senior citizen, or other discounts. Be sure to mention membership in AAA, AARP, frequent-flyer and traveler programs, or trade unions, which may entitle you to special deals as well.

- **Remember the law of supply and demand.** Coastal and resort hotels are most crowded and therefore most expensive on weekends, so discounts are often available for midweek stays. Downtown and business hotels are busiest during the week; expect discounts over the weekend. Avoid high-season stays whenever you can: Planning your vacation just a week before or after official peak season can mean big savings.

- **Dial direct.** When booking a room in a chain hotel, call the hotel's local line and the toll-free number, and see where you get the best deal. A hotel makes nothing on a room that stays empty. The clerk who runs the place is more likely to know about vacancies and will often grant deep discounts in order to fill up.

- **Consider a suite.** If you are traveling with your family or another couple, you can pack more people into a suite (which usually comes with a sofa bed), and reduce your per-person rate. Remember that some places charge for extra guests, some don't.
- **Book an efficiency.** A room with a kitchenette allows you to grocery shop and eat some meals in. Especially during long stays with families, you're bound to save money on food this way.
- **Investigate reservation services.** These outfits usually work as consolidators, buying up or reserving rooms in bulk, and then dealing them out to customers at a profit. They do garner deals that range from 10% to 50% off, but remember, the discounts apply to rack rates—inflated prices that people rarely end up paying. You're probably better off dealing directly with a hotel; but if you don't like bargaining, this is certainly a viable option. Most of them offer online reservation services as well. Here are a few of the more reputable providers.

　　San Diego Hotel Reservations (☎ 800/SAVE-CASH; www. savecash.com); **California Reservations** (☎ 800/576-0003; www.cal-res.com); **Accommodations Express** (☎ 800/950-4685; www. accommodationsxpress.com); **Hotel Reservations Network** (☎ 800/96HOTEL; www.180096HOTEL.com); **Quikbook** (☎ 800/789-9887, includes fax-on-demand service; www. quikbook.com); and **Room Exchange** (☎ 800/846-7000 in the United States, 800/486-7000 in Canada).

　　Note: Rates given here do not include hotel tax, which is an additional 10.5%. Also, you'll notice that some listings mention a free airport shuttle. This is common in San Diego hotels, so before you take a taxi from the airport, check to see what your hotel offers.

1 Downtown

Visitors with business in the city center—including the Convention Center—will find the downtown area convenient. Keep in mind that our "downtown" heading includes hotels in the stylish Gaslamp Quarter, as well as properties conveniently located near the harbor and other leisure attractions.

VERY EXPENSIVE

Embassy Suites. 601 Pacific Hwy. (at N. Harbor Dr.), San Diego, CA 92101. ☎ **800/EMBASSY** or 619/239-2400. Fax 619/239-1520. 337 suites. A/C TV TEL. $189–$300 suite. Rates include full breakfast and afternoon cocktail. Children under 12 stay free in parents' room. AE, DC, DISC, MC, V. Valet parking $12; indoor self-parking $9. Bus: 7. Trolley: Seaport Village.

What might seem like an impersonal business hotel is actually one of the better deals in town. It provides modern accommodations with lots of room for families or claustrophobes. Built in 1988, this neoclassical high-rise is topped with a distinctive neon bulls-eye that's visible from far away. Every room is a suite, with sofa beds in the living/dining areas and convenient touches like microwaves, coffeemakers, refrigerators, and hair dryers. All rooms open onto a 12-story atrium filled with palm trees, koi ponds, and a bubbling fountain; each also has a city or bay view. One block from Seaport Village and five blocks from downtown, the Embassy Suites is the second choice of Convention Center groups (after the pricier Hyatt Regency) and can be fully booked at unexpected times because of that.

Dining/Diversions: Barnett's Grand Cafe, which serves continental cuisine, looks onto the atrium and offers patio seating. Winning Streak Sports and Games Bar serves lunch and dinner, and has a large video screen, sports memorabilia, and video interactive trivia.

Amenities: Indoor pool (open 7am to 11pm), airport pickup, laundry, in-room movies, sauna, weight room, Jacuzzi, sundeck, meeting rooms, gift shop.

✪ **Hyatt Regency San Diego.** 1 Market Place (at Harbor Dr.), San Diego, CA 92101. ☎ **800/233-1234** or 619/232-1234. Fax 619/239-5678. 875 units. A/C MINIBAR TV TEL. $245–$290 double; from $500 suite. Extra person $25. Children under 12 stay free in parents' room. Packages and weekend rates available. AE, CB, DC, DISC, MC, V. Valet parking $16; self-parking $12. Trolley: Seaport Village.

The 40-story Hyatt Regency is generally the first choice of business travelers and convention groups, so the rack rates can be deceptively high—but don't let them scare you off if you want to stay in downtown's best modern high-rise. Weekend rates in particular can be a great deal.

While a behemoth with nearly 900 rooms can't offer very personalized service, you'll enjoy the amenities designed for those expense accounts. All the public spaces and guest rooms are light and airy, and boast stunning views over the city or sea. Built in 1992, the hotel (the tallest waterfront lodging on the West Coast) sports a limestone-and-marble neoclassical theme; guest rooms are quiet and furnished with high-quality but standard Hyatt-issue furnishings. (Trivia buffs: Did you know that virtually every Hyatt in the United States chooses from only *three* corporate-approved furniture styles?) Bathrooms have ample counter space and hair dryers. There's a club

Downtown San Diego Accommodations & Dining

Accommodations:

Best Western Bayside Inn **7**
Clarion Hotel Bay View **26**
Comfort Inn–Downtown **10**
Days Inn Suites **3**
Embassy Suites **32**
Gaslamp Plaza Suites **18**
Holiday Inn on the Bay **8**
Horton Grand **28**
Hyatt Regency San Diego **31**
La Pension Hotel **5**
Keeting House **1**
San Diego Marriott Marina **29**
San Diego Yacht &
  Breakfast Company **2**
Sheraton San Diego Hotel & Marina **2**
Travelodge Hotel Harbor Island **2**
U.S. Grant Hotel **14**
Westgate Hotel **13**

Dining:

Anthony's Star of the Sea **9**
Cafe Lulu **21**
The Cheese Shop **24**
Croce's Restaurants **19**
Dakota Grill and Spirits **16**
Filippi's Pizza Grotto **4**
Fio's **25**
The Fish Market/Top of the Market **12**
Hard Rock Cafe **23**
Kansas City Barbecue **30**
Karl Strauss Brewery & Grill **11**
Old Spaghetti Factory **27**
Osteria Panevino **20**
Panda Inn **15**
Planet Hollywood **10**
Princess Pub & Grille **6**
Rubio's Baja Grill **17**
Sammy's Pizza **23**

37

floor that provides upgraded service. More than 80% of the rooms are designated non-smoking, and the Hyatt gets kudos for superior service for travelers with disabilities (see "Best Hotel Bets," in chapter 1).

Dining: Sally's, a rather formal seafood restaurant, attracts locals as well as guests. There are two other less formal spots (all three offer alfresco dining) and two bars, including one with a spectacular 40th-floor view.

Amenities: State-of-the-art health club and spa, third-story bayview outdoor pool, whirlpool, concierge, 24-hour room service, six tennis courts, dry cleaning, laundry, shoeshine, newspaper delivery, in-room massage, baby-sitting, courtesy car, business center, car-rental desk, beauty salon, gift shop. Boat, water sports, and bicycle rentals.

San Diego Marriott Marina. 333 W. Harbor Dr. (at Front St.), San Diego, CA 92101-7700. ☎ **800/228-9290** or 619/234-1500. Fax 619/234-8678. 1,408 units. A/C MINIBAR TV TEL. $265–$300 double; from $500 suite. Children under 18 stay free in parents' room. Weekend rates, AARP discount, honeymoon and other packages available. AE, CB, DC, DISC, MC, V. Valet parking $18; self-parking $13. Bus: 7. Trolley: Convention Center. Pets accepted.

In the prosperous early '80s, long before San Diego's Convention Center was even a blueprint, this mirrored tower arose. Heck, with more than 1,400 rooms and multiple banquet and ballrooms, the Marriott *was* a convention center. Today, it merely stands next door, garnering a large share of convention attendees. They're drawn by the scenic 446-slip marina, lush grounds, waterfall pool, and breathtaking bay-and-beyond views. The Marriott competes with the much newer Hyatt Regency, and guests benefit from constantly improved facilities and decor. Leisure travelers can also take advantage of greatly reduced weekend rates. Because the Marriott tends to focus on public features and business services, guest quarters are well maintained but plain, and standard rooms are on the small side. Hallway noise can sometimes be disturbing. Rooms have VCRs and in-room movies.

Dining: There are several restaurants, including the Yacht Club, a popular place for informal dining and dancing on the waterfront.

Amenities: Two lagoon-like outdoor pools, two whirlpools, fitness center, sauna, concierge, 24-hour room service, dry cleaning and laundry, newspaper delivery, six lighted tennis courts, bicycle and boat rentals, game room, business center with secretarial services, self-service laundry, car-rental desk, tour desk, hair salon, shops.

The Westgate Hotel. 1055 Second Ave. (between Broadway and C St.), San Diego, CA 92101. ☎ **800/221-3802** or 619/238-1818. Fax 619/557-3604. 223 units. A/C MINIBAR TV TEL. $184–$224 double; from $440 suite. Extra person $10. Children under 19 stay free in parents' room. Weekend rates and packages available. AE, DC, DISC, MC, V. Underground valet parking $10. Bus: 2. Trolley: Civic Center (C St. and Third Ave.).

It's hard not to compare the lavish Westgate with its equally elegant neighbor, the U.S. Grant. But whereas the latter came by its formality during an era when royal treatment was expected, the Westgate might be considered nouveau riche. It was built in 1970 by a wealthy financier whose wife toured Europe collecting the antiques that fill each guest room. Ultimately, the hotel became a money pit for C. Arnholt Smith, but not before it established a standard of luxury—including fruit baskets and deferential service—that today appeals mainly to European and Latin American travelers and dignitaries.

The lobby appears straight out of 18th-century France; it's a precise re-creation of a Versailles anteroom, featuring brocade upholstery, tapestries, luxurious Baccarat crystal chandeliers, and Persian rugs. If you're downtown for a night at the theater or symphony, the Westgate fills the bill, but casual tourists may find the formality a bit stifling.

Dining/Diversions: The Fontainebleau Room offers candlelight dining and bowing, white-gloved waiters; there's a more casual dining room, and a cocktail lounge with piano entertainment.

Amenities: Concierge; 24-hour room service; workout room; sundeck; business services; barbershop; gift shop; valet service; complimentary transportation to airport, downtown appointments, Sea World, and the zoo.

EXPENSIVE

Holiday Inn on the Bay. 1355 N. Harbor Dr. (at Ash St.), San Diego, CA 92101-3385. ☎ **800/HOLIDAY** or 619/232-3861. Fax 619/232-4924. 580 units. A/C TV TEL. $139–$199 double; from $400 suite. Children under 18 stay free in parents' room. Packages and AARP and AAA discounts available. AE, DC, MC, V. Parking $10. Bus: 22, 23, 992. Pets accepted.

This high-rise is basic but well maintained, and located directly on the harbor near the Maritime Museum. It's only 1$^1/_2$ miles from the airport (you can watch planes landing and taking off), and two blocks from the train station and trolley. The rooms are decorated in California contemporary style; some offer harbor views and all have in-room movies. Bathrooms are generally small, but they have separate sinks with a lot of counter space.

Dining: The Elephant and Castle Restaurant, the San Diego branch of the world-famous Ruth's Chris Steakhouse, and Hazelwoods serve lunch and dinner. Elephant and Castle also serves breakfast.

Amenities: Outdoor heated pool, workout equipment, room service (6 to 11am and 5 to 11pm), baby-sitting, laundry, valet, self-service laundry.

Horton Grand. 311 Island Ave. (at Fourth Ave.), San Diego, CA 92101. ☎ **800/542-1886** or 619/544-1886. Fax 619/544-0058. www. hortongrand.com. 132 units. TV TEL. $139–$169 double; $209–$219 minisuite. Packages available. Children under 18 stay free in parents' room. AE, DC, MC, V. Valet parking $10 overnight with unlimited in-out privileges. Bus: 1. Pets accepted; $50 fee.

A cross between an elegant hotel and a charming inn, the Horton Grand combines two hotels that date from 1886—the Horton Grand and the Brooklyn Hotel (which for a time was the Kahle Saddlery Shop). Both were saved from demolition, moved to this spot, and connected by an airy atrium lobby filled with white wicker. The facade, with its graceful bay windows, is original.

Each room is unique and contains antiques and a gas fireplace (on a timer so you can fall asleep in front of it); even the bathrooms, complete with WC and pedestal sink, are genteel. Rooms overlook either the city or the fig tree–filled courtyard. Suites have a microwave, minibar, two TVs and telephones, a sofa bed, and a computer modem hookup. This is an old hotel, and sounds carry more than they might in a modern one; so if you're a light sleeper, request a room with no neighbors.

Dining/Diversions: Ida Bailey's restaurant, named for the well-loved madam whose establishment used to stand on this spot, serves breakfast, lunch, and dinner. It opens onto the hotel's courtyard, which is used for Sunday brunch on warm days. The Palace Bar serves afternoon tea Tuesday through Saturday from 2:30 to 5pm; there's live music Thursday through Saturday evenings and Sunday afternoons.

Amenities: Room service (7am to 10pm), access to nearby pool and weight room, concierge, dry cleaning, baby-sitting.

✪ **San Diego Yacht & Breakfast Company.** Marina Cortez, 1880 Harbor Island Dr., G-Dock, San Diego, CA 92101. ☎ **800/YACHT-DO** or 619/ 297-9484. Fax 619/295-9182. www.yachtdo.com. 12 vessels. TV TEL. May 15– Oct 15 and Dec 10–Jan 5 $135–$295 double; low season $115–$255 double. Extra person $25–$50. Discounts for multi-night stay. Rates include buffet breakfast at nearby Travelodge. AE, DISC, MC, V.

Here's an unusual opportunity to sleep on the water in your own power yacht, sailboat, or floating villa. You fall asleep to the gentle lapping of waves and awaken to the call of seagulls. The vessels are docked in a recreational marina on Harbor Island, near the airport and close to downtown; for an additional charge you can even charter a private cruise aboard your "room" (power- and sailboats only).

The floating villas are 650 square feet and feel like modern condos. Each has one bedroom and $1^1/_2$ bathrooms, and sleeps up to four. They have full kitchens, laundry facilities, comfortable furnishings, two TVs, a VCR, a stereo, and many other comforts. The well-kept power yachts have two staterooms, two heads, a full galley, VCR, stereo system, and TV. Serious sailors may prefer to sleep on a sailboat. They range in length from 25 to 45 feet and accommodate two to four people, but are best suited for one couple. Guests can use the pool at the marina. They receive a 20% discount at Harbor Island restaurants, and discounts on charter rates ($70 to $200 per hour) and on rentals of water toys (such as kayaks).

U.S. Grant Hotel. 326 Broadway (between Third and Fourth aves.), San Diego, CA 92101. ☎ **800/237-5029** or 619/232-3121. Fax 619/232-3626. 340 units. A/C MINIBAR TV TEL. $185–$205 double; from $255 suite. AAA, off-season, and weekend rates ($125–$185 double) available; off-season packages available. Children under 12 stay free in parents' room. AE, CB, DC, MC, V. Parking $13. Bus: 2. Trolley: Civic Center (C St. and Third Ave.). Pets accepted.

In 1910, Ulysses S. Grant, Jr. opened this stately hotel, now on the National Register of Historic Places, in honor of his father. Famous guests have included Albert Einstein, Charles Lindbergh, FDR, and JFK. Resembling an Italianate palace, the hotel is of a style more often found on the East Coast. An elegant atmosphere prevails, with age-smoothed marble, wood paneling, crystal chandeliers, and formal room decor that verges on stuffy. Guest rooms are quite spacious, as are the richly outfitted bathrooms, and include comforts like terry robes, hair dryers, and in-room movies. Extras in the suites make them worth the splurge; each has a fireplace and whirlpool tub, and rates include continental breakfast and afternoon cocktails and hors d'oeuvres. While the hotel has preserved a nostalgic formality, the surrounding neighborhood has become a hodgepodge of chic bistros, wandering panhandlers, and the visually loud Horton Plaza shopping center (Planet Hollywood looms large right across the street).

Dining/Diversions: The prestigious Grant Grill resembles an exclusive private club. In fact, in 1969, eight determined female San

Diegans defied the "gentlemen only" lunch restriction, and a plaque in the restaurant honors their successful effort. The Grill's lounge features live blues and jazz, usually Thursday through Saturday nights. Afternoon tea is served in the lobby Tuesday through Saturday with soft piano music as a backdrop.

Amenities: Concierge, 24-hour room service, 24-hour fitness center with panoramic view of downtown, in-room exercise bike and rowing-machine rentals, access to San Diego Athletic Club, same-day laundry and dry cleaning (except Sunday), turn-down service, baby-sitting, courtesy shuttle to and from the airport and to downtown attractions, limousine service, business services.

MODERATE

Best Western Bayside Inn. 555 W. Ash St. (at Columbia St.), San Diego, CA 92101. ☎ **800/341-1818** or 619/233-7500. Fax 619/239-8060. 122 units. A/C TV TEL. $104–$204 double; $114–$214 harbor-view double. Children under 12 stay free in parents' room. Rates include continental breakfast. Packages and fall, winter, spring weekend rates available. AE, CB, DC, DISC, MC, V. Free covered parking. Trolley: C Street and Kettner.

Though noisy downtown is just outside, this high-rise representative of reliable Best Western offers quiet lodgings. The hotel has an accommodating staff, and stunning city and harbor views. A mecca for business travelers, it's also close to more touristy downtown sites: It's an easy walk to the Embarcadero ("Bayview" would be a more accurate name for the hotel than "Bayside"), a bit farther to Horton Plaza, four blocks to the trolley stop, and five blocks to the train station. Rooms and bathrooms are basic chain-hotel issue, but are well maintained and feature brand-new bedding, towels, and draperies; all have balconies overlooking the bay or downtown (ask for the higher floors).

The hotel's restaurant, the Bayside Bar and Grill, serves breakfast, lunch, and dinner; meals are also available from room service, and many good restaurants and bars are nearby. In-room movies and complimentary airport transportation are provided. You can relax by the outdoor pool or in the Jacuzzi.

Clarion Hotel Bay View San Diego. 660 K St. (at Sixth Ave.), San Diego, CA 92101. ☎ **800/766-0234** or 619/696-0234. Fax 619/231-8199. 312 units. A/C TV TEL. $109–$139 double; $149–$169 suite. Children under 18 stay free in parents' room. Extra person $10. AARP, AAA, and off-season discounts available. AE, DC, DISC, MC, V. Parking $8. Bus: 1. Trolley: Gaslamp/Convention Center.

This relatively new entry on the San Diego hotel scene provides an affordable alternative for those attending meetings at the Convention Center—it's almost as close as the Marriott and the Hyatt, but considerably less expensive. Its location near the Gaslamp Quarter makes it a good choice for those who plan to enjoy the nightlife, but until the Quarter's gentrification spreads a couple of blocks farther south, the Clarion will remain in an industrial and commercial no-man's-land. All units are spacious, bright, and modern, and more than half offer views of San Diego Bay and the Coronado Bridge. Rooms have sliding glass doors and coffeemakers, and many have minibars.

The carpeted rooftop sundeck offers a great view as well as a Jacuzzi, sauna, workout room, and video arcade. Just off the marble-floored lobby is the Gallery Cafe, which serves breakfast, lunch, and dinner daily. There's a big-screen TV in the bar, and "Joey & Maria's Comedy Italian Wedding" dinner theater is popular on Friday and Saturday nights. Amenities include a concierge, room service (6am to 10pm), dry cleaning and laundry, in-room movies, and coin-operated washers and dryers.

Gaslamp Plaza Suites. 520 E. St. (corner of 5th Ave.), San Diego, CA 92101. ☎ **800/874-8770** or 619/232-9500. Fax 619/238-9945. 55 units. AC TV TEL. $93–$139 double; $139–$179 suite. Rates include continental breakfast. AE, CB, DC, DISC, MC, V. Valet parking $11. Bus: 1, 3, 25. Trolley: Fifth Ave.

You can't get closer to the center of the vibrant Gaslamp Quarter than this impeccably restored late Victorian. At 11 stories, it was San Diego's first "skyscraper" in 1913. Built (at great expense) of Australian gumwood, marble, brass, and exquisite etched glass, this splendid building originally housed San Diego Trust & Savings. Various other businesses (jewelers, lawyers, doctors, photographers) set up shop here until 1988, when the elegant structure was placed on the National Register of Historic Places and reopened as a boutique hotel.

You'll be surprised at the timeless elegance, from the dramatic lobby and wide corridors to guest rooms furnished with European flair. Each bears the name of a writer (Emerson, Swift, Zola, Shelley, Fitzgerald, and so on). The bathrooms are impressive, with fine marble and tile, and each room is equipped with microwave, dinnerware, refrigerator, and VCR. Most rooms are spacious. Beware of the few cheapest rooms, however; they are uncomfortably small (although they do have regular-size bathrooms).

Gaslamp Plaza Suites sits atop the popular Dakota Grill (see chapter 5), and hotel guests have the use of the nearby Westin fitness center for a nominal fee. Do remember where you are, and expect to hear some traffic and street noise, even in your room.

INEXPENSIVE

Inexpensive motels line Pacific Highway between the airport and downtown. The **Days Inn Suites** ($49 to $69), 1919 Pacific Hwy. at Grape Street (☎ **800/325-2525** or 619/232-1077), is within walking distance of the Embarcadero, the Maritime Museum, and the Harbor Excursion.

Comfort Inn–Downtown. 719 Ash St. (at Seventh Ave.), San Diego, CA 92101. ☎ **800/228-5150** or 619/232-2525. Fax 619/687-3024. 67 units. AC TV TEL. $79–$84 double. Extra person $5. Children under 18 stay free in parents' room. AARP and AAA discounts, weekly rates available. Rates include continental breakfast. AE, DISC, MC, V. Free parking.

In the northern corner of downtown, this terrific value is popular with business travelers *without* expense accounts and vacationers who just need reliable, safe accommodations. The hotel is surprisingly quiet, partly because the landmark El Cortez Hotel across the street is closed while developers gather funds to transform it into upscale condos and shops. (Oddly enough, even boarded up, its distinctive profile is pleasant to gaze upon.) The Comfort Inn is smartly designed so rooms open onto exterior walkways surrounding the drive-in entry courtyard, lending an insular feel in this less-than-scenic corner of town. There are few frills here, but coffee is always brewing in the lobby, and there's also a Jacuzzi. The hotel operates a free shuttle to the airport and the train and bus stations.

✪ **Keating House.** 2331 Second Ave. (between Juniper and Kalmia sts.), San Diego, CA 92101. ☎ **800/995-8644** or 619/239-8585. Fax 619/239-5774. www.caliburnus.com/keating. 8 units, 3 with bathroom. $65–$95 double. Rates include full breakfast. AE, DISC, MC, V. Bus: 11. From the airport, take Harbor Dr. toward downtown; turn left on Laurel St., then right on Second Ave.

Keating House is a good choice if you'd like a B&B, because gracious owner Larry Vlassoff considers every detail for his guests' comfort. His grand Bankers Hill mansion, between downtown and stylish Hillcrest, has been meticulously restored. It contains splendid turn-of-the-century furnishings and appointments, and offers always-inventive breakfast treats, savvy restaurant recommendations, and a lovingly tended exotic garden. The downstairs entry, parlor, and dining room all have cozy fireplaces, and two rooms (each with a private bathroom) are in the secluded carriage house.

In contrast to many B&Bs in Victorian-era homes, this one eschews dollhouse frills for a classy, sophisticated approach.

✪ **La Pensione Hotel.** 606 W. Date St. (at India St.), San Diego, CA 92101. ☎ **800/232-4683** or 619/236-8000. Fax 619/236-8088. www. lapensionehotel.com. 80 units. TV TEL. $60–$80 double. Packages available. AE, DC, DISC, MC, V. Limited free underground parking. Bus: 5. Trolley: County Center/Little Italy.

This place has a lot going for it: modern amenities, remarkable value, a convenient location within walking distance of the central business district, a friendly staff, and parking (a premium for small hotels in San Diego). The three-story La Pensione is built around a courtyard and feels like a small European hotel; in fact, it's the number one choice of foreign students attending the downtown Language Institute. The decor throughout is modern and streamlined, with plenty of sleek black and metallic surfaces, crisp white walls, and minimal furniture. Guest rooms, while not overly large, make the most of their space and leave you with room to move around. Each room offers a tub-shower combination, ceiling fan, microwave, and small refrigerator; try for a bay or city view rather than the concrete courtyard view. La Pensione is in San Diego's Little Italy and within walking distance of eateries (mostly Italian) and nightspots; there are two restaurants attached to the hotel.

2 Hillcrest/Uptown

Although they're certainly no longer a secret, the gentrified historic neighborhoods north of downtown are still something of a bargain. They're convenient to Balboa Park, with easy access to the rest of town. Filled with chic casual restaurants, eclectic shops, movie theaters, and sizzling nightlife, the area is also easy to navigate.

MODERATE

Balboa Park Inn. 3402 Park Blvd. (at Upas St.), San Diego, CA 92103. ☎ **800/938-8181** or 619/298-0823. Fax 619/294-8070. www. balboaparkinn.com. 26 units. TV TEL. $80–$95 double; $95–$135 suite; $125–$200 specialty suite. Children under 11 stay free in parents' room. Extra person $8. Rates include continental breakfast. AE, CB, DC, DISC, MC, V. Parking available on street. From I-5, take Washington St. east, follow signs to University Ave. E. Turn right at Park Blvd. Bus: 7, 7A/B.

Insiders looking for unusual, well-located accommodations head straight for this small pink inn at the northern edge of Balboa Park. It's a cluster of four Spanish Colonial–style former apartment buildings in a mostly residential neighborhood close to the trendy

Hillcrest area. The hotel caters to a straight clientele as well as gay travelers drawn to Hillcrest's hip restaurants and clubs. All the rooms and suites are tastefully decorated; the "specialty suites," however, are over-the-top. There's the "Tara Suite," as in *Gone With the Wind;* the "Nouveau Ritz," which employs every art deco cliché, including mirrors and Hollywood lighting; and the "Greystoke" suite, a jumble of jungle, safari, and tropical themes with a completely mirrored bathroom and whirlpool tub. All rooms come with refrigerators and coffeemakers, and there's newspaper delivery Monday through Saturday. You can walk to Balboa Park attractions.

✪ **Sommerset Suites Hotel.** 606 Washington St. (at Fifth Ave.), San Diego, CA 92103. ☎ **800/962-9665** or 619/692-5200. Fax 619/692-5299. www.sommerset.com. 80 units. A/C TV TEL. $135–$195 double. Children under 12 stay free in parents' room. Discounts available. Rates include continental breakfast and afternoon refreshments. AE, DC, DISC, MC, V. Free covered parking. Take Washington St. exit off I-5. Bus: 16 or 25.

This all-suite hotel on a busy street was originally built as apartment housing for interns at the hospital nearby. It retains a residential ambiance and unexpected amenities like huge closets, medicine cabinets, and fully equipped kitchens in all rooms (executive suites even have dishwashers). There are poolside barbecue facilities, and a coin-operated laundry. The hotel has a personal, welcoming feel, from the friendly, helpful staff to the snacks, soda, beer, and wine served each afternoon. You'll even get a welcome basket with cookies and microwave popcorn. Rooms are comfortably furnished and have hair dryers, irons and ironing boards, and balconies. Be prepared for noise from the busy thoroughfare below, though. Several blocks of Hillcrest's chic restaurants and shops (plus a movie multiplex) are within easy walking distance. Guest services include a courtesy van to the airport, Sea World, the zoo, and other attractions within a 5-mile radius. *Note:* This hotel's rack rates are misleading; rooms can commonly be had for around $100.

INEXPENSIVE

The Cottage. 3829 Albatross St. (off Robinson Ave.), San Diego, CA 92103. ☎ **619/299-1564.** Fax 619/299-6213. 2 units. TV TEL. $65–$85 double; $85–$105 cottage. Extra person in cottage $10. Rates include continental breakfast. AE, DISC, MC, V.

Built in 1913, the two-room Cottage sits in a secret garden, a private hideaway tucked behind a homestead-style house, at the end of a residential cul-de-sac. There's an herb garden out front, birdbaths, and a flower-lined walkway. The cottage has king-size bed, a living room with a wood-burning stove and a queen-size sofa bed, and a charming kitchen with a coffeemaker. The guest room in the main house features a king-size bed. Both accommodations are filled with fresh flowers and antiques put to clever uses, and each has a private entrance. Owner Carol Emerick (she used to run an antique store—and it shows!) serves a scrumptious breakfast, complete with the morning paper. Guests are welcome to use the dining room and parlor in the main house, where they sometimes light a fire and rev up the 19th-century player piano. The Cottage is close to the cafes of Mission Hills and Hillcrest, and a short drive from Balboa Park.

Crone's Cobblestone Cottage Bed & Breakfast. 1302 Washington Place (2¹/₂ blocks west of Washington St. at Ingalls St.), San Diego, CA 92103. ☎ **619/295-4765.** 2 units. $85 double. Rates include continental breakfast. Minimum 2 nights. No credit cards; checks accepted. From I-5, take Washington St. exit east uphill. Make a U-turn at Goldfinch, then keep right at the "Y" intersection onto Washington Place. Bus: 3.

After just one night at this magnificently restored Craftsman bungalow, you'll feel like an honored guest rather than a paying customer. Artist Joan Crone lives in the architectural award–winning addition to her 1913 home, which is a designated Historic Landmark. Guests have the run of the entire house, including a book-filled, wood-paneled den and antique-filled living room. Both cozy guest rooms have antique beds, goosedown pillows and comforters, and eclectic bedside reading. They share a full bathroom; the Eaton Room also has a private half-bath. Bookmaker and illustrator Crone lends a calm and literary aesthetic to the surroundings, aided by Sam, the cat, who peers in from his side of the house. The quiet, historic Mission Hills neighborhood, just blocks from Hillcrest and Old Town, is one of San Diego's best-kept secrets.

Park Manor Suites. 525 Spruce St. (between Fifth and Sixth aves.), San Diego, CA 92103. ☎ **800/874-2649** or 619/291-0999. Fax 619/291-8844. www.parkmanorsuites.com. 80 units. TV TEL. $69–$89 studio; $89–$129 1-bedroom suite; $139–$179 2-bedroom suite. Children under 12 stay free in parents' room. Extra person $15. Rates include continental breakfast. Weekly rates available. AE, DC, MC, V. Free parking. Bus: 1, 3, 25.

Popular with actors appearing at the Old Globe Theatre in neighboring Balboa Park, this eight-floor Italianate masterpiece was built as a full-service luxury hotel in 1926 on a prime corner overlooking the park. One of the original investors was the family of child actor Jackie Coogan. The Hollywood connection continued—the hotel became a popular stopping-off point for celebrities headed for

Mexican vacations in the 1920s and '30s. Guest rooms are spacious and comfortable, featuring full kitchens, dining rooms, living rooms, and bedrooms with a separate dressing area. A few have glassed-in terraces; request one when you book. The overall feeling is that of a prewar East Coast apartment building, complete with steam heat and lavish moldings. Park Manor Suites does have its weaknesses: Bathrooms have mostly original fixtures and could use some renovation; and the rooftop banquet room, where a simple continental breakfast buffet is served, suffers from a bad '80s rehab with too many mirrors. But prices are quite reasonable for the trendy Hillcrest neighborhood; there's a restaurant on the ground floor, and laundry service is available.

3 Old Town & Mission Valley

Old Town is a popular area for families because of its proximity to Old Town State Historic Park and other attractions that are within walking distance. **Hotel Circle,** on the way to Mission Valley, offers easy freeway access. Its many hotels cater to convention groups, sports fans heading to Qualcomm Stadium, families visiting the University of San Diego or San Diego State University, and leisure travelers drawn by the lower prices and competitive facilities.

MODERATE

Comfort Inn & Suites. 2485 Hotel Circle Place, San Diego, CA 92108. ☎ **800/647-1903** or 619/291-7700. Fax 619/297-6179. 200 units. A/C TV TEL. High season $89–$129 double. Extra person $10. Children under 18 stay free in parents' room. Rates include continental breakfast. Off-season discounts available. AE, CB, DC, DISC, MC, V. Free parking. From I-8, take Hotel Circle exit, follow signs for Hotel Circle north. Bus: 6.

This well-priced, modern, four-story motel at the western, or Old Town, end of Hotel Circle underwent a complete refurbishment in 1996. It enlarged rooms by doing away with balconies (many of which had opened onto the noisy freeway side anyway). Bathrooms are small but well equipped, and all have hair dryers. Rooms and suites are sparingly but adequately outfitted, with standard hotel-issue furnishings and coffeemakers. Suites are the way to go here; all have sleeper sofas in the living room, two TVs, a microwave, refrigerator, and separate vanity area. The heated outdoor pool and Jacuzzi adjoin the parking lot; there's a car-rental desk, game room, and washer and dryer. Stay away from the freeway side, and ask instead for a room looking toward the newly refurbished 18-hole public golf course across the street. The hotel doesn't have a restaurant, but offers room service at dinner from the steakhouse next door.

Hacienda Hotel. 4041 Harney St. (east of San Diego Ave.), San Diego, CA 92110. ☎ **800/888-1991** or 619/298-4707. Fax 619/298-4771. www. haciendahotel-oldtown.com. 170 units. A/C TV TEL. $135–$145 suite. Off-season discounts available. Children under 16 stay free in parents' room. AE, CB, DC, DISC, MC, V. Free underground parking. From I-5 take Old Town Ave. exit; turn left onto San Diego Ave. and right onto Harney St. Bus: 5, 5A.

Perched above Old Town, this Best Western all-suite hotel spreads over several levels. Walkways thread through courtyards with bubbling fountains, palm trees, and bougainvillea-trimmed balconies; but if you have trouble climbing stairs and hills, you'd be wise to stay elsewhere. Aside from that, the place is tops in its price range; every suite has rustic Mexican wood furniture, 20-foot ceilings, a refrigerator, microwave, coffeemaker, and VCR. The unremarkable Acapulco restaurant (yes, it's Mexican) atop the hotel serves breakfast, lunch, and dinner daily. Guests also have signing privileges next door at the Brigantine Restaurant and down the street at Cafe Pacifica (see chapter 5, "Dining"). Amenities include a concierge (Monday through Friday), room service (6:30am to 2pm and 4 to 10pm), complimentary airport and train transportation, movie rentals with complimentary bag of microwave popcorn, heated outdoor pool and spa overlooking Old Town, fitness center, and coin-operated laundry.

Hanalei Hotel. 2270 Hotel Circle North, San Diego, CA 92108. ☎ **800/ 882-0858** or 619/297-1101. Fax 619/297-6049. www.hanaleihotel.com. 416 units. A/C MINIBAR TV TEL. $99–$160 double; $275–$375 suite. Extra person $10. Off-season, AARP, and AAA discounts and golf packages available. AE, CB, DC, DISC, MC, V. Parking $6. From I-8, take Hotel Circle exit, follow signs for Hotel Circle N. Bus: 6. Pets accepted; $50 cleaning fee.

My favorite hotel on Hotel Circle just emerged from a massive renovation and upgrade with its Polynesian theme splendidly intact. Its comfort-conscious sophistication sets it apart from the rest of the pack. Rooms are split between two high-rise towers, set far away from the freeway and cleverly positioned so that the balconies open onto the tropically landscaped pool courtyard or the luxurious links of a formerly private golf club on the Mission Valley floor. The heated outdoor pool is large enough for any luau, as is the oversized whirlpool beside it. The hotel boasts an unmistakable '60s vibe and Hawaiian ambiance—the restaurant and bar have over-the-top kitschy decor, with waterfalls, outrigger canoes, and more. But guest rooms sport contemporary furnishings and features like coffeemakers, hair dryers, irons, ironing boards, and in-room movies. Some have microwaves and refrigerators. There's an all-day casual coffee shop, plus a more expensive dinner-only restaurant. Services include free shuttle to Old Town and other attractions, laundry, and meeting facilities.

✪ **Heritage Park Bed & Breakfast Inn.** 2470 Heritage Park Row, San Diego, CA 92110. ☎ **800/995-2470** or 619/299-6832. Fax 619/299-9465. www.heritageparkinn.com. 12 units. $100–$235 double. Extra person $20. Rates include full breakfast and afternoon tea. AE, DC, DISC, MC, V. Free parking. Take I-5 to Old Town Ave., turn left onto San Diego Ave., then turn right onto Harney St.

This exquisite 1889 Queen Anne mansion is set in a "Victorian park"—an artfully arranged cobblestone cul-de-sac lined with historic buildings saved from the wrecking ball and assembled here, near Old Town, as a tourist attraction. Once inside, that unsettling "fishbowl" feeling subsides as you surrender to the pampering of afternoon tea, candlelight breakfast, and a number of romantic extras (champagne and chocolates, private in-room dinner) available for special celebrations. Like the gracious parlors and porches, each room is outfitted with meticulous period antiques and luxurious fabrics; the staff provides turn-down service. Although the fireplaces are all ornamental, some rooms have whirlpool baths. In the evenings, vintage films are shown in the Victorian parlor.

Vacation Inn. 3900 Old Town Ave., San Diego, CA 92110. ☎ **800/451-9846** or 619/299-7400. Fax 619/299-1619. 124 units. A/C TV TEL. June–Aug $110–$115 double; $130–$175 suite. Sept–May $84–$99 double; $114–$165 suite. Extra person $10. Children under 18 stay free in parents' room. Rates include continental breakfast and afternoon refreshments. AE, CB, DC, DISC, ER, MC, V. Free parking. Bus: 5, 5A.

Just a couple of easy walking blocks from the heart of Old Town, the Vacation Inn has a Colonial Spanish exterior that suits the neighborhood's theme. Inside you'll find better-than-they-have-to-be contemporary furnishings and surprising small touches that make this hotel an affordable option favored by business travelers and families alike. There's nothing scenic on the adjacent streets, so the hotel is smartly oriented toward the inside; request a room whose patio or balcony opens onto the pleasant courtyard. Rooms are thoughtfully and practically appointed, with coffeemakers, microwaves, refrigerators, and writing tables. The lobby, surrounded by

French doors, features a large fireplace, several sitting areas, and a TV. Dry cleaning and laundry service are offered; the hotel also has an outdoor pool and Jacuzzi. The hotel entrance, on Jefferson Street, is hard to find but definitely worth the search.

INEXPENSIVE

Room rates at properties on Hotel Circle are significantly cheaper than those in many other parts of the city. You'll find a cluster of inexpensive chain hotels and motels, including **Best Western Seven Seas** (☎ **800/421-6662** or 619/291-1300), **Mission Valley Center Travelodge** (☎ **800/255-3050** or 619/297-2271), **Ramada Inn** (☎ **800/532-4241** or 619/291-6500), and **Vagabond Inn** (☎ **800/522-1555** or 619/297-1691).

4 Mission Bay & the Beaches

If you plan to enjoy the beach and aquatic activities, this part of town is the right spot. Some hotels are right on Mission Bay, San Diego's water playground; they're always good choices for families, especially those planning to visit Sea World. Ocean Beach, Mission Beach, and Pacific Beach provide a taste of the laid-back surfer lifestyle but can be unpredictable and raucous at times. Don't worry about missing out on the rest of San Diego; even though the beach communities are far removed in atmosphere, downtown is only a 10-minute drive.

VERY EXPENSIVE

Catamaran Resort Hotel. 3999 Mission Blvd. (4 blocks south of Grand Ave.), San Diego, CA 92109. ☎ **800/422-8386** or 619/488-1081; 800/233-8172 in Canada. Fax 619/488-1387. www.catamaranresort.com. 315 units. A/C TV TEL. $165–$225 double; from $265 suite; $190–$235 studio. Children under 18 stay free in parents' room. AE, CB, DC, DISC, MC, V. Valet parking $8; self-parking $6. Take Grand/Garnet exit off I-5 and go west on Grand Ave., then south on Mission Blvd. Bus: 34, 34A/B.

Ideally situated right on Mission Bay, the Catamaran has its own bay and ocean beaches, with water-sports facilities. Built in the 1950s, the hotel has been fully renovated to modern standards without losing its trademark Polynesian theme; the atrium lobby holds a 15-foot waterfall and full-size dugout canoe, and koi-filled lagoons meander through the property. After dark, torches blaze throughout the grounds, with numerous varieties of bamboo and palm sprouting; during the day, the resident tropical birds chirp away. Guest rooms— in a 13-story building or one of the six two-story buildings—have subdued South Pacific decor, and each has a balcony or patio. Tower rooms have commanding views of the bay, the San Diego skyline, La Jolla, and Point Loma. Studios and suites have kitchenettes, and every room has a coffeemaker, hair dryer, and movie channels. The Catamaran is within walking distance of Pacific Beach's restaurant and nightlife. It's also steps away from the bay's exceptional jogging and biking path, and you can rent bikes and jogging strollers at the hotel.

Dining/Diversions: The Atoll restaurant is an upscale hotel dining room, remarkable only for its romantic outdoor bayside seating. The large, lively Cannibal Bar hosts bands and videos. Moray's (named for the moray eels that inhabited its large aquarium until they became too aggressive) is an intimate piano bar.

Amenities: Outdoor heated pool, whirlpool spa, health club, concierge, room service (6:30am to 11pm), dry cleaning and laundry, nightly turn-down, baby-sitting, business center, lifeguard (summer only), supervised children's programs, car-rental desk, tour desk, gift shop.

Hilton San Diego Resort. 1775 E. Mission Bay Dr., San Diego, CA 92109. ☎ **800/445-8667**, 800/962-6307 in California and Arizona, or 619/276-4010. Fax 619/275-7991. 365 units. A/C MINIBAR TV TEL. Summer $205–$335 double; from $500 suite. Off-season $190–$285 double. Extra person $20. Children under 18 stay free in parents' room. Off-season discounts available. AE, CB, DC, DISC, JCB, MC, V. Valet parking $10; free self-parking. Take I-5 to Sea World Dr. exit and turn north on E. Mission Bay Dr. Pets under 25 lbs. accepted; $50 fee.

This sprawling Mediterranean-style resort occupies 18 acres on the east side of Mission Bay and is a quarter-mile from the Visitor Information Center. Room rates have skyrocketed in the past couple of years, but the place is consistently packed. Its main strength is the "no-brainer" aspect—within steps of your room are enough distractions and activities for the duration of your stay. They include a calm beach, tennis courts, charter boats, rental catamarans and water toys (like windsurfers and aquacycles), and an Olympic-plus-size pool. Guests have access to Mission Bay Park's trails and playgrounds, bike rentals, and a bevy of shops and restaurants. All rooms (contained in one eight-story tower and several low-rise buildings) have ceiling fans, a balcony or terrace, refrigerator, coffeemaker, iron and ironing board, hair dryer, makeup mirror, and in-room movies. Rooms are spacious and light, with large, elegant bathrooms and vaguely tropical pastel decor. Sea World is across the bay, and the ocean is 5 miles to the west.

Accommodations & Dining
in Mission Bay & the Beaches

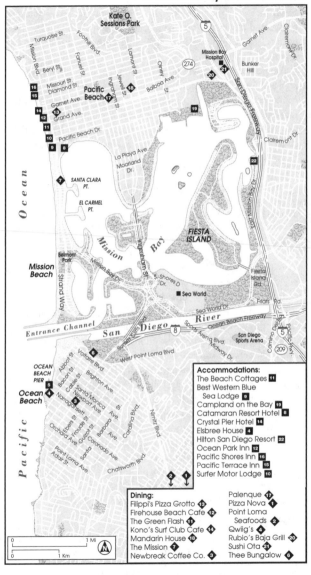

Accommodations:
The Beach Cottages 11
Best Western Blue
  Sea Lodge 9
Campland on the Bay 19
Catamaran Resort Hotel 8
Crystal Pier Hotel 14
Elsbree House 4
Hilton San Diego Resort 22
Ocean Park Inn 12
Pacific Shores Inn 16
Pacific Terrace Inn 15
Surfer Motor Lodge 10

Dining:
Filippi's Pizza Grotto 13
Firehouse Beach Cafe 12
The Green Flash 11
Kono's Surf Club Cafe 14
Mandarin House 18
The Mission 7
Newbreak Coffee Co. 3
Palenque 17
Pizza Nova 1
Point Loma
  Seafoods 2
Qwiig's 4
Rubio's Baja Grill 20
Sushi Ota 21
Thee Bungalow 6

Dining/Diversions: Three restaurants—a casual Southwestern bay-front cafe, a dinner-only Italian restaurant that serves gourmet pizzas, and a Mexican cantina serving tropical drinks and various nachos. The cantina features live entertainment and dancing at night.

Amenities: Giant swimming "lagoon," plus children's wading pool and four Jacuzzis; sauna; weight-training room; five lighted tennis courts; pro shop; putting green; playground; business center; massage; game arcade; meeting rooms; hair salon; concierge; room service (7am to 11pm); dry cleaning and laundry; baby-sitting; children's programs (summer only); free airport transportation.

✪ Pacific Terrace Inn. 610 Diamond St., San Diego, CA 92109. ☎ **800/ 344-3370** or 619/581-3500. Fax 619/274-3341. 73 units. A/C MINIBAR TV TEL. $195–$245 partial-view double; $255–$275 oceanfront double; from $280 suite. 10% AAA discount June 15–Sept 15 (25% Sept 16–June 14). Rates include continental breakfast. AE, CB, DC, DISC, MC, V. Free underground parking. Take I-5 to Grand/Garnet exit and follow Grand or Garnet west to Mission Blvd., turn right (north), then left (west) onto Diamond; inn is at the end of the street on the right. Bus: 34 or 34A.

This pink, condo-like building is the best modern hotel on the boardwalk, a luxury property that stands out from the casual beach pads in the area. With an upscale atmosphere and relaxed ambiance, the hotel provides more peace and quiet than most beachfront lodgings in this desirable but slightly raucous area.

The large, comfortable guest rooms come with balconies or terraces, refrigerators stocked with soft drinks, wall safes, VCRs, and in-room movies; bathrooms have hair dryers, cotton robes, and vanities with separate sinks. About half the rooms have kitchenettes, and top-floor rooms in this three-story hotel enjoy particularly nice views. Management keeps popcorn, coffee, and lemonade at the ready throughout the day; the pool and hot tub face a relatively quiet stretch of beach with fire rings for bonfires or barbecues.

Dining: Five local restaurants allow meals to be billed to the hotel; there's no restaurant on the premises.

Amenities: Outdoor heated pool, whirlpool, daily newspaper, dry cleaning, nightly turn-down, coin-operated laundry.

EXPENSIVE

Best Western Blue Sea Lodge. 707 Pacific Beach Dr., San Diego, CA 92109-5094. ☎ **800/BLUE-SEA** or 619/488-4700. Fax 619/488-7276. www. bestwestern-bluesea.com. 100 units. TV TEL. Mid-June to mid-Sept $149–$179 double; up to $289 suite. Off-season $114–$139 double; up to $219 suite. Children under 13 stay free in parents' room. AAA and AARP discounts available.

AE, CB, DC, DISC, MC, V. Underground and outdoor parking $3. Take I-5 to Grand/Garnet exit, follow Grand Ave. to Mission Blvd. and turn left, then turn right onto Pacific Beach Dr. Bus: 34.

The three-story Blue Sea Lodge is a reliable choice in a prime location. While I'd like to see more meticulous maintenance and decor upgrades, Best Western keeps up with the other bargain properties in the chain. And, despite the rates listed, this is a bargain. There are many ways to get a discount—including just asking. Outfitted in bright florals, each room has a balcony or patio; some have sunken tubs, or kitchenettes with coffeemakers. Rooms with full ocean views overlook the sand and have more privacy than those on the street, but the Pacific Beach boardwalk has never been known for quiet or solitude. Casual beach cafes and grills are nearby, along with several raucous Pacific Beach bars.

Amenities: The lobby offers coffee, tea, and a microwave for guests. The heated pool and Jacuzzi are steps from the beach.

✪ **Crystal Pier Hotel.** 4500 Ocean Blvd. (at Garnet Ave.), San Diego, CA 92109. ☎ **800/748-5894** or 619/483-6983. 26 cottages. TV. Cottages for 2–6 people $115–$305 mid-June to mid-Sept; $95–$250 mid-Sept to mid-June. 3-night minimum in summer. DISC, MC, V. Free parking. Take I-5 to Grand/Garnet exit; follow Garnet to the pier. Bus: 34 or 34A.

This historic property, which dates from 1927, offers a unique opportunity to sleep over the water. Built on a pier over the Pacific Ocean, the hotel offers self-contained cottages with breathtaking beach views. Most cottages date from 1936, and all have been completely renovated. Each comes with a private patio, living room, bedroom, and full kitchen, and has welcoming blue shutters and window boxes. The sound of waves is soothing, but the boardwalk action is only a few steps (and worlds) away. The quietest units are the farthest out on the pier. Guests drive right out and park beside their cottages, a real boon on crowded weekends. There are vending machines and movie rentals. Boogie boards, fishing poles, beach chairs, and umbrellas are also available. The office is open daily from 8am to 8pm. These accommodations book up fast. Besides being a restful place, the pier is a great place to watch the surfers at sunset.

MODERATE

The Beach Cottages. 4255 Ocean Blvd. (1 block south of Grand Ave.), San Diego, CA 92109-3995. ☎ **619/483-7440.** Fax 619/273-9365. 61 units, 17 cottages. TV TEL. July 1–Labor Day $95–$115 double; $125 studio for up to 4; $145–$190 apt for up to 6; $145–$180 cottage for up to 6; $220–$240 2-bedroom suite for up to 6. Off-season discounts and off-season weekly rates available. AE, CB, DC, DISC, MC, V. Free parking. Take I-5 to Grand/Garnet exit, go west on Grand Ave. and right on Mission Blvd. Bus: 34 or 34A.

This family-owned operation has a variety of guest quarters (most geared to the long-term visitor), but the cute little detached cottages steps from the sand give it real appeal. Most other units are perfectly adequate, especially for budget-minded families who want to log major hours on the beach, but stay away from the plain motel rooms—they're just dingy. All accommodations except the motel rooms have fully equipped kitchens. The Beach Cottages are within walking distance of shops and restaurants—look both ways for speeding cyclists before crossing the boardwalk—and have barbecue grills, shuffleboard courts, table tennis, and a laundry. The cottages themselves aren't pristine, but have a rustic charm that makes them popular with young honeymooners and those nostalgic for the golden age of laid-back California beach culture. With one or two bedrooms, each cottage sleeps up to six; each has a patio with tables and chairs.

To make a reservation, call between 9am and 9pm, when the office is open. Reserve the most popular cottages well in advance.

Ocean Park Inn. 710 Grand Ave., San Diego, CA 92109. ☎ **800/231-7735** or 619/483-5858. Fax 619/274-0823. 73 units. A/C TV TEL. Mid-May to mid-Sept $104–$214 double, $179–$304 suite; winter $89–$179 double, $124–$274 suite. Rates include continental breakfast. AE, DC, DISC, MC, V. Free indoor parking. Take Grand/Garnet exit off I-5; follow Grand Ave. to ocean. Bus: 34, 34A/B.

This modern oceanfront motor hotel offers attractive, spacious rooms with well-coordinated contemporary furnishings. Although the inn has a level of sophistication uncommon in this casual, surfer-populated area, you won't find solitude and quiet. The cool marble lobby and plushly carpeted hallways will help you feel a little insulated from the raucous scene outside, though. You can't beat the location (directly on the beach) and the view (ditto), and all rooms are equipped with refrigerators. Rates vary according to view, but all rooms have at least a partial ocean view. Units in front are most desirable, but it can get noisy directly above the boardwalk; try for the second or third floor. The Ocean Park Inn doesn't have its own restaurant, but the casual Firehouse Beach Cafe (see chapter 5, "Dining") is outside the front door.

Pacific Shores Inn. 4802 Mission Blvd. (between Law and Chalcedony sts.), San Diego, CA 92109. ☎ **800/826-0715** or 619/483-6300. Fax 619/483-9276. 55 units. TV TEL. June 15–Sept 15 $103–$108 double, $120 suite. Winter $63–$88 double, $73–$93 suite. Extra person $5. Children under 16 stay free in parents' room. Rates include continental breakfast. AE, DC, DISC, MC, V. Free parking. Bus: 34, 34A. Pets up to 15 lbs. accepted; $25 fee.

If the beach will be a large part of your San Diego vacation, you can't stay in a better location than the one enjoyed by this two-story contemporary motel at the north end of Pacific Beach. It's several blocks from the restaurants, but enjoys a quiet that you won't find at any of the places down the road—and the beach is just 100 yards away. The inn doesn't advertise ocean views, but rooms 23, 29, 31, 33, and 35 have them, and there's also a heated pool by the parking area. Half the units have kitchens; the others offer small refrigerators. The furniture is a little ragged, but carpets, drapes, and bedspreads are brand new. Ask for a room away from the street.

Surfer Motor Lodge. 711 Pacific Beach Dr. (at Mission Blvd.), San Diego, CA 92109. ☎ **800/787-3373** or 619/483-7070. Fax 619/274-1670. 52 units. TV TEL. June 15–Sept 15 $83–$122; winter $70–$93. Extra person $5. Weekly rates available off-season. AE, DC, MC, V. Free parking. Take I-5 to Grand/Garnet, then Grand Ave. to Mission Blvd.; turn left, then right onto Pacific Beach Dr. Bus: 34 or 34A.

Frankly, this property is looking pretty tired, but it's often booked solid during the summer because it offers moderately priced digs right on the boardwalk at the beach, as well as a heated pool. Most rooms in the four-story property have balconies and views and are cooled by ocean breezes, and many have kitchenettes. Hopefully management will consider sprucing the place up a bit, so it doesn't feel so haggard. On the premises is a coin-operated laundry. A popular restaurant serving three meals a day is adjacent.

INEXPENSIVE

Campland on the Bay. 2211 Pacific Beach Dr., San Diego, CA 92109-5699. ☎ **800/4-BAY-FUN** or 619/581-4260. Fax 619/581-4206. www. campland.com. 566 sites, most with hookup. Summer $25–$98 for up to 4 people; off-season $27–$68. Senior rates available. Weekly and monthly rates available off-season. Day use of facilities $5. MC, V. Take I-5 to Grand/Garnet exit, follow Grand to Olney and turn left; turn left again onto Pacific Beach Dr. Dogs accepted; $3 per day.

This bayside retreat is popular with a mixed crowd: RVers, campers (with or without vans), boaters, and their children and pets. At their fingertips are parks, a beach, a bird sanctuary, and a dog walk. Other facilities include pools, a Jacuzzi, catamaran and windsurfer rentals and lessons, bike and boat rentals, a game room, a cafe that serves three meals a day, a market, and a laundry. Planned activities include games and crafts for children; Sea World is 5 minutes away. Reserve popular spots at least six months in advance for spring and summer. The most desirable are the "Bayview" looking into the wildlife reserve. "Beachfront" sites are equally scenic, but noisy during the day.

Elsbree House. 5054 Narragansett Ave., San Diego, CA 92107. ☎ **619/226-4133.** www.oceanbeach-online.com/elsbree/b&b. 7 units. $95 double. 3-bedroom condo $1,250 per week. Room rate includes continental breakfast. MC, V. Bus: 35 or 23 to Narragansett Ave. and Cable St., 1½ blocks away. From airport, take Harbor Dr. west to Nimitz Blvd. to Lowell St., which becomes Narragansett Ave. Bus: 23, 35.

Katie and Phil Elsbree have turned this recently constructed Cape Cod–style building into an immaculate, exceedingly comfortable B&B half a block from the water's edge in Ocean Beach. One condo unit rents only by the week; the Elsbrees occupy another. Each of the six guest rooms has a patio or balcony. Guests share the cozy living room (with a fireplace and TV), breakfast room, and kitchen. Although other buildings on this tightly packed street block the ocean view, sounds of the surf and fresh sea breezes waft in open windows, and beautifully landscaped garden—complete with trickling fountain—runs the length of the house. This Ocean Beach neighborhood is eclectic, occupied by ocean-loving couples, dedicated surf bums, and a sometimes disturbing contingent of punk skater kids who congregate near the pier. Its strengths are proximity to the beach, a limited but pleasing selection of eateries that attract mostly locals, and some of the best antiquing in the city (along Newport Avenue).

5 La Jolla

Some consider La Jolla a jewel, and it's definitely the real thing, not a paste imitation. You'll have a hard time finding bargain accommodations in this upscale, conservative community, but you'll get proximity to a beautiful coastline, as well as a compact downtown village that makes for delightful strolling.

Most of our choices are downtown, with two below the cliffs right on the beach. Chain hotels farther afield include a **Hyatt Regency,** 3777 La Jolla Village Dr. (☎ **800/233-1234** or 858/552-1234). It's a glitzy place whose contemporary decor includes lots of marble—Michael Graves received an American Institute of Architects Onion Award, which recognizes architectural flops, for the design. The **Marriott Residence Inn,** 8901 Gilman Dr. (☎ **800/331-3131** or 858/587-1770), is a good choice for those who want a fully equipped kitchen and more space. Both are near the University of California, San Diego.

A note on driving directions: To reach the places listed here, use the Ardath Road exit from **I-5 north** or the La Jolla Village Drive west exit from **I-5 south,** then follow individual directions.

VERY EXPENSIVE

✪ **Colonial Inn.** 910 Prospect St. (between Fay and Girard), La Jolla, CA 92037. ☎ **800/826-1278** or 858/454-2181. Fax 858/454-5679. www.colonialinn.com. 75 units. TV TEL. $180 double with village view, $205–$275 double with ocean view; from $300 suite. Off-season discounts available. Children under 18 stay free in parents' room. AE, CB, DC, MC, V. Valet parking $7. Take Torrey Pines Rd. to Prospect Place and turn right. Prospect Place becomes Prospect St. Pets under 20 lbs. accepted.

Possessed of an old-world European flair that's more London or Georgetown than seaside La Jolla, the Colonial Inn has garnered accolades for the complete restoration of its polished mahogany paneling, brass fittings, and genteel library and lounge. Guest rooms are quiet and elegantly appointed, with beautiful draperies and traditional furnishings. The hotel is one block from the ocean. Guests who stay here instead of at the more expensive La Valencia, down the street, sacrifice air-conditioning for a ceiling fan, but gain elbow room (and save money). Numerous historic photos on the walls illustrate the inn's fascinating history; the reception desk has a printed sheet with more details of its beginnings as a full-service apartment hotel in 1913. Relics from the early days include oversized closets, meticulously tiled bathrooms, and heavy fire-proof doors suspended in the corridors. The guest rooms have amenities such as hair dryers and refrigerators; terry robes are available on request.

Dining/Diversions: Putnam's restaurant, a former drugstore, now features a popular bar in place of the soda fountain; the clubby dining room serves American and Continental cuisine. A large spray of fresh flowers is the focal point in the lounge, where guests gather in front of the fireplace for drinks.

Amenities: The outdoor heated pool, set in a landscaped garden, is open from sunup to sundown. Walking tours of La Jolla depart from the hotel (see chapter 6). Airport transportation is available for $9 one way. Room service, dry cleaning and laundry, turn-down service on request, baby-sitting, complimentary shoeshine, conference rooms.

✪ **La Valencia Hotel.** 1132 Prospect St. (at Herschel Ave.), La Jolla, CA 92037. ☎ **800/451-0772** or 858/454-0771. Fax 858/456-3921. 103 units. A/C MINIBAR TV TEL. $190–$240 standard double; $375–$400 full ocean-view double; from $475 suite. Extra person $15. AE, DC, DISC, MC, V. Valet parking $8. Take Torrey Pines Rd. to Prospect Place and turn right. Prospect Place becomes Prospect St.

It's not just La Valencia's distinctive pink stucco that brings to mind other gracious historic (and pink) hotels, like the Beverly Hills Hotel and Waikiki's Royal Hawaiian. Within its bougainvillea-draped walls and wrought-iron garden gates, this bastion of gentility does a fine job of resurrecting the elegance of its golden age, when celebrities like Greta Garbo and Charlie Chaplin vacationed alongside the world's moneyed elite. The cliff-top hotel has been the centerpiece of La Jolla since opening in 1926. Today, brides pose in front of the lobby's picture window (against a backdrop of La Jolla Cove and the Pacific), well-coifed ladies lunch in the dappled shade of the garden patio, and neighborhood cronies quaff libations in the clubby Whaling Bar, once a western Algonquin for literary inebriates. One chooses La Valencia for its history and unbeatably scenic location, but you won't be disappointed by the old-world standards of service and style. Rooms are lavishly furnished with rich fabrics and European antique reproductions, though some are on the dark side, and the 1920s bathrooms aren't huge. Rates vary wildly according to view. My advice is to get a cheaper room and enjoy the view from one of the many cozy lounges or serene garden terraces. Linens, towels, and bath accessories are of the finest quality, and rooms also have VCRs, for which you can rent videos.

Dining/Diversions: The elegant rooftop Sky Room serves French cuisine in an intimate setting; the Mediterranean Room and Tropical Patio serves California cuisine. There's also the legendary Whaling Bar & Grill (where Ginger Rogers and Charlton Heston once hung out) and adjoining Cafe La Rue.

Amenities: Outdoor heated pool, shuffleboard courts, Jacuzzi, concierge, 24-hour room service, dry cleaning and laundry, morning newspaper, nightly turn-down, in-room massage, baby-sitting, secretarial services, express checkout, small health club, sauna, access to tennis courts.

The Sea Lodge. 8110 Camino del Oro (at Avenida de la Playa), La Jolla, CA 92037. ☎ **800/237-5211** or 858/459-8271. Fax 858/456-9346. 128 units. A/C TV TEL. Mid-June to mid-Sept $189–$399 double, $429 suite; off-season $139–$269 double, $319–$329 suite. Children under 12 stay free in parents' room. Extra person $15. AE, DC, DISC, MC, V. Free covered parking. Take La Jolla Shores Dr., turn left onto Avenida de la Playa, turn right on Camino del Oro.

This three-story, 1960s hotel in a mainly residential enclave is under the same management as the La Jolla Beach & Tennis Club

La Jolla Accommodations & Dining

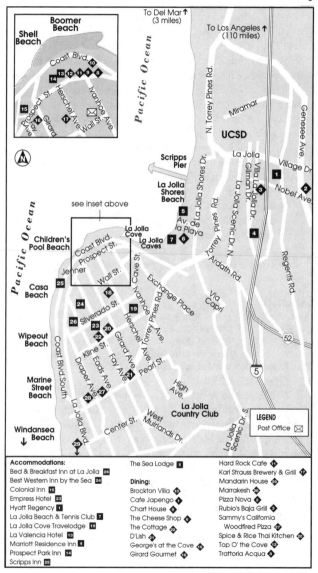

Accommodations:

Bed & Breakfast Inn at La Jolla 26
Best Western Inn by the Sea 24
Colonial Inn 15
Empress Hotel 23
Hyatt Regency 1
La Jolla Beach & Tennis Club 7
La Jolla Cove Travelodge 19
La Valencia Hotel 13
Marriott Residence Inn 4
Prospect Park Inn 14
Scripps Inn 25

The Sea Lodge 5

Dining:

Brockton Villa 10
Cafe Japengo 3
Chart House 9
The Cheese Shop 6
The Cottage 12
D'Lish 21
George's at the Cove 16
Girard Gourmet 18

Hard Rock Cafe 11
Karl Strauss Brewery & Grill 17
Mandarin House 20
Marrakesh 28
Pizza Nova 2
Rubio's Baja Grill 3
Sammy's California
   Woodfired Pizza 22
Spice & Rice Thai Kitchen 26
Top O' the Cove 12
Trattoria Acqua 8

next door. It has an identical on-the-sand location, minus the country club ambiance—there are no reciprocal privileges. Most rooms have some view of the ocean, and the rest look out on the pool or a tiled courtyard. From the Sea Lodge's beach you can gaze toward the top of the cliffs, where La Jolla's village hums with activity (and relentless traffic). The rooms are pretty basic, priced by view and size. Bathrooms feature separate dressing areas with large closets; and all rooms are outfitted with coffeemakers, refrigerators, hair dryers, irons, and ironing boards. Balconies or patios are standard, and some rooms have fully equipped kitchenettes. Like the "B&T," the Sea Lodge is popular with families but also attracts business travelers looking to balance meetings with time on the beach or the hotel's two tennis courts.

Dining: The unremarkable restaurant serves three meals a day; it's convenient, but there are better restaurants within walking distance in the surrounding neighborhood.

Amenities: Lighted tennis courts, heated outdoor pool with whirlpool and kids' pool, fitness room, laundry and dry cleaning, baby-sitting.

EXPENSIVE

The Bed & Breakfast Inn at La Jolla. 7753 Draper Ave. (near Prospect), La Jolla, CA 92037. ☎ **800/582-2466** or 858/456-2066. www.InnLaJolla.com. 15 units. A/C TEL. $109–$225 double; $250 suite. Rates include full breakfast and afternoon wine and cheese. Extra person $25. AE, MC, V. Take Torrey Pines Rd. to Prospect Place and turn right. Prospect Place becomes Prospect St.; proceed to Draper Ave. and turn left.

A 1913 Cubist house designed by prominent local architect Irving Gill—and once occupied by John Philip Sousa and his family—is the setting for this genteel and elegant B&B. Reconfigured for this purpose, the house has lost none of its charm, and appropriately unfrilly period furnishings add to the sense of history. The inn also features lovely enclosed gardens and a cozy library and sitting room. Fresh fruit, sherry, fresh-cut flowers, and terry robes await in every room, some of which feature a fireplace or ocean view. The furnishings are tasteful and cottage-style, with plenty of historic photos of La Jolla.

Dining: The gourmet breakfast is served wherever you desire—dining room, patio, sundeck, or in your room. Picnic baskets (extra charge) are available with a day's notice.

Empress Hotel of La Jolla. 7766 Fay Ave. (at Silverado), La Jolla, CA 92037. ☎ **888/369-9900** or 858/454-3001. Fax 858/454-6387. www.empress-hotel.com. 73 units. A/C TV TEL. $139–$199 double; $349 suite. Extra person

$10. Children under 18 stay free in parents' room. Rates include continental breakfast. Off-season and long-stay discounts available. AE, DC, DISC, MC, V. Valet parking $7. Take Torrey Pines Rd. to Girard Ave., turn right, then left on Silverado St.

The Empress Hotel offers spacious quarters with traditional furnishings a block or two from La Jolla's main drag and the ocean. It's quieter here than at the Colonial Inn or the Prospect Park Inn, and you'll sacrifice little other than direct ocean views. (Many rooms on the top floors afford a partial view.) If you're planning to explore La Jolla on foot, the Empress is a good base, and it exudes a classiness many comparably priced chains lack. Rooms are tastefully decorated (and frequently renovated), and equipped with refrigerators, hair dryers, coffeemakers, irons and ironing boards, and robes. Bathrooms are of average size but exceptionally well appointed, and four "Empress" rooms have sitting areas with full-size sleeper sofas.

Amenities: Room service, valet, laundry service, fitness room with spa and sauna. On nice days, breakfast is set up on a serene sundeck.

✪ **La Jolla Beach & Tennis Club.** 2000 Spindrift Dr., La Jolla, CA 92037. ☎ **800/624-CLUB** or 858/454-7126. Fax 858/456-3805. www.ljbtc.com. 90 units. TV TEL. Mid-June to mid-Sept $165–$289 double; from $229 suite. Off-season $129–$239 double; from $189 suite. Children under 12 stay free in parents' room. Extra person $20. AE, DC, MC, V. Take La Jolla Shores Dr., turn left on Paseo Dorado, and follow to Spindrift Dr.

Pack your best tennis whites for a stay at La Jolla's private "B&T" (as it's locally known), where CEOs and MDs come to relax and recreate. Surprisingly, rates for the club's overnight accommodations aren't that much higher than at the sister hotel next door, but the exclusive atmosphere and extensive amenities are far superior. Guest rooms are unexpectedly plain and frill-free, though they are equipped with hair dryers, coffeemakers, irons, and ironing boards. Most have well-stocked full kitchens that are ideal for families or longer stays. This historic property was founded in the 1920s, when original plans included constructing a private yacht harbor. Today, it's known primarily for tennis. The beach is popular here; the staff sets up comfy sand chairs and umbrellas, and races to supply club members and guests with fluffy towels, beverages, and snacks. Kayaks and water-sport equipment can be rented; there's even a sand croquet court. Surprisingly, there's no room service; besides the on-site dining options, several cozy neighborhood trattorias are two blocks away.

Dining: There's a casual dining room and seasonal beach hut, but don't leave without peeking into the distinctive Marine Room, where waves literally smash against the windows inches away from well-coifed diners. The menu is pricey, but for the price of a cocktail you can enjoy the same astounding view.

Amenities: 12 championship tennis courts and a tennis shop, 9-hole pitch-and-putt course that winds around a lagoon along the stately entry drive, jogging path, playground, table tennis, fitness room, elegant Olympic-size swimming pool, swim instruction, dry cleaning and laundry, turn-down service on request, baby-sitting, swim instruction, massage therapist, coin laundry.

Scripps Inn. 555 Coast Blvd. S. (at Cuvier), La Jolla, CA 92037. ☎ **858/454-3391.** Fax 858/456-0389. 14 units. TV TEL. Memorial Day–Labor Day $155–$200 double, $185–$300 suite; off-season $135–$155 double, $165–$200 suite. Extra person $10. Children under 5 stay free in parents' room. Weekly and monthly rates available off-season. Rates include continental breakfast. AE, DISC, MC, V. Free parking. Take Torrey Pines Rd., turn right on Prospect Place, veer right (downhill) onto Coast Blvd. If you miss the turn, drive through town and turn right at the museum.

It's not easy to find this meticulously maintained inn, tucked away behind the Museum of Contemporary Art, but you're rewarded with seclusion even though the attractions of La Jolla are just a short walk away. Only a small, grassy park comes between the inn and the beach, cliffs, and tide pools; the view from the second-story deck seems to hypnotize guests, who gaze out to sea indefinitely. Rates vary depending on ocean view (all have one, but some are better than others); aside from Room 14, currently being remade into an ultra-deluxe apartment, they're furnished in "early-American comfortable," with new bathroom fixtures and appointments. All rooms have fold-out sofas and refrigerators; two have wood-burning fireplaces, and four have kitchenettes. The inn supplies beach towels, firewood, and French pastries each morning. Repeat guests keep their favorite rooms for up to a month each year, so book ahead for the best choice.

MODERATE

Best Western Inn by the Sea. 7830 Fay Ave. (between Prospect and Silverado sts.), La Jolla, CA 92037. ☎ **800/462-9732,** 800/526-4545 in California and Canada, or 858/459-4461. Fax 858/456-2578. 132 units. A/C TV TEL. $129–$199 double; $175–$450 suite. Off-season discounts available. Rates include continental breakfast. AE, CB, DC, DISC, MC, V. Free parking. Take Torrey Pines Rd. to Prospect Place and turn right. Prospect Place becomes Prospect St.; proceed to Fay Ave. and turn left.

Occupying an enviable location at the heart of La Jolla's charming village, this independently managed property puts guests just a short walk from the cliffs and beach. The low-rise tops out at five stories, with the upper floors enjoying ocean views (and the highest room rates). The Best Western and the more formal Empress, a block away, offer a terrific alternative to pricier digs nearby. Rooms here are Best Western standard issue—freshly maintained, but nothing special. All rooms do have balconies, though, and refrigerators are available at no extra charge; other amenities include a heated pool and whirlpool, free daily newspaper and local phone calls, and room service from the attached IHOP.

Prospect Park Inn. 1110 Prospect St. (at Coast Blvd.), La Jolla, CA 92037. ☎ **800/433-1609** or 858/454-0133. Fax 858/454-2056. 23 units. A/C TV TEL. $120–$185 double; from $275 suite. Rates include continental breakfast and afternoon refreshments. Off-season discounts available. AE, CB, DC, DISC, JCB, MC, V. Free indoor parking ¹/₂ block away. Take Torrey Pines Rd. to Prospect Place and turn right. Prospect Place becomes Prospect St.

This place is a real gem. It's a small property, next door to La Valencia, that offers charming rooms, some with narrow ocean views. Built in 1947 as a boarding house for women, this spotless boutique hotel feels more European than Californian—it has a sparse but functional lobby, a stairway (there's no elevator in the three-story building), and an unexpected combination of frugality and comfort. Fresh fruit and beverages are offered in the library area every afternoon, and breakfast is served on the sundeck, which has a great ocean view. Prospect Park Inn enjoys essentially the same location as La Valencia and the Colonial Inn—the beach, park, shops, and restaurants are within steps—at much lower prices. Beach towels and chairs are provided free of charge for guests.

INEXPENSIVE

La Jolla Cove Travelodge. 1141 Silverado St. (at Herschel Ave.), La Jolla, CA 92037. ☎ **800/578-7878** or 858/454-0791. Fax 858/459-8534. 30 units. A/C TV TEL. $59–$98 double (subject to availability). AE, DC, MC, V. AARP and AAA discounts available. Free off-street parking. Take Torrey Pines Rd. and turn right on Herschel Ave.

While the name is deceptive—the Cove is a 10-minute walk away—this motel is a good value in tony La Jolla. Fitting in with the village's retro feel, the exterior seems unchanged from the 1940s; though rooms have been diligently updated, no one will thrill to the basic motel decor, which features cinder-block walls and small, basic bathrooms. But somehow, the place seems less dreary because it's surrounded by the glamour of La Jolla. Rooms have coffeemakers; some have kitchenettes and microwaves. Management provides the daily newspaper. There isn't a pool, but there is a modest sundeck on the third floor with a view of the ocean, which is about three-quarters of a mile away.

6 Coronado

The "island" (really a peninsula) of Coronado is a great escape. It offers quiet, architecturally rich streets; a small-town, navy-oriented atmosphere, and laid-back vacationing on one of the state's most beautiful and welcoming beaches. Choose a hotel on the ocean side for a view of Point Loma and the Pacific, or stay facing the city for a spectacular skyline vista (especially at night). You may feel pleasantly isolated here, so it isn't your best choice if you're planning to spend lots of time in more central parts of the city.

A note on driving directions: To reach the places listed here, take I-5 to the Coronado Bridge, then follow individual directions. If you have a passenger, stay in the far right lanes to avoid paying the bridge toll.

VERY EXPENSIVE

Coronado Island Marriott Resort. 2000 Second St. (at Glorietta Blvd.), Coronado, CA 92118. ☎ **800/228-9290** or 619/435-3000. Fax 619/435-3032. http://marriotthotels.com/SANCI. 300 units. A/C MINIBAR TV TEL. $195–$325 double; from $395 suite; from $495 villa. Children under 12 stay free in parents' room. Packages available. AE, CB, DC, MC, V. Valet parking $15; self-parking $11. From Coronado Bridge, turn right onto Glorietta Blvd., take first right to hotel. Bus: 901. Ferry: from Broadway Pier.

We're happy to see the new management (Marriott International Inc.) fulfilling its promise to get this former Le Meridien back to high-end status. Elegance and luxury here are understated—without a lot of flash, guests just seem to get whatever they need, be it a lift downtown (by water taxi from the private dock), a tee time at the neighboring golf course, or a prime appointment at the property's spa.

Enduring appeals of the property remain: Its waterfront location, view of the San Diego skyline (but within easy distance of Coronado shopping and dining); casual, airy architecture; lushly planted grounds filled with preening exotic birds; and a wealth of sporting and recreational activities. Guest rooms are generously sized and attractively furnished—actually *decorated*—in colorful French country style; they feature balconies or patios, coffeemakers, hair dryers, and irons, and ironing boards. The superbly designed bathrooms hold an array of toiletries and plush bathrobes. Watch this low-key, comfortable Marriott give competitor Loews a run for its money.

Coronado Accommodations & Dining

Accommodations:
Coronado Inn **13**
Coronado Island Marriott
  Resort **17**
El Cordova Hotel **6**
Glorietta Bay Inn **3**
Hotel del Coronado **4**
Loews Coronado Bay Resort **1**
The Village Inn **8**

Dining:
Azzura Point ◆
Bay Beach Cafe **15**
The Brigantine **16**
Chameleon Cafe/
  Lizard Lounge ◆
Chart House ◆
Chez Loma ◆

Kensington Coffee Co. **14**
Miguel's Cocina ◆
Peohe's ◆
Primavera Pastry Caffé **11**
Primavera Ristorante **12**
Prince of Wales Grill ◆
Rhinoceros Cafe & Grill ◆

Dining/Diversions: L'Escale, a Mediterranean brasserie, serves breakfast, lunch, and dinner. The hotel's cocktail lounge is worth a visit for its jazzy, moody ambiance.

Amenities: Sporting a new contemporary image, the Spa intends to be Marriott's main attraction; clients can choose from Swiss beauty treatments, Hawaiian and Asian holistic therapies, and expanded fitness, yoga, and tennis programs. Other features include three outdoor heated pools (including a lap pool), two outdoor whirlpools, six lighted tennis courts, bicycle rental, water sports, a jogging trail and bike path, concierge, 24-hour room service, laundry, valet, turn-down service, baby-sitting, business center, complimentary shuttle to Horton Plaza, airport shuttle ($9 each way).

Glorietta Bay Inn. 1630 Glorietta Blvd. (near Orange Ave.), Coronado, CA 92118. ☎ **800/283-9383** or 619/435-3101. Fax 619/435-6182. www. gloriettabayinn.com. 100 units. A/C TV TEL. Mansion $225–$245 double, $275–$425 suite; annex $135–$225 double, from $245 suite. Children under 19 stay free in parents' room. Extra person $10. Rates include continental breakfast. AE, MC, V. Free parking. From Coronado Bridge, turn left on Orange Ave. After 2 miles, turn left onto Glorietta Blvd.; inn is across the street from the Hotel del Coronado.

Right across the street and somewhat in the (figurative) shadow of the Hotel del Coronado, this pretty white hotel consists of the charmingly historic John D. Spreckels mansion (1908) and two younger, motel-style buildings. Only 11 rooms are in the mansion, which boasts original fixtures, a grand staircase, and old-fashioned wicker furniture; the guest rooms are also decked out in antiques, and have a romantic and nostalgic ambiance.

Rooms in the modern annexes are less expensive but much plainer. All units are equipped with refrigerators, coffeemakers, in-room movies, and hair dryers; some have kitchenettes. Wherever your room is, you'll gather for breakfast on the main house's sunny veranda. In addition to offering rental bikes and boat rentals on Glorietta Bay across the street, the hotel is within easy walking distance of the beach, golf, tennis, water sports, shopping, and dining. Rooms in the mansion get booked early, but are worth the extra effort and expense.

Dining: Only continental breakfast is available.

Amenities: Heated swimming pool, whirlpool, in-room movies, laundry and dry cleaning, baby-sitting, coin laundry.

✪ **Hotel del Coronado.** 1500 Orange Ave., Coronado, CA 92118. ☎ **800/468-3533** or 619/435-8000. Fax 619/522-8238. www.hoteldel.com. 700 units. MINIBAR TV TEL. From $200 standard; from $245 deluxe; from $330 ocean view; from $435 oceanfront; from $500 suite. Packages available. Children under 18 stay free in parents' room. AE, CB, DC, DISC, MC, V. Valet parking $16; self-parking $12. From Coronado Bridge, turn left onto Orange Ave. Bus: 901. Ferry: from Broadway Pier.

Opened in 1888 and designated a National Historic Landmark in 1977, the "Hotel Del," as it's affectionately known, is the last of California's grand old seaside hotels. Legend has it that the Duke of Windsor met his duchess here, and Marilyn Monroe frolicked around the hotel in *Some Like It Hot*. This monument to Victorian grandeur boasts tall cupolas, red turrets, and gingerbread trim, all spread out over 26 acres. Rooms run the gamut from compact to extravagant, and all are packed with antique charm; most have custom-made furnishings. The best rooms have balconies fronting the ocean and large windows that take in one of the city's finest white-sand beaches. If you're a stickler for detail, ask to stay in the original building rather than in the contemporary tower additions.

During the shelf life of this guide—and probably the next edition, too—the hotel will be undergoing painstaking restoration. Purists will rejoice to hear that historical accuracy is paramount; as the infrastructure is upgraded, public spaces and Victorian wing rooms are being returned to their turn-of-the-century splendor. Inquire when you book, so you can avoid construction areas, enjoy vintage rooms before they're worked on, or take advantage of just-completed improvements. Even if you don't stay here, don't miss a stroll through the grand, wood-paneled lobby or along the pristine wide beach.

Dining/Diversions: The hotel has nine dining areas; the most charming is the Prince of Wales Grill, newly remodeled from a dark, clubby room to a golden-hued salon with ocean views. The upscale menu puts a Pacific Rim twist on Continental favorites. The sunny, breezy Ocean Terrace offers alfresco bistro fare; cocktails and afternoon tea are served in the wood-paneled lobby and adjoining conservatory lounge. There's music and dancing nightly, ranging from quiet piano tinkling to amplified dance music.

Amenities: Two outdoor pools, whirlpools, massage, six tennis courts, bicycle rental, concierge, 24-hour room service, turn-down service, laundry and dry cleaning, valet, baby-sitting, beauty salon and spa, limousine service, guided tours of the hotel (they're fun), 24-hour deli, children's activities, airport shuttle ($10), shopping arcade, signature shop with appealing logo items.

✪ **Loews Coronado Bay Resort.** 4000 Coronado Bay Rd., Coronado, CA 92118. ☎ **800/81-LOEWS** or 619/424-4000. Fax 619/424-4400. 437 units. A/C MINIBAR TV TEL. $235–$285 double; from $425 suite. Children under 18 stay free in parents' room. Packages available. AE, CB, DC, DISC, MC, V. Valet parking $14; covered self-parking $12. From Coronado Bridge, go left onto Orange Avenue, continue 8 miles down Silver Strand Hwy. Turn left at Coronado Bay Rd., entrance to the resort. Pets under 25 lbs. accepted.

This luxury resort opened in 1991 on a secluded 15-acre peninsula, slightly removed from downtown Coronado and San Diego. It's perfect for those who prefer a self-contained resort in a get-away-from-it-all location, and is surprisingly successful in appealing to business travelers, convention groups, vacationing families, and romance-minded couples. All units offer terraces that look onto the hotel's private 80-slip marina, the Coronado Bay Bridge, or San Diego Bay. A private pedestrian underpass leads to nearby Silver Strand Beach. Rooms boast finely appointed marble bathrooms, plus VCRs, for which you can rent videos. At press time Loews was in the midst of refurnishing the guest rooms, which had become far too outdated and worn for a hotel of this caliber.

Dining: Azzura Point, facing the San Diego skyline, has Mediterranean decor and sophisticated California-Mediterranean cuisine. There's also a casual cafe, lobby lounge, poolside bar and grill, and specialty food market.

Amenities: A highlight here is The Gondola Company (☎ **619/429-6317**), which offers romantic and fun gondola cruises through the canals of tony Coronado Cays. The seasonal Commodore Kids Club, for children 4 to 12, offers supervised half-day, full-day, and evening programs with meals. Other features include three outdoor swimming pools; a fitness center with saunas and whirlpools; five lighted tennis courts and a pro shop; bicycle, skate, and water-sports rentals; concierge; 24-hour room service; laundry/valet; newspaper delivery; turn-down service; in-room massage; baby-sitting; business center; fax machines in suites; car-rental desk; beauty salon.

MODERATE

El Cordova Hotel. 1351 Orange Ave. (at Adella Ave.), Coronado, CA 92118. ☎ **800/229-2032** or 619/435-4131. Fax 619/435-0632. 40 units. TV TEL. $95 double; $115–$125 studio with kitchen; $145–$185 1-bedroom suite; $220–$295 2-bedroom suite. Children under 12 stay free in parents' room. Weekly and monthly rates available off-season. AE, DC, DISC, MC, V. No off-street parking. From Coronado Bridge, turn left onto Orange Ave. Parking available on street.

This Spanish hacienda across the street from the Hotel del Coronado began life as a private mansion in 1902. By the 1930s it had become a hotel, the original building augmented by a series of attachments housing retail shops along the ground-floor arcade. Shaped like a baseball diamond and surrounding a courtyard with meandering tiled pathways, flowering shrubs, a swimming pool, and patio seating for Miguel's Cocina Mexican restaurant, El Cordova hums pleasantly with activity.

Each room is a little different from the next—some sport a Mexican colonial ambiance, while others evoke a comfy beach cottage. All feature ceiling fans and brightly tiled bathrooms, but lack the frills that command exorbitant rates. El Cordova has a particularly inviting aura, and its prime location makes it a popular option; I advise reserving several months in advance, especially for the summer.

Facilities include a heated pool, barbecue area with a picnic table, and a laundry room.

INEXPENSIVE

Coronado Inn. 266 Orange Ave. (corner of 3rd St.), Coronado, CA 92118. ☎ 800/598-6624 or 619/435-4121. www.coronadoinn.com. 30 units (most with shower only). A/C TV TEL. Memorial Day through Labor Day $98–$125 up to 4 people; winter $85–$110. Rates include continental breakfast. Discounts available. AE, MC, V. Free parking. From Coronado Bridge, stay on 3rd St. Pets accepted; $10 per night.

Well-located and terrifically priced, this renovated 1940s courtyard motel has such a friendly ambiance; it's like staying with old friends. Iced tea, lemonade, and fresh fruit are even provided poolside on summer days. It's still a motel, though—albeit with brand-new paint and fresh tropical floral decor—so rooms are pretty basic. The six rooms with bathtubs also have small kitchens. There are laundry facilities on the property, and refrigerators and microwaves are available. Rooms close to the street are noisiest, so ask for one toward the back. The Coronado shuttle stops a block away; it serves the shopping areas and Hotel Del.

The Village Inn. 1017 Park Place (at Orange Ave.), Coronado, CA 92118. ☎ 619/435-9318. 14 units. Summer $90–$95 double; winter and weekly rates available. Rates include continental breakfast. AE, MC, V. Parking available on street. From Coronado Bridge, turn left onto Orange Ave., then right on Park Place.

Its location a block or two from Coronado's main sights—the Hotel Del, the beach, shopping, and cafes—is this inn's most appealing feature. Historic charm runs a close second; a plaque outside identifies the three-story brick-and-stucco hotel as the once-chic Blue Lantern Inn, built in 1926. The charming vintage lobby sets the mood in this European-style hostelry; each simple but well-maintained room holds antique dressers and armoires, plus lovely Battenberg lace bedcovers and shams. Front rooms enjoy the best view, and coffee and tea are available all day in the kitchen where breakfast is served. The appealing inn's only Achilles' heel is tiny, tiny bathrooms, so cramped that you almost have to stand on the toilet to use the small-scale sinks. Surprisingly, some have been updated with whirlpool tubs.

7 Near the Airport

San Diego's airport has the unusual distinction of being virtually *in* downtown. While locals grouse about the noise and decreased property values, it's good news for travelers: Most of the accommodations in the "Downtown," "Hillcrest," and "Old Town" (including Hotel Circle) neighborhoods are only 5 to 10 minutes from the airport.

For those who must stay as close as possible to the airport, there are two good choices literally across the street. The 1,045-room **Sheraton San Diego Hotel and Marina,** 1380 Harbor Island Dr. (☎ **800/325-3535** or 619/291-2900), offers rooms from $150 to $280. At the 208-room **Travelodge Hotel–Harbor Island,** 1960 Harbor Island Dr. (☎ **800/255-3050** or 619/291-6700), rooms go for $129 to $149. Both hotels offer marina views, a health club, a pool, and proximity to downtown San Diego.

5

Dining

*T*he city's dining scene, once a bastion of rich continental and heavy American cuisine, has come into its own during the past decade. The explosion of a transplant population and the diversification of San Diego neighborhoods have sparked a new spirit of experimentation and style. An improved economy helped, too, motivating folks to step out and exercise their palates. The restaurant scene races to keep up with current trends and desires. One positive sign is that the culinary bible, the *Zagat Survey,* now publishes an edition exclusively for San Diego and its environs.

San Diego offers terrific seafood, far more so than in the equally oceanfront Los Angeles, for example. Whether at unembellished market-style restaurants that let freshness take center stage or at upscale restaurants that feature extravagant presentations, the ocean's bounty is everywhere.

Those traditional mainstays, American and Continental cuisine, are (metaphorically speaking) still carrying their share of the weight in San Diego. But, with increasing regularity, they're mating with lighter, more contemporary, often ethnic styles. The movement is akin to the eclectic "fusion" cuisine that burst onto the scene in the early 1990s. That's not to say traditionalists will be disappointed— San Diego still has the most clubby steak-and-potatoes stalwarts on the West Coast.

If you love Italian food, you're in luck. Not only does San Diego boast a strong contingent of old-fashioned Sicilian-style choices, but these days you can't turn a corner without running into a trattoria. The Gaslamp Quarter corners the market, with upscale Northern Italian bistros on virtually every block. Hillcrest, La Jolla, and other neighborhoods also boast their fair share. They cater mostly to locals, and their menus usually include gourmet pizzas baked in wood-fired ovens, a trend that shows no signs of slowing down (see "Only in San Diego," at the end of this chapter).

Ethnic foods are rising in popularity even as this book is being written. Number 1 on everyone's list of favorites is Mexican—a logical choice given the city's history and location. You'll find lots of

A Note on Smoking

In January 1998, California law made it illegal to smoke in all restaurants and bars, except in outdoor seating. Almost immediately,
opponents scrambled to appeal the legislation, so the situation may
have changed by the time you visit—be sure to inquire before you
light up.

highly Americanized fare along with a few hidden jewels, like
Palenque and Berta's, that serve true south-of-the-border cuisine.
The most authentic Mexican food may be the humble fish taco (see
"Only in San Diego," at the end of this chapter). The Baja import,
faithfully re-created by Rubio's, has become San Diego's favorite fast
food. Asian cuisine runs a close second, with Thai and Vietnamese
restaurants starting to catch up with Chinese and Japanese. Many
intrepid chefs fuse Asian ingredients and preparations with more
familiar Mediterranean or French menus, and sushi bars are on the
rise.

For diners on a budget, the more expensive San Diego restaurants
are accommodating if you want to order a few appetizers instead of
a main course, and many offer more reasonably priced lunch menus.
Dress tends to be pretty casual, even in pricey places; some notable
exceptions are La Jolla's more expensive restaurants and the hotels
on Coronado, where jeans are a no-no and gentlemen generally wear
jackets.

A note on parking: Unless a listing specifies otherwise, drivers can
expect to park within 2 or 3 blocks of the restaurants listed here. If
you can't find a free or metered space on the street, you can seek out
a garage or lot (see "Parking" under Getting Around in chapter 3).

1 Restaurants by Cuisine

AMERICAN

Bay Beach Cafe (Coro-
    nado, *M*)
Chart House (Coronado, La
    Jolla, *E*)
Corvette Diner (Hillcrest/
    Uptown, *I*)

Croce's Restaurant &
    Nightclubs (Down-
    town, *E*)
Dakota Grill and Spirits
    (Downtown, *M*)
Firehouse Beach Cafe (Pacific
    Beach, *I*)

Key to abbreviations: *E* = Expensive; *M* = Moderate; *I* = Inexpensive

The Green Flash (Pacific Beach, *M*)
Hard Rock Cafe (La Jolla, *I*)
Hob Nob Hill (Hillcrest/ Uptown, *M*)
Kansas City Barbecue (Downtown, *I*)
Karl Strauss Brewery & Grill (Downtown, La Jolla, *M*)
Kono's Surf Club (Pacific Beach, *I*)
Rhinoceros Cafe & Grill (Coronado, *M*)

BREAKFAST

The Cottage (La Jolla, *I*)
Brockton Villa (La Jolla, *I*)
Café Lulu (Downtown, *I*)
Hob Nob Hill (Hillcrest/ Uptown, *M*)
Kono's Surf Club (Pacific Beach, *I*)
The Mission (Pacific Beach, *I*)
Old Town Mexican Cafe (Old Town, *I*)
Primavera Pastry Caffé (Coronado, *I*)

CALIFORNIA

Azzura Point (Coronado, *E*)
Brockton Villa (La Jolla, *M*)
Cafe Pacifica (Old Town, *E*)
California Cuisine (Hillcrest/Uptown, *E*)
The Cottage (La Jolla, *I*)

D'Lish (La Jolla, *I*)
George's at the Cove (La Jolla, *E*)
George's Ocean Terrace and Cafe/Bar (La Jolla, *M*)
Mixx (Hillcrest/Uptown, *M*)
Prince of Wales Grill (Coronado, *E*)
Qwiig's (Ocean Beach, *E*)
Wolfgang Puck Cafe (Mission Valley, *M*)

CHINESE

Mandarin House (Hillcrest, Pacific Beach, La Jolla, *I*)
Panda Inn (Downtown, *M*)

COFFEE & TEA

Garden House Coffee & Tea (Old Town, *I*)
The Mission (Pacific Beach, *I*)
Newbreak Coffee Co. (Hillcrest/Uptown, Ocean Beach, *I*)

CONTINENTAL

Thee Bungalow (Ocean Beach, *E*)
Top O' the Cove (La Jolla, *E*)

DESSERTS

Extraordinary Desserts (Hillcrest/Uptown, *I*)

ECLECTIC

Chameleon Cafe & Lizard Lounge (Coronado, *I*)

Croce's Restaurant & Nightclubs (Downtown, *E*)

ENGLISH

Princess Pub & Grille (Downtown, *I*)

FRENCH

Cafe Eleven (Hillcrest, *M*)
Chez Loma (Coronado, *E*)
Laurel (Hillcrest/Uptown, *E*)
Liaison (Hillcrest/Uptown, *M*)
Thee Bungalow (Ocean Beach, *E*)

INTERNATIONAL

The Mission (Pacific Beach, *I*)
Mixx (Hillcrest/Uptown, *M*)

ITALIAN

D'Lish (La Jolla, *I*)
Filippi's Pizza Grotto (Downtown, Pacific Beach, and other locations, *I*)
Fio's (Downtown, *E*)
Old Spaghetti Factory (Downtown, *I*)
Osteria Panevino (Downtown, *M*)
Primavera Ristorante (Coronado, *E*)
Trattoria Acqua (La Jolla, *E*)

JAPANESE/SUSHI

Cafe Japengo (La Jolla, *E*)
Ichiban (Hillcrest/Uptown, *I*)
Sushi Ota (Mission Bay, *M*)

LATIN AMERICAN

Berta's Latin American Restaurant (Old Town, *M*)

LIGHT FARE

Bread & Cie. Bakery and Cafe (Hillcrest/Uptown, *I*)
Kensington Coffee Company (Coronado, *I*)
Newbreak Coffee Co. (Hillcrest/Uptown, Ocean Beach, *I*)
Primavera Pastry Caffé (Coronado, *I*)

MEDITERRANEAN

Bread & Cie. Bakery and Cafe (Hillcrest/Uptown, *I*)
Laurel (Hillcrest/Uptown, *E*)

MEXICAN

Casa de Bandini (Old Town, *M*)
Casa de Pico (Old Town, *I*)
Old Town Mexican Cafe (Old Town, *I*)
Miguel's Cocina (Coronado, *M*)
Palenque (Pacific Beach, *I*)

MOROCCAN

Marrakesh (La Jolla, *E*)

PACIFIC RIM

Azzura Point (Coronado, *E*)
Cafe Japengo (La Jolla, *E*)
Peohe's (Coronado, *E*)

SEAFOOD

Anthony's Star of the Sea Room (Downtown, *E*)

Bay Beach Cafe (Coronado, *M*)

Brigantine Seafood Grill (Old Town, Coronado, *E*)

The Fish Market/Top of the Market (Downtown, *E*)

Peohe's (Coronado, *E*)

SOUTHWESTERN

Croce's Restaurant & Nightclubs (Downtown, *E*)

Dakota Grill and Spirits (Downtown, *M*)

THAI

Celadon (Hillcrest/ Uptown, *M*)

Spice & Rice Thai Kitchen (La Jolla, *M*)

VEGETARIAN

Café Lulu (Downtown, *I*)

The Vegetarian Zone (Hillcrest/ Uptown, *I*)

2 Downtown

Downtown dining tends to be more formal than elsewhere, because of the business clientele and evening theater- and opera-goers. Once the domain of high-priced and highfalutin Continental and American restaurants, downtown was turned on its ear when chic spots began filling the Gaslamp Quarter's restored Victorian buildings. If you stroll down Fifth Avenue between E Street and K Street, you'll find a month's worth of restaurants, all packed with a hip local crowd. The Embarcadero, a stretch of waterfront along the bay, is also home to several great eating spots, all of which capitalize on their bay views.

Note: To locate these restaurants, please see the "Downtown San Diego Accommodations & Dining" map on page 37.

EXPENSIVE

Anthony's Star of the Sea Room. Harbor Dr. and Ash St. ☎ **619/ 232-7408.** Reservations required. Jacket and tie suggested. Main courses $16.50–$32.50. AE, CB, DC, MC, V. Daily 5:30–10:30pm. Closed major holidays. Valet parking $4. Bus: 2. Trolley: America Plaza or Seaport Village. SEAFOOD.

An institution since 1965, Anthony's specializes in service, style, and seafood—all superbly delivered under the attentive eye of manager and maître d' Mario Valerio, who has been with the restaurant since it opened. The "newest" waiter has worked here for more than 25 years. The restaurant is set over the water on pilings, and its arched window wall and raised booths ensure that all diners can enjoy the view. Candles glow and crystal glistens, setting the stage for white-gloved and silver-domed-platter service that seems pretentious for all but the most special occasions. Popular appetizers are clams Genovese tossed with béchamel sauce and topped with Parmesan cheese, and lobster scampi della casa. Other seafood dishes that get top billing are baked sole à l'admiral (stuffed with lobster, shrimp, and crab) and swordfish, both prepared for two. Come with a hearty appetite—portions are quite large.

✪ **Croce's Restaurants & Nightclubs.** 802 Fifth Ave. (at F St.). ☎ **619/233-4355.** www.croces.com. Reservations not accepted; call for same-day "priority seating" (before walk-ins). Main courses $14–$23. AE, DC, DISC, MC, V. Daily 5pm–midnight. Valet parking $6 with validation. Bus: 3, 5, 16, or 25. Trolley: Gaslamp Quarter. AMERICAN/SOUTHWESTERN/ECLECTIC.

Ingrid Croce, widow of singer-songwriter Jim, was instrumental in the resurgence of the once-decayed Gaslamp Quarter, and her establishment has expanded to fill every corner of this 1890 Romanesque building. Croce's is the primary restaurant, featuring a menu that fuses Southern soul food and Southwestern spice with Asian flavors and Continental standards. Croce's West is more casual in ambiance, but not in price; the menu is virtually identical save for a few more Southwestern touches (a jalapeño here, an avocado there). Add the raucous Top Hat Bar & Grille and the intimate Jazz Bar, and the complex is the hottest ticket in town, with crowds lining up for dinner tables and nightclub shows.

An evening in the Gaslamp Quarter isn't complete without at least strolling by the Croce's corner; expect a festive good time any night of the week. Those who dine at the full-service restaurants can enter the two nightspots (see chapter 8 for a full listing) without paying the cover charge.

✪ **Fio's.** 801 Fifth Ave. (at F St.). ☎ **619/234-3467.** www.fioscucina.com. Reservations recommended for dinner. Main courses $11–$25. AE, DC, DISC, MC, V. Mon–Thurs 5–10:30pm, Fri–Sat 5–11pm, Sun 5–10pm. Valet parking $6 with validation. Bus: 3, 5, 16, or 25. Trolley: Gaslamp Quarter. NORTHERN ITALIAN.

Fio's has been *the* spot to see and be seen in the Gaslamp Quarter since it opened, and it's the granddaddy of the new wave of trendy Italian restaurants. Set in an 1881 Italianate Victorian that once housed chic Marston's department store, Fio's has a sophisticated ambiance and is *always* crowded. Once cutting-edge, the upscale trattoria menu is now practiced and consistently superior. It features jet-black linguini tossed with the freshest seafood, delicate angel hair pasta perfectly balanced with basil and pine nuts, and gourmet pizzas served at regular tables and the special pizza bar. The menu pleases both light eaters (with antipasti and pastas) and heartier palates— the impressive list of meat entrees includes mustard-rosemary rack of lamb, veal shank on saffron risotto, and delicately sweet hazelnut-crusted pork loin with Frangelico and peaches. If you stop by without a reservation, you can sit at the elegant cocktail bar and order from the complete menu.

The Fish Market/Top of the Market. 750 N. Harbor Dr. ☎ **619/232-FISH** (Fish Market), or 619/234-4TOP (Top of the Market). www.thefishmarket.com. Reservations not accepted at the Fish Market, recommended for Top of the Market. Main courses $9–$25 (Fish Market); $15–$32 (Top of the Market). AE, CB, DC, DISC, MC, V. Daily 11am–10pm. Valet parking $4. Bus: 7/7B. Trolley: Seaport Village. SEAFOOD.

The red building perched on the end of the G Street Pier at the Embarcadero houses two of San Diego's most popular seafood restaurants: The Fish Market and its pricier cousin, Top of the Market. Both offer superb fresh seafood and menus that change daily. The chalkboard out front tells you what's freshest, be it Mississippi catfish, Maine lobster, Canadian salmon, or Mexican yellowtail. The ground-level Fish Market, a market and casual restaurant, has oyster and sushi bars and a cocktail lounge. Upstairs, the elegant Top of the Market looks like a private club, with teakwood touches, mounted fish trophies, and historic photographs. The panoramic view encompasses the bay, the Coronado Bay Bridge, and, sometimes, aircraft carriers (the restaurant provides binoculars). Besides seafood, you can order homemade pasta and choose from a wine list as extensive as the menu. This lofty place inspires some to dress up and make a reservation, but you can also drop by just to have a drink and enjoy the view. Outdoor seating is directly above the water. You can spend a moderate amount downstairs, and a lot more upstairs.

There is another Fish Market Restaurant in **Del Mar** at 640 Via de la Valle (☎ **858/755-2277**).

MODERATE

Dakota Grill and Spirits. 901 Fifth Ave. (at E St.). ☎ **619/234-5554.** Reservations recommended. Main courses $9–$18. AE, DC, DISC, MC, V. Mon–Fri 11:30am–2:30pm; Mon–Thurs 5–10pm, Fri–Sat 5–11pm, Sun 5–9pm. Valet parking (after 5pm) $5; self-parking in the area $7. Bus: 3, 5, 16, or 25. Trolley: Gaslamp Quarter. AMERICAN/SOUTHWESTERN.

This downtown business lunch favorite is always busy and noisy; the Southwestern cowboy kitsch matches the cuisine but can be a little too theme-y for some. Little pistols on the menu indicate the most popular items, which include shrimp tasso (sautéed with Cajun ham and sweet peas in ancho chili cream), spit-roasted chicken with orange chipotle glaze or Dakota barbecue sauce, and mixed grill served with roasted garlic and grilled red potatoes. When the kitchen is on, Dakota's innovation makes it one of San Diego's best, but an occasional dud results from the overzealous combination of too many disparate ingredients. Still, it's not losing any ground as one of the Gaslamp Quarter's star eateries, and the raucous, casual atmosphere fits the lively cuisine. A pianist plays weekend nights.

Karl Strauss Downtown Brewery & Grill. 1157 Columbia St. (between B and C sts.). ☎ **619/234-BREW** (2739). Main courses $7–$15. MC, V. Sun–Wed 11:30am–10pm (beer and wine until 11pm), Thurs–Sat 11:30am–midnight (beer and wine until 1am). Bus: 5. Trolley: America Plaza. AMERICAN.

Brewmaster Karl Strauss put San Diego on the microbrewery map with this unpretentious factory setting. The smell of hops and malt wafts throughout, and the stainless-steel tanks are visible from the bar. Brews, all on tap, range from pale ale to amber lager. Five-ounce samplers are 85¢ each; if you like what you taste, 12-ounce glasses, pints, and hefty schooners stand chilled and ready. There's also non-alcoholic beer, and wine by the glass. Accompaniments include Cajun fries, hamburgers, German sausage with sauerkraut, fish-and-chips, and other greasy bar food, but that's secondary to the stylish suds. Beer-related memorabilia and brewery tours are available.

Osteria Panevino. 722 Fifth Ave. (between F and G sts.). ☎ **619/595-7959.** Reservations recommended. Main courses $9–$21. AE, CB, DC, DISC, MC, V. Sun–Thurs 11:30am–10pm, Fri–Sat 11:30am–11:30pm. Valet parking $6. Bus: 3, 5, 16, or 25. Trolley: Gaslamp Quarter. ITALIAN.

Expertly prepared, intricate dishes set Osteria Panevino apart from the Gaslamp Quarter's ubiquitous trattorias. The setting is welcoming, a New York–like space with bare brick walls and a small sidewalk-seating area. The unselfconscious atmosphere belies the sophistication of the menu, which peaks with homemade pastas in rich, complex sauces. Antipasti are so satisfying that they are almost minimeals; I recommend mozzarella wrapped in prosciutto and baked over sautéed spinach, or filet mignon carpaccio topped with hearts of palm, avocado, goat cheese, and olive oil. Fish and meat entrees are equally enticing, bathed in rich reduction sauces and

Where to Find Theme Restaurants

San Diego's branch of **Planet Hollywood,** 197 Horton Plaza, corner of Broadway and 5th Avenue (☎ 619/702-STAR), is in the heart of the Gaslamp Quarter, downtown. There's nearly always a line of folks waiting to eat here and ogle the movie memorabilia; the staff regularly pacifies diners with free movie posters and theater passes.

There's also a **Hard Rock Cafe,** at 909 Prospect St., La Jolla (☎ 858/454-5101). Replete with rock 'n' roll memorabilia and great burgers, this branch defers to conservative La Jolla by *not* mounting its trademark Caddy on the roof.

---

accented with inventive flavors. A good wine list is made better with special themed trios of 2-ounce tastings. Sometimes the hostess, clad in evening gown and heels, warmly greets passersby from the doorway like a high-class circus barker. The atmosphere is cozy or crowded, depending on how close you like to be to your fellow diners.

✪ **Panda Inn.** Horton Plaza (top floor). ☎ **619/233-7800.** Reservations recommended. Main courses $8–$18. AE, DC, DISC, JCB, MC, V. Sun–Thurs 11am–10pm, Fri–Sat 11am–10:30pm. Trolley: American Plaza. CHINESE.

Circus-like Horton Plaza holds many restaurants, but this stylish, upscale choice is on the opposite end of the spectrum from your average Hot-Dog-on-a-Stick. Its elegant interior—decorated with modern art and Chinese pottery—matches the gourmet selection of Mandarin and Szechuan dishes. Standouts include lemon scallops, honey-walnut shrimp, and enoki-mushroom chicken. The dining room has a view of the city skyline, and the lounge area has a full bar. Some will find the location convenient for shopping and movie-going, while others will be irritated at dealing with parking and the crowded shopping mall maze—Panda Inn is really one of San Diego's best, though.

INEXPENSIVE

✪ **Café Lulu.** 419 F St. (near Fourth Ave.). ☎ **619/238-0114.** Main courses $3–$7. No credit cards. Sun–Thurs 9am–2am, Fri and Sat 9am–4am. Bus: 3, 5, 16, or 25. Trolley: Gaslamp Quarter. VEGETARIAN.

Smack-dab in the heart of the Gaslamp Quarter, Café Lulu aims for a hip, Bohemian mood despite its location half a block from commercial Horton Plaza. Ostensibly a coffee bar, the cafe makes a terrific choice for casual dining; if the stylishly metallic interior is too harsh for you, watch the street action from a sidewalk table. The food is health-conscious, prepared with organic ingredients and no meat. Soups, salads, cheese melts, and veggie lasagne are on the menu; breads come from the incomparable Bread & Cie., uptown (see the entry later in this chapter). Eggs, granola, and waffles are served in the morning, but anytime is the right time to try one of the inventive coffee drinks, like cafe Bohème (mocha with almond syrup) or cafe L'amour (iced latte with a hazelnut tinge). Beer and wine are also served.

✪ **Filippi's Pizza Grotto.** 1747 India St. (between Date and Fir sts.), Little Italy. ☎ **619/232-5095.** Fax 619/695-8591. Main courses $4.75–$12.50. AE, DC, DISC, MC, V. Sun–Thurs 11am–10pm, Fri–Sat 11am–11pm. Free parking. Bus: 5. Trolley: County Center/Little Italy. ITALIAN.

Think Little Italy, and this is the picture that comes to mind. To get to the dining area, decorated with Chianti bottles and red-checked tablecloths, you walk through an Italian grocery store and deli strewn with cheeses, pastas, wines, bottles of olive oil, and salamis. You might even end up eating behind shelves of canned olives, but don't feel bad—this has been a tradition since 1950. The intoxicating smell of pizza wafts into the street; Filippi's has more than 15 varieties (including vegetarian), plus Old World spaghetti, lasagne, and other pasta. Children's portions are available, and kids will feel right at home.

The original of a dozen branches, this Filippi's has free parking; other locations include 962 Garnet Ave., Pacific Beach (☎ **619/483-6222**); Kearny Mesa; East Mission Valley; and Escondido.

Kansas City Barbecue. 610 W. Market St. ☎ **619/231-9680.** Reservations accepted only for parties of 8 or more. Main courses $8.75–$11.50. MC, V. Daily 11am–1am. Trolley: Seaport Village. AMERICAN.

Kansas City Barbecue's honky-tonk mystique was fueled by its appearance as the fly-boy hangout in the movie *Top Gun.* Posters from the film share wall space with county-fair memorabilia, old Kansas car tags, and a photograph of official "bar wench" Carry Nation. This homey dive is right next to the railroad tracks and across from the tony Hyatt Regency. The spicy barbecue ribs, chicken, and hot links are slow-cooked over an open fire and served with sliced Wonder bread and your choice of coleslaw, beans, fries, onion rings, potato salad, or corn on the cob. The food is okay, but the atmosphere is the real draw.

Old Spaghetti Factory. 275 Fifth Ave. (at K St.). ☎ **619/233-4323.** Main courses $4.25–$8.10. DISC, MC, V. Mon– Fri 11:30am–2pm and 5–10pm, Sat– Sun noon–10pm. Bus: 1. Trolley: Gaslamp Quarter. ITALIAN.

It's lively, it's family-friendly, and it's a great deal—no wonder folks are always waiting for tables. The menu is basic spaghetti-and-meatball fare; for the price of a main course, you also get salad, sourdough bread, ice cream, and coffee or tea (with refills). Table wines are available by the glass or decanter. Part of a chain that always has creative settings; the restaurant is in a former printing factory, with some tables enclosed in a 1917 trolley car. The decor is lavish early bordello—fun for adults and stimulating for kids, who can frolic in the small play area.

Princess Pub & Grille. 1665 India St. (at Date St.). ☎ **619/702-3021.** www.princesspub.com. Main courses $6–$11. DISC, MC, V. Daily 11:30am–1am. Bus: 5. Trolley: Santa Fe Depot. ENGLISH.

This local haunt is great for Anglophiles and others hungry for a ploughman's plate, Cornish pasty, steak-and-kidney pie, fish-and-chips, or bangers in hefty portions. Formerly known as the Princess of Wales, the bar still has photos and commemorative plates of Princess Diana hanging everywhere, along with flags from England, a well-worn dartboard, and a photo of the Queen Mother downing a pint. You can usually find a copy of the *Union Jack* (a newspaper published in the United States for British expats), too. Among the English beers available are Bass, Fuller's, and Watney's. For a taste of Ireland, order a Guinness; the Princess also serves hard Devon cider. Friday and Saturday nights are particularly busy.

3 Hillcrest/Uptown

Hillcrest and the other fashionable uptown neighborhoods are jam-packed with great food for any palate (and any wallet). Some are old standbys filled nightly with loyal regulars; others are cutting-edge experiments that might be gone next year. Ethnic food, French food, health-conscious bistro fare, retro comfort food, specialty cafes and bakeries, California cuisine (as in the restaurant of the same name)—they're all done with the panache you'd expect in the trendiest part of town.

EXPENSIVE

California Cuisine. 1027 University Ave. (east of 10th St.). ☎ **619/543-0790.** Reservations recommended for dinner. Main courses $13–$20; 3-course theater menu (daily 5–7pm) $20. AE, DISC, MC, V. Tues–Fri 11am–10pm, Sat–Sun 5–10pm. Bus: 8, 11, 16, or 25. CALIFORNIA.

While this excellent restaurant's name is no longer as cutting-edge as when it opened in the early '80s, the always-creative menu keeps up with contemporary trends. A quiet, understated dining room and delightfully romantic patio set the stage as the smoothly professional and respectful staff proffers fine dining at moderate prices to a casual crowd.

The menu changes daily and contains mouth-watering appetizers like sesame-seared ahi with hot-and-sour raspberry sauce, or caramelized onion and Gruyère tart on balsamic baby greens. Main courses are, more often than not, stacked in trendy towers, and their flavors are composed with equal care: Blackened beef tenderloin sits atop sun-dried mashed potatoes surrounded by bright tomato puree, and Chilean sea bass is poached in saffron broth with tangy capers and buttery Yukon Gold potatoes. Early birds and bargain seekers will appreciate the theater menu, which is a great deal. Parking can be scarce along this busy stretch of University. You'll spot the light-strewn bushes in front of the restaurant.

✪ **Laurel.** 505 Laurel St. (at Fifth Ave.). ☎ **619/239-2222.** Reservations recommended. Main courses $15–$22. AE, CB, DC, DISC, JCB, MC, V. Sun–Thurs 5–10pm, Fri–Sat 5–11pm. Valet parking $4. Bus: 1, 3, or 25. FRENCH/MEDITERRANEAN.

Given its sophisticated decor, pedigreed chefs, prime Balboa Park location, and well-composed menu of country French dishes with a Mediterranean accent, it's no wonder this relatively new restaurant was an instant success. It's also popular with theater-goers, offering shuttle service to the Old Globe followed by an after-performance dessert. Live piano music adds to the glamour of dining in this swank room on the ground floor of a new office building. Start by choosing from an extensive selection of tantalizing appetizers, including saffron-tinged red pepper–and–shellfish soup, veal sweetbreads with portabella mushrooms and grainy mustard sauce, and warm caramelized onion and Roquefort tart. Main courses include crisp Muscovy duck confit, roasted salmon with tangy red-beet vinaigrette, and venison in a rich shallot–port wine sauce. One of the most stylish choices near often-funky Hillcrest, Laurel has an almost New York ambiance coupled with moderate prices.

MODERATE

Celadon. 3628 Fifth Ave. (between Brookes and Pennsylvania aves.). ☎ **619/295-8800.** Reservations recommended. Main courses $8–$15. AE, MC, V. Mon–Fri 11:30am–2pm; Mon–Sat 5–10pm. Bus: 1, 3, or 25. THAI.

Celadon fills a niche with moderately priced yet elegant dining. When it opened in the mid-'80s, this sleek, modern eatery was a pioneer, bringing gourmet Thai to a city unfamiliar with the cuisine. Because the restaurant is still known for beautifully prepared and presented dishes, it seems unfair to grouse about the dated mauve decor. Specialties include shrimp in spicy, creamy coconut sauce; sautéed scallops in "burnt" sauce with a touch of garlic; *mee krob,* caramelized noodles with chicken and shrimp; and vegetarian pad Thai with deep-fried tofu. Appetizers range from sweet and savory to hot and spicy; a favorite is Bangkok summer salad, composed of roasted pork with cilantro, mint, and lime juice.

Hob Nob Hill. 2271 First Ave. (at Juniper St.). ☎ **619/239-8176.** Breakfast and lunch menu items $3.25–$8.55; dinner main courses $8–$14. AE, DC, DISC, MC, V. Daily 7am–9pm. Bus: 1, 3, or 25. AMERICAN.

This homey coffee shop and deli began as a 14-stool lunch counter in 1944, and has grown into one of the most popular neighborhood hangouts in the city. At any given time it's a sure bet no patron lives farther than 5 miles away; this is no "destination" restaurant. You'll find comfort food at its best, priced reasonably enough for many regulars to dine here more often than in their own homes. The career waitresses are accustomed to plenty of hobnobbing professionals conducting power breakfasts over beef hash, oatmeal with pecans, or fried eggs with thick, hickory-smoked bacon. Stick-to-your-ribs meals appear at lunch and dinner—old favorites like chicken and dumplings, roast turkey, prime rib, or liver grilled with onions. It's a great place to bring the kids, especially on Sunday, when many local families observe a multigeneration dinner tradition.

Liaison. 2202 Fourth Ave. (at Ivy St.). ☎ **619/234-5540.** Main courses $10.75–$19.75; fixed-price dinner $46 per couple. AE, CB, DC, DISC, MC, V. Tues–Sun 5–10:30pm. Bus: 1, 3, or 25. FRENCH.

The cuisine and decor at this cozy, inviting cafe evoke a Gallic farmhouse kitchen. It has stone walls, blue-and-white tablecloths, candlelit tables, and copper pots hanging from the rafters. Conveniently located for Balboa Park theatergoers, this fave has a hearty French country menu that includes lamb curry, medallions of pork or beef, coquilles St. Jacques, roast duckling à l'orange, salmon with crayfish butter, and more. The nightly fixed price dinner—pâté, soup, salad, main course, dessert, and wine for two—is a great deal. The house specialty dessert costs extra: a Grand Marnier chocolate or amaretto soufflé for two, at $5 per person. Ooh la la!

Mixx. 3671 Fifth Ave. (at Pennsylvania Ave.). ☎ **619/299-6499.** Reservations recommended, especially on weekends. Main courses $11–$19. AE, CB, DC, DISC, MC, V. Sun–Thurs 5–10pm, Fri–Sat 5–11pm. Bus: 1, 3, or 25. CALIFORNIA/INTERNATIONAL.

Aptly named for its subtle global fusion fare, Mixx embodies everything good about Hillcrest dining: an attractive, relaxing room; a sophisticated crowd; thoughtfully composed dinners; and polished, friendly service. It's easy to see why hip locals gravitate to Mixx's wood-paneled street-level cocktail lounge and the often-jovial dining room above. Menu standouts include a starter of pepper-seared ahi over ginger-jicama slaw, duck and wild mushroom ravioli, and pepper filet mignon on truffle mashed potatoes with an armagnac, cream, and port wine reduction. Even carnivores should check out chef Josh McGinnis' surprisingly inventive nightly vegetarian special. Prepared, plated, and presented with finesse, one meal here will quickly convince you that Mixx cares about style, substance, *and* value. Allow time to search for that elusive Hillcrest parking space!

INEXPENSIVE

✪ **Bread & Cie. Bakery and Cafe.** 350 University Ave. (between Third and Fourth sts.). ☎ **619/683-9322.** Sandwiches and light meals $3–$6. No credit cards. Mon–Fri 7am–7pm, Sat 7am–6pm, Sun 8am–6pm. Bus: 8, 11, or 16. LIGHT FARE/MEDITERRANEAN.

Delicious aromas permeate this cavernous Hillcrest bakery, where the city's most unusually flavored breads are baked before your eyes all day long. The traditions of European artisan bread-making and attention to the fine points of texture and crust quickly catapulted Bread & Cie. to local stardom. Mouthwatering favorites include anise and fig, black olive, *panella dell'uva* (grape bread), and rye currant (weekends only). Even the relatively plain sourdough batard is tart, chewy perfection. Ask for a free sample, or order one of the many Mediterranean-inspired sandwiches on the bread of your choice. Try tuna niçoise on potato dill; mozzarella, roasted peppers, and olive tapenade on rosemary olive oil; or roast turkey with hot pepper cheese on jalapeño. The specialty coffee drinks make a perfect accompaniment to a light breakfast of fresh scones, muffins, and fruit turnovers. Seating is at bistro-style metal tables in full view of the busy ovens.

Corvette Diner. 3946 Fifth Ave. (between Washington St. and University Ave.). ☎ **619/542-1001.** Reservations not accepted. Main courses $4.50–$9.95. AE, DC, DISC, MC, V. Sun–Thurs 11am–10pm, Fri–Sat 11am–midnight. Valet parking free weekdays, $4 evening and weekend. Bus: 1, 3, or 25. AMERICAN.

Time travel back into the rockin' '50s at this theme diner, where the jukebox is loud, the gum-snapping waitresses slide into your booth to take your order, and the decor is vintage Corvette to the highest power. Equal parts *Happy Days* hangout and Jackrabbit Slim's (from *Pulp Fiction*), the Corvette Diner is a comfy time warp in the midst of trendy Hillcrest, and the eats ain't bad, either. Burgers, sandwiches, appetizer munchies, blue-plate specials, and salads share the menu with a *very* full page of fountain favorites. Beer and wine are served, and there's a large bar in the center of the cavernous dining room. The party jumps a notch at night, with DJs and even a magician providing more entertainment (on top of the already entertaining atmosphere).

✪ **Extraordinary Desserts.** 2929 Fifth Ave. (between Palm and Quince sts.). ☎ **619/294-7001.** Desserts $2–$6. MC, V. Mon–Thurs 8:30am–11pm, Fri 8:30am–midnight, Sat 11am–midnight, Sun 2–11pm. Bus: 1, 3, or 25. DESSERTS.

If you're a lover of sweets—heck, if you've ever eaten a dessert at all—you owe it to yourself to visit this unique cafe. Chef and proprietor Karen Krasne's name features prominently on the sign, as well it should: Krasne's talent surpasses the promise of her impressive pedigree, which includes a *Certificate de Patisserie* from Le Cordon Bleu in Paris. Dozens of divine creations are available daily, and even the humble carrot cake is savory enough to wow naysayers. Others include a raspberry linzer torte layered with white-chocolate buttercream; Grand Marnier chocolate cheesecake on a brownie crust, sealed with bittersweet ganache; and 24-karat chocolate praline dacquoise—crunchy chocolate praline mousse balanced by Frangelico-soaked hazelnut meringues and coated with dark chocolate and gold leaf. Originally educated in Hawaii, Krasne likes to incorporate island touches like macadamia nuts, ultra-fresh coconut, passion fruit, and pure Kona coffee. Her Parisian experience is also represented; the shop sells tea and accoutrements from the fine salon Mariage Frères. If you're trying to moderate your diet, eat at The Vegetarian Zone next door (see below)—it helps justify dessert!

Mandarin House. 2604 Fifth Ave. (at Maple St.). ☎ **619/232-1101.** Reservations recommended. Most main courses $6.50–$10. AE, DC, MC, V. Mon–Sat 11am–10pm, Sun 2–10pm. Bus: 1, 3, or 25. CHINESE.

Practiced Mandarin and Szechuan fare at reasonable prices is the prevailing theme of this Hillcrest mainstay, the bulk of whose business is local takeout. The dining room is comfortable, quiet, and softly lit; I'd gladly trade the bland pastel decor, though, for the kitschy red lacquer–and–dragon style usually associated with the classic Chinese restaurant. It would certainly be in keeping with the ornate Polynesian cocktails Mandarin House serves in specialty glasses (hula girls, Buddhas, and so forth); sweet and not too potent, they're a bargain at $3.75. The comprehensive menu probably contains your favorite dish—there are several show-stopping sizzling platters, and a nice selection of meat-free choices. Anything marked hot and spicy can have its heat turned down (or up) a notch according to taste. While vegetable and chicken dishes are evenly good, those featuring beef or pork don't always use the best grade of meat.

Mandarin House also has locations in La Jolla, at 6765 La Jolla Blvd. (☎ **858/454-2555**), and Pacific Beach, at 1820 Garnet Ave. (☎ **619/273-2288**).

Newbreak Coffee Co. 523 University Ave. ☎ **619/295-1600.** Menu items $1.25–$5. No credit cards. Mon–Thurs 6am–11pm, Fri 6am–midnight, Sat 7am–midnight, Sun 7am–11pm. Bus: 1 or 3. COFFEE & TEA/LIGHT FARE.

It changes ownership—and names—too often to keep track, but this centrally located coffeehouse is essential to the Hillcrest scene. Ocean Beach's Newbreak Coffee Company recently took over from the San Diego coffee gurus Pannikin, but changed little else. The large, casual main lounge is strewn with newspapers and people at leisure, enjoying Newbreak's gourmet bagel spreads, light sandwiches, scones, sweets, and coffee fresh from the in-store roaster. Those seeking solitude can be found nestled in the cozy upstairs lounge, and even busy Hillcrest residents stop in for freshly ground coffee sold by the pound.

There's a branch in Ocean Beach, at 1830 Sunset Cliffs Blvd. (☎ **619/226-4471**).

✪ **The Vegetarian Zone.** 2949 Fifth Ave. (between Palm and Quince sts.). ☎ **619/298-7302**, or 619/298-9232 for deli and takeout. Reservations not accepted. Main courses $5–$10. AE, DC, DISC, MC, V. Mon–Thurs 11:30am–9pm, Fri 11:30am–10pm, Sat 8:30am–10pm, Sun 8:30am–9pm; deli, daily 10am–9pm. Free parking. Bus: 1, 3, or 25. VEGETARIAN.

San Diego's only strictly vegetarian restaurant is a real treat, and word has gotten around—it's nearly always crowded, and everyone knows about it. Even if you're wary of tempeh, tofu, and meat substitutes, there are plenty of veggie ethnic selections on the menu. Greek spinach-and-feta pie has crispy edges and buttery phyllo layers; Indian turnovers are sweet and savory, flavored with pumpkin and curry; and the Mediterranean roasted-vegetable sandwich is accented with smoky mozzarella cheese. If you're ordering salad, don't miss the tangy miso-ginger dressing. In business since 1975, the Vegetarian Zone has opened a deli next door. There's seating indoors and on a casual patio; soothing music creates a pleasant ambiance enjoyed by trendy Hillcrest types, business lunchers, and the health-conscious from all walks of life. Wine is served by the glass. In case you feel deserving of a treat after such a healthful meal, the heavenly Extraordinary Desserts (see above) is next door.

4 Old Town

Visitors usually have at least one meal in the Old Town area. San Diego's oldest historic district is also its most touristy, and most restaurants here follow suit—Mexican food and bathtub-size margaritas are the big draw, as are mariachi music and colorful decor. For a change of pace, try Cafe Pacifica or Berta's; the Garden House also offers a pleasant respite.

EXPENSIVE

Brigantine Seafood Grill. 2444 San Diego Ave. ☎ **619/298-9840.** Reservations recommended on weekends. Main courses $7.95–$29.95; early-bird special (Sun–Thurs 5–7pm) $10–$14. AE, CB, DC, MC, V. Mon–Thurs 11am–10:30pm, Fri–Sat 11am–11pm, Sun 10am–10:30pm. Bus: 5/5A. Trolley: Old Town. SEAFOOD.

The Brigantine is best known for its oyster-bar happy hour from 4 to 7pm (until 9:30pm on Mondays). Beer, margaritas, and food are heavily discounted, and you can expect standing room only. Early-bird dinners include seafood, steak, or chicken served with several side dishes and bread. The food is good but not great; it's above average for a chain, but the congenial atmosphere seems the primary draw. Inside, the decor is upscale and nautical; outside, there's a pleasant patio with a fireplace to take the chill off the night air. At lunch, you can get everything from crabcakes or fish-and-chips to fresh fish or pasta. Lunch specials come with sourdough bread and two side dishes. The bar and oyster bar are open daily until midnight.

There's also a Brigantine Seafood Grill on Coronado, at 1333 Orange Ave. (☎ **619/435-4166**).

Cafe Pacifica. 2414 San Diego Ave. ☎ **619/291-6666.** www.cafe pacifica. com. Reservations recommended. Main courses $12–$22. AE, CB, DC, DISC, MC, V. Mon–Sat 5:30–10pm, Sun 5–9:30pm. Valet parking $4. Bus: 5/5A. Trolley: Old Town. CALIFORNIA.

You can't tell a book by its cover: Inside this cozy Old Town casita, the decor is cleanly contemporary (but still romantic) and the food anything but Mexican. Established in 1980 by the now revered duo of Kipp Downing and Deacon Brown, Cafe Pacifica serves upscale, imaginative seafood and produces kitchen alumni who go on to enjoy local fame. Among the temptations on the menu are crab-stuffed portabella mushroom topped with grilled asparagus, anise-scented bouillabaisse, and daily fresh-fish selections served grilled with your choice of five sauces. Signature items include Hawaiian ahi with shiitake mushrooms and ginger butter, griddled mustard catfish, and the "Pomerita," a pomegranate margarita. Patrons tend to dress up, though it's not required. To avoid the crowds, arrive in the early evening.

MODERATE

✪ **Berta's Latin American Restaurant.** 3928 Twiggs St. (at Congress St.). ☎ **619/295-2343.** Main courses $5–$7 at lunch, $11–$13 at dinner. AE, MC, V. Daily 11am–10pm (lunch menu till 3pm). Bus: 5/5A. Trolley: Old Town. LATIN AMERICAN.

Berta's is a welcome change from the nacho-and-fajita joints that dominate Old Town dining, though it can attract large a crowd on weekends. Housed in a charming, basic cottage tucked away on a side street, Berta's faithfully re-creates the sunny flavors of Central America, where slow cooking mellows the heat of chiles and other spices. Everyone starts with a basket of fresh flour tortillas and mild salsa verde, which usually vanishes before you're done contemplating such mouthwatering dishes as Guatemalan *chilimal*, a rich pork-and-vegetable casserole with chiles, tomatoes, cornmeal masa, coriander, and cloves. Try the Salvadoran *pupusas* (at lunch only)— dense corn-mash turnovers with melted cheese and black beans, their texture perfectly offset with crunchy cabbage salad and one of Berta's special salsas. Or opt for a table full of Spanish-style *tapas*, grazing alternately on crispy empanadas (filled turnovers), strong Spanish olives, or *Pincho Moruno*, skewered lamb and onion redolent of spices and red saffron.

Casa de Bandini. 2754 Calhoun St. (opposite Old Town Plaza). ☎ **619/297-8211.** Reservations not accepted. Main courses $6–$15. AE, CB, DC, DISC, MC, V. Daily 11am–9pm (till 10pm in summer). Free parking. Bus: 5/5A. Trolley: Old Town. MEXICAN.

As much an Old Town tradition as the mariachi music that's played here on weekends, Casa de Bandini is the most picturesque of several Mexican restaurants with predictable food and birdbath-size margaritas. It fills the nooks and crannies of an adobe hacienda built in 1823 for Juan Bandini, a local merchant and politician. The superbly renovated enclosed patio has iron gates, flowers blooming around a bubbling fountain, and umbrella-shaded tables for year-round alfresco dining. Some of the dishes are gourmet Mexican, others simple south-of-the-border fare. The crowd consists mainly of out-of-towners, but the ambiance and towering tostada salads draw a lunchtime crowd. The setting makes this restaurant extra-special, and makes it worth a mediocre meal.

Casa de Pico. 2754 Calhoun St. ☎ **619/296-3267.** Reservations not accepted. Main courses $5–$14. AE, DC, MC, V. Sun–Thurs 10am–9pm, Fri–Sat 10am–9:30pm. Free parking. Bus: 5/5A. Trolley: Old Town. MEXICAN.

The heartbeat of Bazaar del Mundo, Casa de Pico has a carnival atmosphere and a colorful courtyard complete with fountain, flags, umbrellas, and mariachis who will serenade your table on request. The restaurant sits on the original site of the home of General Pío Pico, the last governor of Mexican California. Diagrammed explanations of Mexican dishes on the menu are a tip-off to the touristy element, but plenty of visitors are eager to dine at the heart of Old Town's historic center. A selection of bodacious margaritas helps keep things lively. The menu holds no surprises to anyone familiar with enchiladas, tacos, and burritos; a popular selection is the Mexican sampler, "La Especial de Juan," with chimichangas, enchiladas, and fajitas. To avoid standing in line for a table, try coming here before 5pm or after 8pm Sunday through Thursday.

INEXPENSIVE

Garden House Coffee & Tea. 2480 San Diego Ave. ☎ **619/220-0723.** Menu items $1–$3. No credit cards. Mon–Thurs 7am–6pm, Fri–Sat 7am–9pm, Sun 7am–7:30pm (shorter hours in winter). Bus: 5/5A. Trolley: Old Town. COFFEE & TEA.

Set off San Diego Avenue along a brick walkway beside the Whaley House, this gourmet shop in an old wooden cottage is always good for a cup of fresh-brewed coffee (any variation or size). You get 10¢ off if you bring your own cup the way the locals do; refills are half price. Muffins and pastries are also available. While it's mostly a takeout place, there are a few chairs on the porch, and some benches nearby. This is a great place to rest in the shade of the wizened pepper trees. It's next to the Old Town Drug Store Museum.

✪ **Old Town Mexican Cafe.** 2489 San Diego Ave. ☎ **619/297-4330.** Reservations accepted only for parties of 10 or more. Main courses $7.50–$11.50.

AE, DISC, MC, V. Sun–Thurs 7am–11pm, Fri–Sat 7am–midnight; bar service until 2am. Bus: 5/5A. Trolley: Old Town. MEXICAN.

This place is so popular that it's become an Old Town tourist attraction in its own right. It keeps expanding into additional colorful dining rooms and outdoor patios, but the wait for a table is still often 30 to 60 minutes. Pass the time gazing in from the sidewalk as tortillas are hand-patted the old-fashioned way, soon to be a hot-off-the-grill treat accompanying every meal. Once inside, order what some consider the best margarita in town, followed by one of the cafe's two specialties: carnitas, the traditional Mexican dish of deep-fried pork served with tortillas, guacamole, sour cream, beans, and rice; or rotisserie chicken with the same trimmings. It's loud and crowded and the *cerveza* flows like, well, beer, but this Old Town mainstay is best in the city for traditional Mexican.

5 Mission Bay & the Beaches

Generally speaking, restaurants at the beach exist primarily to provide an excuse for sitting and gazing at the water. Because this activity is most commonly accompanied by steady drinking, it stands to reason that the food isn't often remarkable. We've tried to balance the most scenic of these typical hangouts with places actually known for outstanding food—with a little effort, they can be found.

Note: To locate these restaurants, please see the "Accommodations & Dining in Mission Bay & the Beaches" map on page 53.

EXPENSIVE

Thee Bungalow. 4996 W. Point Loma Blvd. (at Bacon St.), Ocean Beach. ☎ **619/224-2884.** www.theebungalow.com. Reservations recommended. Main courses $14–$23; early-bird specials $10–$13. AE, DC, DISC, MC, V. Mon–Thurs 5:30–9:30pm, Fri–Sat 5–10pm, Sun 5–9pm. Free parking. Bus: 26 or 34B. FRENCH/CONTINENTAL.

This small cottage stands alone at the edge of Robb Field near the Ocean Beach channel, a romantic hideaway beckoning diners for consistently good Continental cuisine augmented by a well-chosen, well-priced wine list. By far the fanciest restaurant in laid-back Ocean Beach, Thee Bungalow endears itself to the local crowd with daily early-bird specials ($10–$13). The house specialty is crispy roast duck, served with your choice of sauce (the best are black cherry or spiced pepper rum), ideally followed by one of the decadent, made-to-order dessert soufflés for two (chocolate or Grand Marnier). Another menu standout is *osso buco*–style lamb shank adorned with shallot–red-wine puree. Equally appealing first courses include brie and asparagus baked in puff pastry, and warm chicken salad (stuffed with sun-dried tomatoes and basil, then presented with feta cheese and fruit, it also doubles as a light meal). There's always a sampler plate featuring house-made pâtés with Dijon, cornichons, capers, and little toasts.

Qwiig's. 5083 Santa Monica St. (at Abbott St.), Ocean Beach. ☎ **619/ 222-1101.** Reservations suggested. Main courses $12–$21. AE, MC, V. Mon– Fri 11:30am–9pm, Sat 5–10pm, Sun 5–9pm. Bus: 23 or 35. CALIFORNIA.

It's taken more than a sunset view overlooking the Ocean Beach Pier to keep this upscale bar and grill going since 1985; the restaurant owes its consistent popularity to first-rate food served without pretense. Every table faces the sea, but the best view is from slightly elevated crescent-shaped booths (ask for one when reserving). Even the after-work crowd that gathers at the bar to munch on fried calamari, artichokes, and oysters can see to the pier; only sushi bar patrons in the corner miss out on the view.

Large and welcoming, Qwiig's hums pleasantly with conversation and serves food that's better than any other view-intense oceanfront spot in this area. The fresh-fish specials are most popular—choices often include rare ahi with braised spinach and sesame-sherry sauce, and Chilean sea bass with lime, tequila, and roasted garlic. Several seafood pastas are offered. Meat and poultry dishes include prime rib, an outstanding $1/2$-pound burger, and nightly specials that always shine. Wines are well matched to the cuisine, and there are imaginative special cocktails each night. The restaurant got its strange name from a group of Ocean Beach surfers nicknamed "qwiigs."

MODERATE

The Green Flash. 701 Thomas Ave. (at Mission Blvd.), Pacific Beach. ☎ **619/ 270-7715.** Reservations recommended. Main courses $10–$20; sunset specials Sun–Thurs 4:30–7pm. AE, CB, DC, DISC, MC, V. Mon–Thurs 8am–9:30pm, Fri 8am–10pm, Sat 7:30am–10pm, Sun 7:30am–9:30pm. Bus: 34/34A. AMERICAN.

Known throughout Pacific Beach for its location and hip, local clientele, the Green Flash serves reasonably good (and typically beachy) food at decent prices. The menu includes plenty of grilled and deep-fried seafood, straightforward steaks, and giant main-course salads. You'll also find platters of shellfish (oysters, clams, shrimp) and ethnic appetizers. On the glassed-in patio, locals congregate every evening to catch a glimpse of the optical phenomenon for which this boardwalk hangout is named. It has something to do with the color spectrum at the moment the sun disappears below the horizon, but the scientific explanation becomes less important—and the decibel level rises—with every round of drinks.

✪ **Palenque.** 1653 Garnet Ave. (at Jewell St.), Pacific Beach. ☎ **619/ 272-7816.** Reservations not accepted. Main courses $4–$8 at lunch, $9–$15 at dinner. AE, MC, V. Daily 11:30am–2:30pm; Sun–Thurs 5–9pm, Fri–Sat 5–10pm. Bus: 27. MEXICAN.

Often described as a hole-in-the-wall and a hidden treasure, this casual, family-run restaurant is both—and well worth the search. Behind a foliage-laden fence on busy Garnet Avenue, Palenque has a pleasant outdoor patio and casual dining room where piñatas and paper birds dangle from the thatched, skylit ceiling. You'll start with crispy chips accompanied by two homemade salsas whose fresh perfection is representative of every dish on the menu. From earthy *mole* sauce (the best in San Diego) and freshly patted corn tortillas to carafes of refreshing lemonade, everything tastes as if it was lovingly prepared by your Mexican grandma. Drawing on regional traditions from Mexico's interior, the menu features a long list of unique appetizers that are good for sharing, plus exceptionally good layered enchiladas. At dinner, meats like *tinga poblano* (pork flavored with chipotle peppers), beef *panile* (with peanut-pasilla chile sauce), and chicken *mole poblano* are served platter-style with tortillas and all the fixings. Some dishes pack quite a spicy kick.

✪ **Sushi Ota.** 4529 Mission Bay Dr. (at Bunker Hill), Mission Bay. ☎ **619/ 270-5670.** Reservations recommended on weekends. Main courses $8–$15; sushi $2.50–$8. AE, MC, V. Tues–Fri 11:30am–2pm; daily 5:30–10:30pm. JAPANESE.

If you like statistics, you should know that chef-owner Yukito Ota's masterful sushi garnered a nearly perfect food rating in the San Diego *Zagat Survey*. This sophisticated, traditional restaurant (no Asian fusion here) is a minimalist bento box with stark white walls and black furniture, softened by indirect lighting. The sushi menu is short, because savvy regulars look first to the 8 to 10 daily specials posted behind the counter. The city's most experienced chefs, armed with nimble fingers and very sharp knives, turn the day's fresh catch into artful little bundles accented with mounds of wasabi and ginger. The rest of the varied menu features seafood, teriyaki-glazed meats, feather-light tempura, and a variety of small appetizers perfect to accompany a large sushi order.

This restaurant is difficult to find, mainly because it's hard to believe that such outstanding dining would hide behind a Laundromat and convenience store in the rear of a mini-mall that's perpendicular to the street. It's also in a nondescript part of Pacific

Beach, nearer to I-5 than the ocean, but none of that should discourage you from seeking it out.

INEXPENSIVE

Firehouse Beach Cafe. 722 Grand Ave., Pacific Beach. ☎ **619/272-1999.** Reservations recommended on weekends. Main courses $6–$13. AE, DISC, MC, V. Sun–Thurs 7am–9pm, Fri–Sat 7am–10pm. Free parking. Bus: 34/34A. AMERICAN.

Ceiling fans stir the air in this cheerful, comfortably crowded place, and there's pleasant rooftop dining with an ocean view if you're lucky enough to snag a seat. Just off the Pacific Beach boardwalk, the cafe sees a lot of foot traffic and socializing locals. Those in the know go for great breakfasts—choices include Mexican-style eggs and breakfast burritos, French toast, and omelets. During happy hour (4 to 6pm), you'll find bargain prices on drinks and finger-lickin' appetizers. The rest of the menu is adequate, running the gamut from fish tacos to Tex-Mex fajitas to lasagne and all-American burgers.

The Mission. 3795 Mission Blvd. (between Pacific Beach Dr. and Mission Bay Way), Mission Beach. ☎ **619/488-9060.** Menu items $4.50–$8. AE, MC, V. Mon–Fri 7am–3pm, Sat–Sun 7am–4pm. Bus: 27, 34, 34A, or 34B. COFFEE-HOUSE/INTERNATIONAL.

Located alongside the funky surf shops, bikini boutiques, and alternative galleries of Bohemian Mission Beach, the Mission is this neighborhood's central meeting place. But it's good enough to attract more than just locals, and now has an upscale sister location east of Hillcrest that serves dinner. At the beach, the menu features all-day breakfasts (from traditional pancakes to nouvelle egg dishes and Latin-flavored burritos and quesadillas), plus light lunch sandwiches and salads. Standouts include tamales and eggs with tomatillo sauce, chicken-apple sausage with eggs and a mound of rosemary potatoes, and cinnamon French toast with blackberry puree. Seating is casual, comfy, and conducive to lingering (tons of students, writers, and diarists hang out here), if only with a soupbowl-size caffe latte.

The other location is in North Park, at 2801 University Ave. (☎ **619/220-8992**).

6 La Jolla

As befits an upscale community with time (and money) on its hands, La Jolla seems to have more than its fair share of good restaurants. Happily, they are mostly affordable, and more ethnically diverse than you might expect in a community that still supports a haberdashery called "The Ascot Shop." While many eateries are clustered in the village, on Prospect Street and the few blocks directly east, you can also cruise down La Jolla Boulevard or up by the La Jolla Beach & Tennis Club for additional choices.

Note: To locate these restaurants, please see the "La Jolla Accommodations & Dining" map on page 61.

EXPENSIVE

Cafe Japengo. At the Hyatt Regency La Jolla, 8960 University Center Lane. ☎ **858/450-3355.** Reservations recommended. Main courses $12–$20. AE, DC, DISC, MC, V. Mon–Fri 11:30am–2:30pm; Sun–Thurs 5–10pm, Fri–Sat 5–10:30pm. Sushi bar open till 11pm Mon–Thurs, 11:30pm Fri–Sat. Valet parking $3, validated self-parking free. From I-5, take La Jolla Village Dr. E. PACIFIC RIM/SUSHI.

Despite being contrived and self-conscious, Cafe Japengo is worth a trip for the food alone. With subdued lighting and a highly stylized Asian atmosphere, this restaurant is the best of several attached to the Golden Triangle's behemoth Hyatt Regency Hotel. The beautiful people know they look even more so among the warm woods and leafy shadows here, so there's lots of posing and people-watching. It's always packed; patrons come from all over the county for Japengo's Pacific Rim fusion cuisine, which incorporates South American and even European touches.

Some offerings, like the pot-stickers in tangy coriander-mint sauce or lemongrass-marinated swordfish, are superb; others, like the seared ahi "Napoleon," suffer from extra ingredients that just make the dish fussy. Sushi here is the same way; Japengo features the finest and freshest fish, but churns out enormously popular "specialty" rolls (combinations wrapped in even more ingredients, often drenched in sauce and garnished even further). The dramatic, colorfully presented inventions are enormously popular, but sushi purists will be happiest sticking to the basics.

George's at the Cove. 1250 Prospect St. ☎ **858/454-4244.** Reservations recommended. Main courses $9–$15 at lunch, $21–$31 at dinner. AE, DC, DISC, MC, V. Mon–Fri 11:30am–2:30pm, Sat–Sun 11:30am–3pm; Mon–Thurs 5:30–10pm, Fri–Sat 5–10:30pm, Sun 5–10pm. Valet parking $5–$6. CALIFORNIA.

You'll find host and namesake George Hauer at his restaurant's door most nights; he greets loyal regulars by name, and his confidence assures newcomers that they'll leave impressed with this beloved La Jolla tradition. Voted most popular in the *Zagat* restaurant survey,

George's wins consistent praise for impeccable service, gorgeous views of the cove, and outstanding California cuisine.

The menu, in typical San Diego fashion, presents many inventive seafood options. Appetizers range from baked Carlsbad mussels to phyllo-wrapped prawns flavored with cumin and ginger. The healthful smoked chicken, broccoli, and black-bean soup is a mainstay. Main courses combine many flavors with practiced artistry; applewood-smoked and cedar-roasted king salmon is paired with crisp polenta and subtle nuances of ginger, and tenderloin fillet is wrapped in bacon and finished with a gorgonzola-tinged reduction. As an alternative to dinner's pricey main courses, try the tasting menu, which offers a seasonally composed five-course sampling for around $38 per person; or try the more reasonably priced lunch menu. The informal Ocean Terrace Cafe is upstairs.

Marrakesh. 634 Pearl St. (at Draper Ave.). ☎ **858/454-2500.** Reservations recommended on weekends. Main courses $15–$19.95; 5-course "feasts" $16.50–$23. AE, CB, DC, DISC, MC, V. Sun–Thurs 5–10pm, Fri–Sat 5–11pm. Free parking. MOROCCAN.

One of several Southern California Marrakesh locations, this "total experience" restaurant evokes its origins in the 1960s, when many of its ilk were inspiring decorators with banquette seating and ethnic prints. Step inside and you enter a Moroccan palace, where guests eat in the traditional style—fingers only, no utensils—at low tables in tent-like surroundings. The padded walls and seats are rich with dark tapestries and North African prints. Exotic mood music, soft lighting, and (on weekends only) a strolling belly dancer complete the experience—along with authentic Moroccan fare that's available à la carte or as a complete feast. Appetizers include Middle Eastern tabouleh and hommus, as well as traditional Moroccan bastilla (a pastry filled with chicken, egg, and crushed almonds, then topped with powdered sugar and cinnamon). There's also a seafood bastilla. Most dinners feature brochettes of beef, lamb, chicken, or seafood, while the "feasts" offer choices of lemon chicken, lamb in honey sauce, quail, rabbit, or fish stew. Finish with a simple dessert of fruit, nuts, and baklava. While some consider food-as-entertainment passé, Marrakesh is still a great choice for the uninitiated or a festive group meal.

✪ **Top O' the Cove.** 1216 Prospect St. ☎ **858/454-7779.** www.topofthecove.com. Reservations recommended. Jackets suggested for men at dinner. Main courses $10–$17 at lunch, $25–$32 at dinner; Sun brunch $18.50. AE, CB, DC, MC, V. Mon–Sat 11:30am–10:30pm, Sun 10:30am–10:30pm. Valet parking $5. CONTINENTAL.

Always voted "most romantic" in annual diner surveys, Top O' the Cove is traditionally where San Diegans go for special occasions—first dates, marriage proposals, anniversaries. They're banking that its timeless elegance will enhance the evening's mood, and they're rarely disappointed. The finely proportioned historic cottage is one of the last remaining along Prospect Street, and it's shaded by 100-year-old Australian fig trees. Fireplaces glow on chilly evenings, and a gazebo and patio make the perfect setting for balmy summer dining or Sunday brunch.

The menu is peppered with French names, but the cuisine has distinct California overtones, often with Asian flavors (blackened ahi sashimi, salmon spring rolls, pan-seared tuna with wasabi). Classic standouts include green-peppercorn tenderloin dressed with Cognac and cream, veal piccata, medallion of elk with wine-shallot sauce, and fresh swordfish prepared differently each day. Sorbet is served between courses. Lunch is lighter, with salads and sandwiches joining selections from the dinner menu. The dessert specialty is a bittersweet chocolate box filled with cream and fruit in a raspberry sauce—try it with a liqueur-laced house coffee. Aficionados will thrill to the extensive wine list, but its steep markup threatens to spoil the mood.

✪ **Trattoria Acqua.** 1298 Prospect St., on Coast Walk. ☎ **858/454-0709.** www.trattoriaacqua.com. Reservations recommended. Main courses $13–$22. AE, MC, V. Daily 11:30am–2:30pm; Sun–Thurs 5–9:30pm, Fri–Sat 5–10:30pm. Validated self-parking free. ITALIAN.

Nestled on tiled terraces close enough to catch ocean breezes, this excellent Northern Italian spot has a more relaxed ambiance than similarly sophisticated Gaslamp Quarter trattorias. Rustic walls and outdoor seating shaded by flowering vines evoke a romantic Tuscan villa. A mixed crowd of suits and well-heeled couples gather to enjoy expertly prepared seasonal dishes; every table starts with bread served with an indescribably pungent Mediterranean spread. Acqua's pastas (all available as appetizers or main courses) are as good as it gets—rich, heady flavor combinations like spinach, chard, and four-cheese gnocchi, or veal- and-mortadella tortellini in fennel cream sauce. Other specialties include *saltimbocca con funghi* (veal scaloppini with sage, prosciutto, and forest-mushroom sauce), cassoulet (traditional Toulouse-style duck confit, sausage, and braised lamb baked with white beans, tomato, and fresh thyme), and *salmone al pepe* (roasted peppercorn-crusted Atlantic salmon served over lentils with sherry-and-shallot vinaigrette). The well-chosen wine list has received *Wine Spectator* accolades several years in a row.

MODERATE

✪ **Brockton Villa.** 1235 Coast Blvd. (across from La Jolla Cove). ☎ **858/ 454-7393.** Reservations recommended (call by Thurs for Sun brunch). Breakfast $4–$7.25; dinner main courses $10–$20. AE, DISC, MC, V. Mon 8am–3pm, Tues–Sun 8am–9pm (later in summer). BREAKFAST/CALIFORNIA.

In a restored 1894 beach bungalow, this charming cafe has a history as intriguing as its varied, eclectic menu. Named for an early resident's hometown (Brockton, Mass.), the cottage is imbued with the spirit of artistic souls drawn to this breathtaking perch overlooking La Jolla Cove. Rescued by the trailblazing Pannikin Coffee Company in the 1960s, the restaurant is now independently run by a Pannikin alum.

The biggest buzz is at breakfast, when you can enjoy inventive dishes such as soufflé-like "Coast Toast" (the house take on French toast) and Greek "steamers" (eggs scrambled with an espresso steamer, then mixed with feta cheese, tomato, and basil). The dozens of coffee drinks include the "Keith Richards"—four shots of espresso topped with Mexican hot chocolate (Mother's Little Helper indeed!). Lunch stars include homemade soups and salads, plus unusual sandwiches like turkey meat loaf on toasted sourdough bread with spicy tomato-mint chutney. The constantly expanding dinner menu includes salmon *en croute* (wrapped in prosciutto, Gruyère, and sage, with a grainy mustard sauce), plus pastas, stews, and grilled meats. Steep stairs from the street limit access for wheelchair users.

George's Ocean Terrace and Cafe/Bar. 1250 Prospect St. ☎ **858/ 454-4244.** Reservations not accepted. Main courses $10–$15 at lunch, $9.50–$14.95 at dinner. AE, DC, DISC, MC, V. Sun–Thurs 11am–10pm, Fri–Sat 11am–10:30pm. Valet parking $5–$6. CALIFORNIA.

The legendary main dining room at George's has won numerous awards for its haute cuisine. But George's also accommodates those seeking good food and a spectacular setting with a more reasonable price tag—the upstairs Ocean Terrace and Cafe prepares similar dishes as well as new creations in the same kitchen as the high-priced fare. The two areas offer indoor and outdoor seating overlooking La Jolla Cove, and the same great service as the main dining room. For dinner, you can choose from several seafood or pasta dishes, or have something out of the ordinary like George's meat loaf served with mushroom-and-corn mashed potatoes. The award-winning smoked chicken, broccoli, and black-bean soup appears on both menus.

Spice & Rice Thai Kitchen. 7734 Girard Ave. ☎ **858/456-0466.** Reservations recommended. Main courses $7–$13. AE, MC, V. Mon–Thurs 11am–3pm and 5–10pm, Fri 11am–3pm and 5–11pm, Sat 5–11pm, Sun 5–10pm. THAI.

A fairly recent entry into the La Jolla mix, this stylish Thai restaurant is a couple of blocks from the village's tourist crush—far enough to ensure effortless parking. The lunch crowd consists of shoppers and curious tourists, while dinner is quieter; all the local businesses have shut down and many diners are going to the old-fashioned Cove movie theater next door. The food is excellent, with polished presentations and expert renditions of the classics like pad Thai, satay, curry, and glazed duck. The starters often sound as good as the entrees—consider making a grazing meal of house specialties like "gold bags" (minced pork, vegetables, and herbs wrapped in crispy rice paper and served with earthy plum sauce) or minced roast duck spiced with chiles and lime juice; spicy calamari is flavored with ginger, cilantro, lime, and chili sauce. The romantically lit covered front patio has a secluded garden feel, and inside tables also have indirect lighting. I'm predicting this all-around satisfying insider's secret will soon explode with popularity.

INEXPENSIVE

✪ **The Cottage.** 7702 Fay Ave. (at Kline St.). ☎ **858/454-8409.** www. cottagelajolla.com. Reservations accepted for dinner only. Breakfast and lunch $5–$7; dinner main courses $7–$12. AE, DISC, MC, V. Daily year-round 7:30am–3pm; May 15–Sept 30 Tues–Sat 5–9:30pm. BREAKFAST/CALIFORNIA.

La Jolla's best—and friendliest—breakfast is served at this turn-of-the-century bungalow on a sunny village corner. Newly modernized, the cottage is light and airy, but most diners opt for tables outside, where a charming white picket fence encloses the trellis-shaded brick patio. Omelets and egg dishes feature Mediterranean, Asian, or classic American touches; my favorite has creamy mashed potatoes, bacon, and melted cheese folded inside. The Cottage bakes its own muffins, breakfast breads, and—you can quote me on this—the best brownies in San Diego. While "breakfast" dishes are served all day, toward lunch the kitchen begins turning out freshly made, healthful soups, light meals, and sandwiches. Summer dinners (never heavy, always tasty) are a delight, particularly when you're seated before dark on a balmy seaside night.

D'Lish. 7514 Girard Ave. (at Pearl St.). ☎ **858/459-8118.** Reservations recommended on weekends. Main courses $7–$11. AE, DC, DISC, MC, V. Sun–Thurs 11:30am–10pm, Fri–Sat 11:30am–11pm. Free underground parking. ITALIAN/CALIFORNIA.

Located on one of La Jolla's busiest intersections (in what some consider the ugliest building in town), D'Lish is a casual crowd-pleaser. The menu offers something for everyone. The specialty is pizza—

the trendy, wood-fired variety. There's also an impressive selection of equally inventive pastas, and you could just as easily choose a steak grilled with wild mushrooms, Santa Fe chicken wrap with chipotle and salsa, or meal-sized Thai chicken salad. The service is friendly and polished, even when the place is packed, and the food is reliably good enough to make up for the lack of atmosphere. Booths and tables are clustered downstairs around a wide bar, and on an upstairs mezzanine that tends to be stuffy in summer's heat.

7 Coronado

Rather like the conservative, old-school navy aura that pervades the entire "island," Coronado's dining options are reliable and often quite good, but the restaurants aren't breaking new culinary ground.

Some notable exceptions are the resort dining rooms, which seem to be waging a little rivalry over who can attract the most prestigious, multiple–award-winning executive chef. If you're in the mood for a special-occasion meal that'll knock your socks off, consider **Azzura Point,** in Loews Coronado Bay Resort, or the **Prince of Wales Grill** at the Hotel del Coronado. Of course, such culinary expertise doesn't come cheap. And if you seek ethnic or funky food, better head back across the bridge. Mexican fare (gringo-style, but well practiced) is served on the island at popular **Miguel's Cocina,** inside El Cordova hotel (☎ **619/437-4237**). A branch of the **Brigantine Seafood Grill** (see "Old Town," above) is at 1333 Orange Ave. (☎ **619/435-4166**).

Note: To locate these restaurants, please see the "Coronado Accommodations & Dining" map on page 67.

EXPENSIVE

Chart House. 1701 Strand Way. ☎ **619/435-0155.** Reservations recommended. Main courses $9–$25. AE, CB, DC, DISC, MC, V. Daily 5–10pm. Free parking. Bus: 901. AMERICAN.

Perched at the edge of Glorietta Bay, this restaurant resembles a cupola that must have escaped from the Hotel del Coronado, up the hill. It has been here, in the Del's former boathouse, since 1968. The upscale Chart House chain is known for restoration of historic structures, and this project is a beauty; it holds 38 antique tables and the largest collection of Tiffany lamps in Southern California (about 20 at last count). Enjoy dinner on the deck in summer or in the upstairs lounge; the mahogany, teak, and stained-glass bar came from Atlanta and dates from 1880.

A Cocktail Hour Tip

If you're longing for great appetizers that are more sophisticated than popcorn shrimp and potato skins, then the new **Chameleon Cafe & Lizard Lounge,** 1301 Orange Ave., Coronado (☎ **619/437-6677**), is your answer. It's the latest venture of chef Ken Irvine, the local superstar of Chez Loma fame. The casual, eclectic eatery is half cocktail lounge—fitting, because the menu is half appetizers. The "first plates" range in price from $4 to $9, and are generously sized and suitable for sharing. Relax and watch the activity along Orange Avenue while nibbling on Asian delicacies (lobster-crab pot-stickers, smoked salmon–and–avocado sushi), Southwestern spice (goat-cheese tamales, pork empanadas), or Mediterranean standards (grilled pizzas with smoked chicken and fontina cheese or portabella mushrooms). The bar features premium vodkas and aged tequilas; we recommend eschewing the restaurant's pricier main courses and having a "grazing" meal in the bar, which stays open from lunchtime till closing.

The fare is straightforward—seafood and steaks, with plenty of fresh-fish specials daily. Tourist-oriented and overpriced by local standards, the Chart House still guarantees the best prime rib or Australian lobster tail you'll find. The view from the restaurant encompasses Glorietta Bay, the Coronado Yacht Club, and the Coronado Bay Bridge.

There's also a branch in La Jolla, at 1270 Prospect St. (☎ **858/ 459-8201**).

Chez Loma. 1132 Loma (off Orange Ave.). ☎ **619/435-0661.** Reservations recommended. Main courses $18–$26. AE, DC, MC, V. Daily 5–10pm; Sun 10am–2pm. Bus: 901. FRENCH.

You'd be hard pressed to find a more romantic dining spot than this intimate Victorian cottage filled with antiques and subdued candlelight. The house dates from 1889, the French-Continental restaurant from 1975. Tables are scattered throughout the house and on the enclosed garden terrace; an upstairs wine salon, reminiscent of a Victorian parlor, is a cozy spot for coffee or conversation.

Among the creative entrees are salmon with smoked-tomato vinaigrette, and roast duckling with green-peppercorn sauce. All main courses are served with soup or salad, rice or potatoes, and fresh vegetables. California wines and American microbrews are available. Follow dinner with a creamy crème caramel or Kahlúa crème brûlée. Chez Loma's service is attentive, the herb rolls addictive, and early birds enjoy specially priced meals.

Peohe's. 1201 First St. (Ferry Landing Marketplace). ☎ **619/437-4474.** Reservations recommended. Main courses $7–$15 at lunch, $16–$29 at dinner. AE, CB, DC, DISC, MC, V. Mon–Sat 11:30am–2:30pm, Sun 10:30am–2:30pm; Mon–Thurs 5:30–9pm, Fri 5:30–10pm, Sat 5–10pm, Sun 4:30–9pm. Bus: 901 or 904. PACIFIC RIM/SEAFOOD.

With over-the-top Polynesian decor of which Disneyland would be proud, Peohe's is definitely touristy and definitely overpriced—but there's no denying the awesome view across the bay or the excellent Hawaiian-style seafood and Pacific Rim–accented cuisine. Every table in the giant, light- and plant-filled atrium has a view; there are even better tables on the wooden deck at the water's edge. Dinner main courses include acclaimed crunchy coconut shrimp; island-style halibut sautéed with banana, macadamia nuts, and Frangelico liqueur; and rack of New Zealand lamb with Hunan barbecue sauce. Lunchtime options include more casual sandwiches and salads, and the tropical fantasy desserts are delectably rich. For those who love theme restaurants and Polynesian kitsch, Peohe's is a worthwhile splurge.

Primavera Ristorante. 932 Orange Ave. ☎ **619/435-0454.** Reservations recommended. Main courses $8–$12 at lunch, $13–$27 at dinner. AE, CB, DC, DISC, MC, V. Mon–Fri 11am–2:30pm; daily 5–10:30pm. Bus: 901. ITALIAN.

Located among the most fashionable Orange Avenue businesses, Primavera is the only Italian restaurant worth noting on Coronado. Residents of this conservative enclave continue to rave about the excellent fare, which noncommittally straddles the line between traditional Northern Italian and the trendy variety in evidence at San Diego's newer trattorias. The restaurant's unremarkable pastel tapestry decor brings banquet rooms to mind, but that hardly seems to matter, considering the reliably excellent food and polished service—albeit at somewhat steep prices. Old-fashioned is represented by seven traditional veal dishes, the most intriguing of which pairs tender medallions and scampi sautéed with wild mushrooms and shallots in Madeira sauce. Saffron-seafood risotto or spinach tortellini under porcini mushroom and tomato-cream sauce will appeal to more contemporary tastes. If you have room for dessert, Primavera is known for perfectly balanced tiramisu. Look for plenty of button-down military types and well-coifed socialites in the dinner crowd; at lunch, you'll see shoppers, military bigwigs who get to leave the base, and escapees from the "mainland."

MODERATE

Bay Beach Cafe. 1201 First St. (Ferry Landing Marketplace). ☎ **619/435-4900.** Reservations recommended for dinner on weekends. Main courses $9–$18; pub menu $6–$10. AE, DISC, MC, V. Mon–Fri 7–10:30am and 11am–4pm, Sat–Sun 7–11:30am and noon–4pm; daily 5–10:30pm. Free parking. Bus: 901 or 904. AMERICAN/SEAFOOD.

This loud, friendly gathering place isn't on the beach at all, but enjoys a prime perch on San Diego Bay. Seated indoors or on a glassed-in patio, diners gaze endlessly at the city skyline, which is dramatic by day and breathtaking at night. The cafe is quite popular at happy hour, when the setting sun glimmers on downtown's mirrored high-rises. The ferry docks at a wooden pier a few steps away, discharging passengers into the complex of gift shops and restaurants with a New England fishing-village theme. At the Bay Beach Cafe, the food takes a back seat to the view, but the pub menu of burgers, sandwiches, salads, and appetizers is inexpensive and satisfying. Dinner entrees aren't quite good enough for the price.

Rhinoceros Cafe & Grill. 1166 Orange Ave. ☎ **619/435-2121.** Main courses $8.95–$17.95. AE, DISC, MC, V. Mon–Fri 11am–2:45pm, Sat–Sun 8am–2:45pm; daily 5–9pm. Bus: 901. AMERICAN.

With its quirky name and something-for-everyone menu, this light, bright bistro is a welcome addition to the Coronado dining scene. It's more casual than it looks from the street and offers large portions, though the kitchen is a little heavy-handed with sauces and spices. At lunch, every other patron seems to be enjoying the popular penne à la vodka in creamy tomato sauce; favorite dinner specials are monkfish cioppino over spaghettini, Southwestern-style meat loaf, and simple herb-roasted chicken. Plenty of crispy fresh salads balance out the menu. There's a good wine list, or you might decide to try Rhino Chaser's American Ale.

INEXPENSIVE

Kensington Coffee Company. 1106 First St. ☎ **619/437-8506.** Menu items $1.50–$4.50. AE, DISC, MC, V. Daily 6am–11pm. Bus: 901 or 904. LIGHT FARE.

Dropping by here is a great way to start or end the day—or take a break. This popular coffee and tea emporium at the island's east end features five fresh brews daily, and specialty espresso drinks. Munchies include bagels, croissants, filled pastries, muffins, and scones—plus tempting brownies and cakes. Light fare, such as burritos and salads, is served at lunchtime. Tables are set up outdoors and in, scattered amongst displays of coffee and tea paraphernalia, gifts, and postcards.

The friendly staff knows almost everyone by name and is extra nice to newcomers.

Primavera Pastry Caffé. 956 Orange Ave. ☎ **619/435-4191.** Main courses $4–$6. No credit cards. Daily 6:30am–6pm. Bus: 901. SANDWICHES/LIGHT FARE.

If the name sounds familiar, it's because this fantastic little cafe— the best of its kind on the island—is part of the family that includes Primavera Ristorante, up the street. In addition to fresh-roasted coffee and espresso drinks, it serves omelets and other breakfast treats (till 1:30pm), burgers and deli sandwiches on the delicious house bread, and a daily fresh soup. It's the kind of spot where half the customers are greeted by name. Locals rave about the "Yacht Club" sandwich, a croissant filled with yellowfin tuna, and the breakfast croissant, topped with scrambled ham and eggs and cheddar cheese. I can't resist Primavera's fat, gooey cinnamon buns.

8 Only in San Diego

WOOD-FIRED PIZZA

It all started with Wolfgang Puck, that crafty Austrian chef who dazzled Hollywood restaurant-goers at Spago and went on to build a dynasty of California cuisine. By now, everyone is familiar with the building block of that empire; heck, you can even get it in the frozen food section. We're talking about pizza, of course. Not the marinara-and-pepperoni variety found in other pizza meccas like New York and Chicago—for a whole generation of Californians, pizza will always mean barbecued chicken, tomato-basil, or goat cheese and sun-dried tomato. Gourmet pizzas appear to have overtaken the traditional variety in popularity, and kitchens all over San Diego stoke their wood-fired ovens to keep up with the demand.

Most of the Italian restaurants in this chapter feature at least a handful of individual-size pizzas. **D'Lish** in La Jolla (☎ **858/ 459-8118**) has almost 20 eclectic topping variations borrowed from various ethnic cuisine. Always tops in San Diego polls is **Sammy's California Woodfired Pizza,** at 770 Fourth Ave., at F Street, in the Gaslamp Quarter (☎ **619/230-8888**); 702 Pearl St., at Draper Street, La Jolla (☎ **858/456-8018**); and 12925 El Camino Real, at Del Mar Heights Road, Del Mar (☎ **858/259-6600**). Conveniently located and always frustratingly crowded, Sammy's serves creations like duck sausage, potato garlic, or Jamaican jerk shrimp atop 10-inch rounds. It also excels at enormous salads, making it easy to share a meal and save a bundle.

A similar menu is available at **Pizza Nova,** a similarly stylish minichain with a similarly vibrant atmosphere. Despite being alike, each chain thrives by covering the neighborhoods the other doesn't. You'll find Pizza Nova at 3955 Fifth Ave., north of University Avenue, Hillcrest (☎ **619/296-6682**); 5120 N. Harbor Dr., west of Nimitz Boulevard, Point Loma (☎ **619/226-0268**); and 8650 Genesee Ave., at Nobel Drive, in La Jolla's Golden Triangle (☎ **858/458-9525**).

If you're a purist, or unfamiliar with this trend's granddaddy, head to Mission Valley and San Diego's new branch of **Wolfgang Puck Cafe,** 1640 Camino del Rio N., in Mission Valley Center (☎ **619/295-9653**). Like its cousins throughout Southern California, the casual cafe has dizzying decor, loud music, and an army of fresh-faced staffers ferrying much more than pizza. (Another of Puck's excellent signature dishes is bacon-wrapped meat loaf served on a bed of mashed potatoes.)

BAJA FISH TACOS

One of San Diego's culinary ironies is that, although the city is conscious of its Hispanic roots—not to mention within visual range of the Mexican border—it's hard to find anything other than gringoized combo plates in most local Mexican restaurants.

Perhaps the most authentic recipes are those at humble **Rubio's Baja Grill.** Actually, it's not so humble anymore, since proprietor Ralph Rubio began branching out into every corner of Southern California with his enormously successful yet deceptively simple fare. You can now find Rubio's in Phoenix, Las Vegas, and Los Angeles, and even edging out hot dogs in the stands at Qualcomm Stadium. In 1983, it was an achievement for local surfer Rubio to come in off the beach just long enough to open a tiny walk-up taco stand on busy Mission Bay Drive.

After years of scarfing down cheap beers and fish tacos in the Mexican fishing village of San Felipe, Ralph secured the "secret" recipe for this quintessential Baja treat: batter-dipped, deep-fried fish fillets folded in corn tortillas and garnished with shredded cabbage, salsa, and tangy *crema* sauce. Thatched-roof shacks along Baja's beach roads sell the tacos, and in the past decade they've taken this side of the border by storm. The menu at Rubio's has expanded to include beefy *carne asada,* marinated pork carnitas, chargrilled mahi mahi, and homemade guacamole, all accented by the distinctively Baja flavors of fresh lime and cilantro. Unlike the food at your average McDrive-thru, at Rubio's you can wash it all down with an icy-cold beer. Because many of the newer locations have a homogenous fast-food look to them, it's fun to stop by the original stand, at 4504 E. Mission Bay Dr., at Bunker Hill Street (☎ **619/272-2801**), if you're in the neighborhood.

Rubio's also has locations in the Gaslamp Quarter, 901 Fourth St., at E Street (☎ **619/231-7731**); Hillcrest, 3900 Fifth Ave., at University Avenue (☎ **619/299-8873**); La Jolla, 8855 Villa La Jolla Dr., at Nobel Drive (☎ **858/546-9377**); Pacific Beach, 910 Grand Ave. (☎ **619/270-4800**); and Point Loma, 3555 Rosecrans St., at Midway Drive (☎ **619/223-2631**).

PICNIC FARE

San Diego's benign climate lends itself to dining alfresco. An excellent spot to pick up sandwiches is the **Cheese Shop,** a gourmet deli with locations downtown at 401 G St. (☎ **619/232-2303**) and in La Jolla Shores at 2165 Avenida de la Playa (☎ **858/459-3921**). Other places to buy picnic fare include **Girard Gourmet,** 7837 Girard Ave., La Jolla (☎ **858/454-3321**); **Boudin Sourdough Bakery and Cafe** and the **Farmer's Market,** both in Horton Plaza; and **Old Town Liquor and Deli,** 2304 San Diego Ave. (☎ **619/291-4888**).

Another spot that's very popular with San Diegans is **Point Loma Seafoods,** on the water's edge in front of the Municipal Sportfishing Pier, at 2805 Emerson near Scott Street, south of Rosecrans and west of Harbor Drive (☎ **619/223-1109**). There's a fish market here, and you can pick up seafood sandwiches, fresh sushi, and salads to go. If you decide to make your own sandwiches, the best bread in the county comes from **Bread & Cie. Bakery and Cafe,** 350 University Ave., Hillcrest (☎ **619/683-9322**), and **Primavera Pastry Caffé,** 956 Orange Ave., Coronado (☎ **619/435-4191**).

6

What to See & Do

*Y*ou won't run out of things to explore in San Diego. The San Diego Zoo, Sea World, and the Wild Animal Park are the three top drawing cards, but many other activities—lots of them free!—also await.

1 The Three Major Animal Parks

Looking for wild times? San Diego supplies them as no other city can. Its world-famous zoo is home to more than 4,000 animals, many of them rare and exotic. A sister attraction, the San Diego Wild Animal Park, offers another 2,500 creatures representing 275 species in an *au naturel* setting. And Shamu and his friends form a veritable chorus line at Sea World—waving their flippers, waddling across an ersatz Antarctica, and blowing killer-whale kisses—in more than a dozen shows a day.

✪ **San Diego Zoo.** Park Blvd. and Zoo Place, Balboa Park. ☎ **619/234-3153.** TDD 619/233-9639. Panda-viewing hot line 888/MY-PANDA. www. sandiegozoo.org. Admission $16 adult, $7 children 3–11, military in uniform free. Deluxe package (admission, guided bus tour, round-trip Skyfari aerial tram) $24 adults, $21.60 seniors 60 and over, $13 children. Combination Zoo and Wild Animal Park package (deluxe zoo package, Wild Animal Park admission) $35.15 adults, $20.75 children; valid for 5 days from date of purchase. DISC, MC, V. Daily year-round 9am–4pm (grounds close at 5pm); summer 9am–9pm (grounds close at 10pm). Bus: 7/7B.

More than 4,000 animals reside at this world-famous zoo, which was founded in 1916 with a handful of animals originally brought here for the 1915–16 Panama–California International Exposition. Many of the buildings you see in surrounding Balboa Park were built for the exposition. The zoo's founder, Dr. Harry Wegeforth, a local physician and lifelong animal lover, once braved the fury of an injured tiger to toss medicine into its roaring mouth.

In the early days of the zoo, "Dr. Harry" traveled around the world and bartered native Southwestern animals such as rattlesnakes and sea lions for more exotic species. The loan of two giant pandas

San Diego Area Attractions

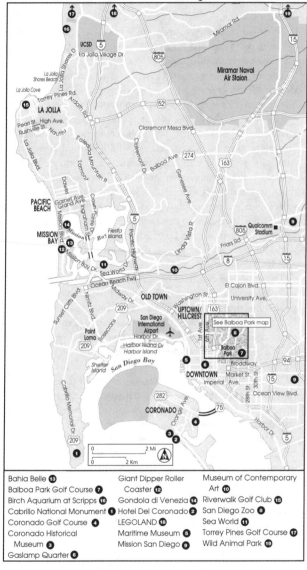

Bahia Belle **13**	Giant Dipper Roller Coaster **12**	Museum of Contemporary Art **10**
Balboa Park Golf Course **7**	Gondola di Venezia **14**	Riverwalk Golf Club **15**
Birch Aquarium at Scripps **16**	Hotel Del Coronado **2**	San Diego Zoo **8**
Cabrillo National Monument **1**	LEGOLAND **18**	Sea World **11**
Coronado Golf Course **4**	Maritime Museum **5**	Torrey Pines Golf Course **17**
Coronado Historical Museum **3**	Mission San Diego **9**	Wild Animal Park **19**
Gaslamp Quarter **6**		

from the People's Republic of China is a twist on the long-standing tradition—instead of exchanging exotic species, the San Diego Zoo agreed to pay $1 million for each year that the pandas are here, to aid the conservation effort in China.

The zoo is also an accredited botanical garden, representing more than 6,000 species of flora from many climate zones, all installed to help simulate the animals' native environments.

The giant pandas are the big attention-getters, but the zoo has many other rare and exotic species: cuddly koalas from Australia, long-billed kiwis from New Zealand, wild Przewalski horses from Mongolia, lowland gorillas from Africa, and giant tortoises from the Galapagos. Of course, the zoo's regulars—lions, elephants, giraffes, tigers, and bears—prowl around as well, and the zoo is home to a great number of tropical birds. Most of the animals are housed in barless, moated enclosures that resemble their natural habitats. The habitats include Australasia, Tiger River, Sun Bear Forest, two of the world's largest walk-through bird aviaries, Flamingo Lagoon, Gorilla Tropics, Hippo Beach, and Polar Bear Plunge.

The zoo offers two types of bus tours. Both provide a narrated overview and allow you to see 75% of the park. On the **35-minute guided bus tour,** you get on the bus and complete a circuit around the zoo. It costs $4 for adults, $3 for kids 3 to 11, and is included in the deluxe package. The **Kangaroo Bus Tour** allows you to get on and off the bus as many times as you want at any of the eight stops—you can even go around more than once. It costs $8 for adults and $5 for children. In general, it's better to take the tour early in the morning or late in the afternoon, when the animals are more active. The last tour starts an hour before closing—it's not as crowded as the others, but you won't see the elephants because it's their feeding time. Call the **Bus Tour Hot Line** (☎ **619/685-3264**) for information about these tours, as well as Spanish-language tours, a comedy tour, and signed tours for the hearing impaired.

You can also get an aerial perspective from the **Skyfari,** which costs $1 per person each way. The ride lasts about 5 minutes—but, because it doesn't get particularly close to the animals, it's better for a bird's-eye view of Balboa Park and a survey of the zoo.

The **Children's Zoo** is scaled to a youngster's viewpoint. There's a nursery with baby animals and a petting area where kids can cuddle up to sheep, goats, and the like. The resident wombat is a special favorite here.

Money-Saving Tip

If you plan to go to the Zoo and Wild Animal Park, you might want to consider buying a **Zoological Society Membership,** which costs $68 a year for two adults living in the same household. Membership gives each cardholder unlimited entrance to the Zoo and Wild Animal Park, plus two adult-admission passes, six discounted admission passes, and four two-fer bus tickets, plus a subscription to *Zoo News* magazine. A **Koala Club** membership for a child costs $15 and provides unlimited entry for a year. If you don't buy the annual pass, the best discount is the one for **AAA members.** The next-best deal is using the coupons in the *Super Savings Coupon Book* available from the International Visitor Information Center.

Wild Animal Park. 15500 San Pasqual Valley Rd., Escondido. ☎ **760/ 747-8702.** TDD 760/738-5067. www.sandiegozoo.org. Admission $19.95 adults, $17.95 seniors 60 and over, $12.95 children 3–11, free for children under 3 and military in uniform. Combination Zoo and Wild Animal Park package (includes deluxe zoo package) $35.15 adults, $20.75 children; valid for 5 days from date of purchase. DISC, MC, V. Daily 9am–4pm (grounds close at 5pm); extended hours during summer and Festival of Lights in December. Parking $3 per car. Take I-15 to Via Rancho Pkwy.; follow signs for about 3 miles.

Just 30 miles north of San Diego, in the San Pasqual Valley, the Wild Animal Park transports you to the African plains and other landscapes. Some 3,200 animals, many of them endangered species, roam freely over the park's 1,800 acres. In a reversal of roles, the humans are enclosed here instead of the animals. This living arrangement encourages breeding colonies, so it's not surprising that more than 80 white rhinoceroses have been born here. Several species of rare animals that had vanished from the wild, such as cheetahs and Przewalski wild horses, have been reintroduced to their natural habitats from stocks bred by the park. Approximately 650 baby animals are born every year in the park, which also serves as a botanical preserve with more than 2 million plants, including 300 endangered species.

The best way to see the animals is by riding the 5-mile **monorail** (included in the price of admission); for the best views, sit on the right-hand side. During the 50-minute ride, you'll pass through areas resembling Africa and Asia, and you'll learn interesting tidbits—did you know that rhinos are susceptible to sunburn and mosquito bites? Trains leave every 20 minutes; you can watch informative videos while you wait in the stations.

If you'd like to get a little closer to the animals, the park offers several alternative ways to explore the area. On the 1³/₄-mile **Kilimanjaro self-guided safari walk,** you'll see tigers, elephants, and cheetahs close up, as well as the Australian rain forest and views of East Africa. You can also journey into the **Heart of Africa** (the park's newest feature) on a ³/₄-mile self-guided trail that takes walkers through dense forest, flourishing wetlands, sprawling savannas, and open plains to discover Africa's biodiversity. It encompasses 30 acres and is home to about 300 animals representing nearly 30 species. Photographers will get a click out of **photo caravan tours,** which venture into the field enclosures. The photo tours run Wednesday through Sunday, and they cost $65 or $90 depending on the tour. Stroller and wheelchair rentals are available. Take a jacket along; it can get cold in the open-air monorail.

The most intriguing development at the Wild Animal Park is the **Roar and Snore** program, which runs from May through September. It offers a chance to camp out in the park compound and observe the nocturnal movements of rhinos, tigers, and other animals, which are often more active at night than during the day. The park provides equipment, the camp staff sets up tents, and dinner is cooked for you on a camp stove—well, an industrial-strength version. The camping is secondary, though, to the opportunity to sit around the campfire listening to tales of animal behavior, then be lulled to sleep (or from it, for the skittish) by the extraordinary animal calls emanating from every corner of the park. In the morning, enjoy a pancake breakfast, monorail ride, and Heart of Africa visit, and spend the rest of the day exploring the park. The camp-overs take place on Friday, Saturday, and Sunday nights; some are restricted to adults, while others are family events. Prices are $87.50 for adults, $67.50 for kids 8 to 11; children under 8 are not permitted. To request Roar and Snore information by mail, call ☎ **760/738-5049;** reservations can be made by calling ☎ **800/ 934-CAMP.**

Sea World. 500 Sea World Dr., Mission Bay. ☎ **619/226-3901.** TDD 619/ 226-3907. www.seaworld.com. Admission $38 adults, $29 children 3–11, free for children under 3. DISC, JCB, MC, V. Parking $6 per car, $3 per motorcycle, $8 per RV. Guided 90-min. behind-the-scenes tours, $8 adults, $7 children 3– 11. Ticket sales stop ¹/₂ hr. before closing. June–Aug daily 9am–10pm; Sept–May daily 10am–5pm. Bus: 9. By car from I-5, take Sea World Dr. exit; from I-8, take W. Mission Bay Dr. exit to Sea World Dr.

One of the best-promoted attractions in California, Sea World may be your main reason for coming to San Diego. The 150-acre, multimillion-dollar aquatic playground is a showplace for marine life, made politically correct with a nominally "educational" atmosphere. Several successive 4-ton black-and-white killer whales have functioned as the park's mascot, Shamu. At its heart, Sea World is a family entertainment center where the performers are dolphins, otters, sea lions, walruses, and seals. Shows run continuously throughout the day, while visitors can rotate through the various theaters.

The 2-acre hands-on area called **Shamu's Happy Harbor** encourages kids to handle everything—and features everything from a pretend pirate ship, with plenty of netted towers, to tube crawls, slides, and chances to get wet. The newest attraction is **Wild Arctic,** a virtual-reality trip to the frozen North, complete with polar bears, beluga whales, walruses, and harbor seals. Other draws include **Baywatch at Sea World,** a water-ski show named for the popular TV show, and **Shamu Backstage,** where visitors can get up close and personal with killer whales.

The **Dolphin Interaction Program** creates an opportunity for people to meet bottlenose dolphins. Although the program stops short of allowing you to swim with the dolphins, it does offer the opportunity to wade waist-deep, and plenty of time to stroke the mammals and give commands like the trainers. This 2-hour program (1 hour of education and instruction, 15 minutes of wet-suit fitting, 45 minutes in the water with the dolphins) costs $125 per person, which includes admission to Sea World on the day of your program, as well as another day within a week. Space is limited to eight people per day, so reservations are required. Participants must be age 13 or older.

Although Sea World is best known as Shamu's home, the facility also plays an important role in rescuing and rehabilitating beached animals found along the West Coast—including more than 300 seals, sea lions, marine birds, and dolphins in a year. Following the successful rescue and 1998 release of a young California gray whale, Sea World turned its attention to the manatee, an unusual aquatic mammal rarely seen outside Florida's tropical waters. At press time, the manatees were on display at the park.

2 San Diego's Beaches

San Diego County is blessed with 70 miles of sandy coastline and more than 30 beaches that attract surfers, snorkelers, swimmers, and sunbathers. In summer, the beaches teem with locals and visitors alike. The rest of the year, when the water is cooler, they are popular places to walk and jog, and surfers don wet suits to pursue their passion.

Here's a list of San Diego's most accessible beaches, each with its own personality and devotees. They are listed geographically from south to north. *Note:* All beaches are good for swimming unless otherwise indicated.

IMPERIAL BEACH

Half an hour south of San Diego by car or trolley, and only a few minutes from the Mexican border, lies Imperial Beach. Besides being popular with surfers, it plays host to the annual U.S. Open Sandcastle Competition each August. The world-class sand creations range from sea scenes to dragons to dinosaurs.

✪ CORONADO BEACH

Lovely, wide, and sparkling white, this beach is conducive to strolling and lingering, especially in the late afternoon. It fronts Ocean Boulevard and is especially pretty in front of the Hotel del Coronado. The islands visible from here, "Los Coronados," are 18 miles away and belong to Mexico.

OCEAN BEACH

The northern end of Ocean Beach Park is officially known as "Dog Beach," and is one of only two in San Diego where your pooch can roam freely on the sand (and frolic with several dozen other people's pets). Surfers generally congregate around the Ocean Beach Pier, mostly in the water but often at the snack shack on the end. Rip currents are strong here and discourage most swimmers from venturing beyond waist depth. Facilities at the beach include rest rooms, showers, picnic tables, and plenty of metered parking lots. To reach the beach, take West Point Loma Boulevard all the way to the end.

BONITA COVE/MARINER'S POINT & MISSION POINT

Facing Mission Bay in South Mission Beach, with calm waters, grassy areas for picnicking, and playground equipment, these spots are perfect for families.

PACIFIC BEACH

There's always some action at Mission Beach, particularly along **Ocean Front Walk,** a paved promenade featuring a human parade akin to that at L.A.'s Venice Beach boardwalk. It runs along Ocean

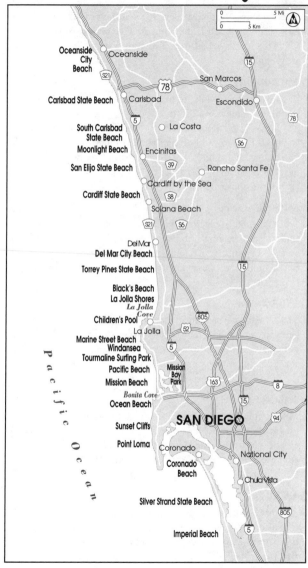

San Diego Beaches

Oceanside City Beach
Oceanside

San Marcos

Carlsbad State Beach
Carlsbad

Escondido

South Carlsbad State Beach
La Costa

Moonlight Beach
Encinitas

San Elijo State Beach
Rancho Santa Fe

Cardiff State Beach
Cardiff by the Sea

Solana Beach

Del Mar
Del Mar City Beach

Torrey Pines State Beach

Black's Beach
La Jolla Shores
La Jolla Cove
Children's Pool
La Jolla

Marine Street Beach
Windansea
Tourmaline Surfing Park
Pacific Beach
Mission Bay Park
Mission Beach
Bonita Cove
Ocean Beach

SAN DIEGO

Sunset Cliffs

Point Loma
Coronado
National City

Coronado Beach
Chula Vista

Silver Strand State Beach

Imperial Beach

Pacific Ocean

Boulevard (just west of Mission Boulevard), north of Pacific Beach Drive. Pacific Beach is the home of **Tourmaline Surfing Park,** where the sport's old guard gathers to surf waters where swimmers are prohibited.

✪ MISSION BAY PARK

In this 4,600-acre aquatic playground, you'll find 27 miles of bayfront, 17 miles of oceanfront beaches, picnic areas, children's playgrounds, and paths for biking, roller-skating, and jogging. The bay lends itself to windsurfing, sailing, riding personal watercraft, waterskiing, and fishing. There are dozens of access points; one of the most popular is off I-5 at Clairemont Drive, where there's a visitor information center.

MISSION BEACH

While Mission Bay Park is a body of salt water surrounded by land and bridges, Mission Beach is actually a beach on the Pacific Ocean. Surfing is popular year-round here. The long beach and boardwalk extend from Pacific Beach Drive south to Belmont Park and beyond to the jetty.

✪ WINDANSEA

The fabled locale of Tom Wolfe's *Pump House Gang,* Windansea is legendary to this day among California's surf elite. Reached by way of Bonair Street (at Neptune Place), Windansea has no facilities, and street parking is first-come, first-served. Come to surf, watch surfers, or soak in the camaraderie and party atmosphere.

CHILDREN'S POOL

Much of the sand near the point of La Jolla's peninsula is cordoned off for the resident sea lion population; the rest is inhabited by curious shutterbugs and families taking advantage of the same calm conditions that keep the sea lions around. The beach is at Coast Boulevard and Jenner Street; there's limited free street parking.

✪ LA JOLLA COVE

The protected, calm waters—praised as the clearest along the California coast—attract swimmers, snorkelers, scuba divers, and families. There's a small sandy beach, and on the cliffs above, the **Ellen Browning Scripps Park.** The cove's "look but don't touch" policy protects the colorful Garibaldi, California's state fish, plus other marine life, including abalone, octopus, and lobster. The unique Underwater Park stretches from here to the northern end of Torrey

Pines State Reserve and incorporates kelp forests, artificial reefs, two deep submarine canyons, and tidal pools. La Jolla Cove is accessible from Coast Boulevard.

LA JOLLA SHORES BEACH

The wide, flat mile of sand at La Jolla Shores is popular with joggers, swimmers, and beginning body and board surfers, as well as families. Weekend crowds can be enormous, though, quickly occupying both the sand and the metered parking spaces in the lot. There are rest rooms, showers, and picnic areas here.

BLACK'S BEACH

The area's unofficial (and illegal) nude beach, it lies between La Jolla Shores Beach and Torrey Pines State Beach. Located below some steep cliffs, it is out of the way and not easy to reach. To get here, take North Torrey Pines Road, park at the Glider Port, and walk from there. *Note:* Although the water is shallow and pleasant for wading, this area is known for its rip currents.

DEL MAR

After a visit to the famous fairgrounds that are home to the Del Mar Thoroughbred Club, you may want to make tracks for the beach, a long stretch of sand backed by grassy cliffs and a playground area. Del Mar is about 15 miles from downtown San Diego.

NORTHERN SAN DIEGO COUNTY

Those inclined to venture farther north in San Diego County won't be disappointed. Pacific Coast Highway leads to some inviting beaches, such as these in Encinitas: peaceful **Boneyards Beach, Swami's Beach** for surfing, and **Moonlight Beach,** popular with families and volleyball buffs. Farthest north is Oceanside, which has one of the West Coast's longest wooden piers, wide sandy beaches, and several popular surfing areas.

3   Attractions in Balboa Park

Balboa Park's 1,174 acres encompass walkways, gardens, historic buildings, restaurants, an ornate pavilion with the world's largest outdoor organ, a high-spouting fountain, an OMNIMAX theater, a nationally acclaimed theater, and the world-famous zoo (see section 1 of this chapter for a complete listing). The park's most distinctive features are the architectural beauty of the Spanish-Moorish buildings lining El Prado, its main street, and the outstanding and diverse museums contained within it.

Money-Saving Tip

Many Balboa Park attractions are free on certain days; see "Free of Charge & Full of Fun," in section 5. If you plan to visit all or most of the museums in the park, consider buying the **Passport to Balboa Park.** The $19 passport, which represents a $56 value, is a coupon booklet that allows one entrance to each of 11 museums and is valid for a week. You can buy yours at any participating museum, the Balboa Park Visitor Center, or the Times Arts Tix Booth in Horton Plaza.

Free **tram** transportation within the park runs Monday through Friday from 8am to 5pm and Saturday and Sunday from 11am to 4pm. Ask at the Visitor Center about free walking and museum **tours.**

✪ **San Diego Aerospace Museum.** Pan-American Plaza. ☎ **619/ 234-8291.** www.aerospacemuseum.org. Admission $6 adults, $2 children 6– 17, free for active military with ID and children under 6. Free 4th Tues of each month. Sept–May daily 10am–4:30pm; June–Aug daily 10am–5:30pm (last admission ¹/₂ hour before closing). Closed Thanksgiving, Dec 25. Bus: 7/7B, 16, or 25.

The Aerospace Museum, with its International Aerospace Hall of Fame, provides an overview of the nation's air and space history, from the days of hot-air balloons to the space age. It emphasizes local aviation history, including the construction here of the *Spirit of St. Louis.* The cylindrical Ford Building, built by the Ford Motor Company for the California Pacific International Exposition of 1935, houses the museum. Behind-the-scenes restoration tours are available.

Museum of Art. 1450 El Prado. ☎ **619/232-7931.** www.sdmart.com. Admission $8 adults; $6 seniors 65 and over, military, and students with ID; $3 children 6–17; free for children under 6. Admission to traveling exhibits varies. Free 3rd Tues of each month. Tues–Sun 10am–4:30pm. Bus: 7/7B, 16, or 25.

This museum has outstanding collections of Italian Renaissance and Dutch and Spanish baroque art, along with contemporary paintings and sculptures. The Grant–Munger Gallery on the ground floor features works by Monet, Toulouse-Lautrec, Renoir, Pissarro, van Gogh, and Dufy. Upstairs in the Fitch Gallery is El Greco's *Penitent St. Peter* and in the Gluck Gallery, Modigliani's *Boy with Blue Eyes* and Braque's *Coquelicots.* The traveling exhibit *Norman Rockwell: Pictures For The American People* will run in the fall of

Balboa Park

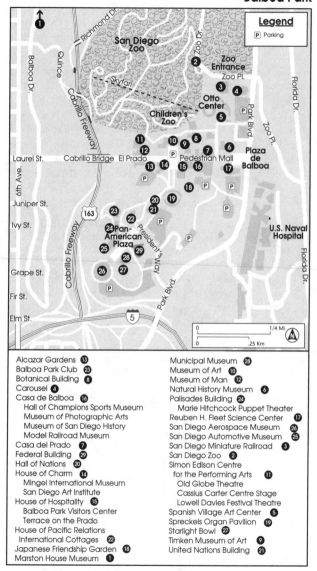

Alcazar Gardens ⑬
Balboa Park Club ㉓
Botanical Building ⑧
Carousel ④
Casa de Balboa ⑯
  Hall of Champions Sports Museum
  Museum of Photographic Arts
  Museum of San Diego History
  Model Railroad Museum
Casa del Prado ⑦
Federal Building ㉙
Hall of Nations ⑳
House of Charm ⑭
  Mingei International Museum
  San Diego Art Institute
House of Hospitality ⑮
  Balboa Park Visitors Center
  Terrace on the Prado
House of Pacific Relations
  International Cottages ㉒
Japanese Friendship Garden ⑱
Marston House Museum ①

Municipal Museum ㉘
Museum of Art ⑩
Museum of Man ⑫
Natural History Museum ⑥
Palisades Building ㉔
  Marie Hitchcock Puppet Theater
Reuben H. Fleet Science Center ⑰
San Diego Aerospace Museum ㉖
San Diego Automotive Museum ㉕
San Diego Miniature Railroad ③
San Diego Zoo ②
Simon Edison Centre
  for the Performing Arts ⑪
  Old Globe Theatre
  Cassius Carter Centre Stage
  Lowell Davies Festival Theatre
Spanish Village Art Center ⑤
Spreckels Organ Pavilion ⑲
Starlight Bowl ㉗
Timken Museum of Art ⑨
United Nations Building ㉑

2000. The museum has a shop, sculpture garden, and cafe with out-door seating. Its rotunda features a striking Spanish-style tile staircase.

Museum of Photographic Arts. 1649 El Prado. ☎ **619/238-7559.** Admission $4 adults, free for children under 13 with adult. Free 2nd Tues of each month. Daily 10am–5pm. Bus: 7/7B, 16, or 25.

This is one of the few museums in the country dedicated exclusively to photographic arts, and the exhibits span the 150-year history of the medium. The extensive permanent collection of 3,600 images includes work by Edward Weston, Duane Michals, Ansel Adams, Max Yavno, Manual Alvarez Bravo, Mary Ellen Mark, Margaret Bourke-White, Sebastiao Salgado, and many others. There are also six to eight changing exhibitions every year.

Natural History Museum. 1788 El Prado. ☎ **619/232-3821.** www.sdnhm.org. Admission $6 adults, $5 seniors and active-duty military, $3 children 6–17, free for children under 6. Free 1st Tues of each month. Daily 9:30am–4:30pm, open later in summer. Bus: 7/7B, 16, or 25.

The museum focuses on the flora, fauna, and mineralogy of the Southwest. Kids marvel at the animals they find here and enjoy exploring the Desert Lab, home to live snakes and tarantulas. Upcoming exhibits include **"Dinosaurs of the Lost World"** (March 3 to September 4, 2000).

Reuben H. Fleet Science Center. 1875 El Prado. ☎ **619/238-1233.** www.rhfleet.org. Admission to Science Center $5 adults, $4 seniors 65 and over, $3 kids 3–12. Free to all 1st Tues of each month. Combination tickets available for admission plus Space Theater, SciTours, or Planetarium. MC, V. Mon–Tues 9:30am–6pm, Wed–Thurs and Sun 9:30am–9pm, Fri–Sat 9:30am–10pm. Bus: 7/7B, 16, or 25.

The Reuben H. Fleet Science Center houses the world's first OMNIMAX theater, a 76-foot tilted-dome screen that shows breathtaking IMAX/OMNIMAX films. The Science Center features five galleries with hands-on exhibits as intriguing for grown-ups as kids, and in 1998 it added **SciTours,** a simulator ride that explores space and the worlds of science and biology. To avoid waiting in line, you can buy tickets in advance; this is especially useful on week-ends, which tend to be busy.

Museum of Man. 1350 El Prado. ☎ **619/239-2001.** www.museumofman.org. Admission $5 adults, $4.50 seniors, $3 children 6–17, free for children under 6. Free 3rd Tues of the month. Daily 10am–4:30pm. Bus: 16 or 25.

In a landmark building just inside the park entrance at the Cabrillo Bridge, this museum is devoted to anthropology, with an emphasis on the peoples of North and South America. Favorite exhibits include life-size replicas of a dozen varieties of *Homo sapiens,* from Cro-Magnon and Neanderthal to Peking Man. Don't overlook the annex across the street, which houses more exhibits. The museum's annual **Indian Fair,** held in June, features American Indians from the Southwest demonstrating tribal dances and selling ethnic food, arts, and crafts.

Mingei International Museum. 1439 El Prado, in the House of Charm. ☎ **619/239-0003.** Admission $5 adults, $2 children 6–17 and students with ID, free for children under 6. AE, MC, V. Free 3rd Tues of each month. Tues–Sun 10am–4pm.

This museum (pronounced Min-gay—"art of the people" in Japanese) offers changing exhibitions celebrating human creativity. It's manifested in textiles, costumes, jewelry, toys, pottery, paintings, and sculpture—all crafted from natural materials. Displays represent countries all over the world. Martha Longenecker, a potter and professor emeritus of art at San Diego State University, founded the museum in 1977. It is one of only two major museums in the United States devoted to folk crafts on a worldwide scale (the other is in Santa Fe, New Mexico).

San Diego Automotive Museum. 2080 Pan American Plaza. ☎ **619/231-2886.** Admission $6 adults, $5 seniors and active military, $2 children 6–15, free for children under 6. Free 4th Tues of each month. MC, V. Sept 5–May 31 daily 10am–4:30pm, June 1–Sept 4 daily 10am–5:30pm. Last admission 1/2 hour before closing. Bus: 7/7B, 16, or 25.

Classic, antique, and exotic cars and motorcycles are on display here in changing shows. The museum has an extensive gift shop and a full automotive research library. On your visit you might see a 1927 Bentley, a 1931 Duesenberg Model J, a 1931 Rolls-Royce Phaeton, and the late actor Steve McQueen's 1953 Allard, as well as the ill-fated 1948 Tucker and 1981 DeLorean.

Botanical Building and Lily Pond. El Prado. Free admission. Fri–Wed 10am–4pm. Bus: 7/7B, 16, or 25.

Within a serene park, ivy, ferns, orchids, impatiens, begonias, and other plants—about 1,200 tropical and flowering varieties—are sheltered beneath the domed lath house. The building, part of the 1915 Panama–California Exposition, measures 250 feet long by 75 feet wide by 60 feet high, and is one of the world's largest wood lath structures. The lily pond out front attracts sun worshipers and street entertainers.

Hall of Champions. 2133 Pan American Plaza. ☎ **619/234-2544.** Admission $5 adults, $3 seniors 65 and older and military, $1 children 6–17, free for children under 6. Free 2nd Tues of each month. Daily 10am–4:30pm. Bus: 7/7B, 16, or 25.

One of the country's few multisport museums, Hall of Champions has been popular with sports fans since 1961. The museum highlights more than 40 professional and amateur sports. More than 25 exhibits surround a centerpiece statue, the *Discus Thrower.* One particularly interesting exhibit is devoted to athletes with disabilities. The museum moved to this spacious new location in 1999.

House of Pacific Relations International Cottages. Adjacent to Pan-American Plaza. ☎ **619/234-0739.** Free admission; donations welcome. Sun 12:30–4:30pm, 4th Tues of each month 11:30am–3pm. Bus: 7/7B, 16, or 25.

This cluster of one- and two-room cottages disseminates information about the culture, traditions, and history of 31 countries. Light refreshments are served, and outdoor lawn programs are presented March through October.

Japanese Friendship Garden. Adjacent to the Organ Pavilion. ☎ **619/232-2780.** Admission $2 adults; $1 seniors 65 and older, military, people with disabilities, and children 7–17; $5 family; free for children under 7. Free 3rd Tues of each month. Tues and Fri–Sun 10am–4pm. Bus: 7/7B, 16, or 25.

Of the 11$\frac{1}{2}$ acres designated for the garden, only an acre—a beautiful, peaceful one—has been developed. The garden's Information Center shows a model of the future installation, San-Kei-En (Three-Scenery Garden). It will eventually include a shallow lake with a shoreline of Japanese irises; a pastoral scene, such as a meadow abloom with springtime trees; and a rushing mountain waterfall and a stream filled with colorful koi. A self-guided tour is available at the main gate. From the gate, a crooked path (to confound evil spirits, who move only in a straight line) threads its way to the information center in a Zen-style house; here you can view the most ancient kind of garden, the sekitei, made only of sand and stone. Refreshments are served on a Japanese-style deck to the left of the entrance. Japanese holidays are celebrated here, and the public is invited.

Marston House Museum. 3525 Seventh Ave. (northwest corner of Balboa Park at Balboa Dr. and Upas St.). ☎ **619/298-3142.** Guided tour $3, $5 in combination with Villa Montezuma, free for children under 13. Fri–Sun noon–4:30pm (last tour at 3:45pm). Bus: 1, 3, 16, or 25.

The noted San Diego architect Irving Gill designed this house in 1905 for George Marston, a local businessman and philanthropist. A classic example of Craftsman-style architecture, reminiscent of Frank Lloyd Wright's work, the house is now managed by the San Diego Historical Society. Some of its interesting features are wide hallways, brick fireplaces, and redwood paneling. Opened to the public in 1991, it contains few original pieces, but does exhibit Roycroft, Stickley, and Lampert furniture and is slowly being furnished with Craftsman-era pieces or copies as funds become available. Tours take about 45 minutes. Enter at the left. There's a small bookstore and gift shop.

✪ **Model Railroad Museum.** Casa de Balboa Building, El Prado. ☎ **619/ 696-0199.** www.sdmodelrailroadm.com. Admission $3 adults, free for children under 15. Senior, student, and military (with ID) discounts. Free 1st Tues of each month. Tues–Fri 11am–4pm, Sat–Sun 11am–5pm. Bus: 7, 7A/B, 16, or 25.

Four permanent, scale-model railroads depict Southern California's transportation history and terrain, including San Diego County's Grand Canyon, the Carriso Gorge. Children will enjoy the hands-on Lionel trains, and train buffs of all ages will appreciate the interactive multimedia exhibits. The gift shop sells rail-related items, including toys, mugs, signs, and kids' overalls and shirts.

Museum of San Diego History. 1649 El Prado, in Casa del Balboa. ☎ **619/ 232-6203.** Admission $4 adults, $3 seniors and military with ID, $3 for groups of 10 or more, $1.50 children 5–12, free for children under 5. Free 2nd Tues of each month. Tues–Sun 10am–4:30pm. Bus: 7/7B, 16, or 25.

A good place to start if you are a newcomer to San Diego, the recently remodeled museum offers permanent and changing exhibits on topics related to the history of the region, from pioneer outposts in the 1800s to the present day. Many of the museum's photographs depict Balboa Park and the growth of the city. Docent tours are available; call ☎ **619/232-6203**, ext. 117, for information and reservations. Books about San Diego's history are available in the gift shop.

Spreckels Organ Pavilion. South of El Prado. ☎ **619/226-0819.** Free 1-hr. concerts Sun year-round; free Summer Festival concerts July–Aug, 8pm Mon and 6:15pm Tues–Thurs. Bus: 7/7B, 16, or 25.

Given to San Diego citizens in 1914 by brothers John D. and Adolph Spreckels, the ornate, curved pavilion houses a magnificent organ with 4,445 individual pipes. They range in length from less than a half-inch to more than 32 feet. With only brief interruptions, the organ has been in continuous use in the park, and today visitors can enjoy free hour-long concerts on Sundays at 2pm. There's seating for 2,400.

Timken Museum of Art. 1500 El Prado. ☎ **619/239-5548.** gort.ucsd.edu/ sj/timken. Free admission. Tues–Sat 10am–4:30pm, Sun 1:30–4:30pm. Closed Sept. Bus: 7/7B, 16, or 25.

Called the "Jewel of the Park," this museum houses the Putnam Foundation's collection of 19th-century American paintings and works by European old masters, as well as an outstanding display of Russian icons.

4 More Attractions

DOWNTOWN & BEYOND

✪ **Cabrillo National Monument.** 1800 Cabrillo Memorial Dr., Point Loma. ☎ **619/557-5450.** www.nps.gov/cabr. Admission $5 per vehicle, $2 for walk-ins, free for children under 17 and American citizens age 62 and older with Golden Age Passport. Daily 9am–5:15pm. Take I-5 or I-8 to Highway 209/ Rosecrans St. and follow signs. Bus: 26.

Breathtaking views mingle with the early history of San Diego, which began when Juan Rodríguez Cabrillo arrived in 1542. His statue dominates the tip of Point Loma, which is also a vantage point for watching migrating gray whales en route from the Arctic Ocean to Baja California from December through March. The restored lighthouse (1855) allows a glimpse of what life was like here in the past century. The road into the monument passes Fort Rosecrans National Cemetery, with row after row of white markers. National Park Service rangers lead walks at the monument, and there are tide pools that beg for exploration. Free 30-minute films on Cabrillo, tide pools, and California gray whales are shown on the hour daily from 10am to 4pm. Cabrillo National Monument welcomes almost 1.2 million visitors annually, making it one of the country's most visited national monuments. Only a half-hour ride from downtown, the trip is worth your time. Gray Line tours also offers an excursion to the monument (see "Organized Tours," later in this chapter).

Children's Museum of San Diego. 200 W. Island Ave. ☎ **619/233-KIDS.** Admission $6 adults and children, $3 seniors, free for children under 2. Tues–Fri 10am–3pm, Sat–Sun 10am–4pm. Trolley: Convention Center; museum is a block away. All-day parking (across the street) about $3.

This interactive attraction, which encourages participation, is a home away from home for kids. It provides ongoing supervised activities, as well as a monthly special celebration, recognizing important issues such as earth awareness or African-American history. The indoor-outdoor art studio is a big draw for kids ages 2 to 10. There is also a theater with costumes for budding actors to don, plus an observation walk above the exhibits that kids climb on and exit by way of a spiral slide. The museum shop is filled with toys, games, crafts, and books. School groups come in the morning, so you might want to schedule your visit for the afternoon.

Firehouse Museum. 1572 Columbia St. (at Cedar St.). ☎ **619/232-FIRE.** Admission $2 adults, $1 seniors and military in uniform, $1 youths 13–17, free for children under 13. Wed–Fri 10am–2pm, Sat–Sun 10am–4pm. Bus: 5, 16, or 105.

Appropriately housed in San Diego's oldest firehouse, the museum features shiny fire engines, including hand-drawn and horse-drawn models, a 1903 steam pumper, and memorabilia such as antique alarms, fire hats, and foundry molds for fire hydrants. There's also a small gift shop.

✪ **Maritime Museum.** 1306 N. Harbor Dr. ☎ **619/234-9153.** www.sdmaritime.com. Admission $5 adults, $4 seniors over 62 and youths 13–17, $2 children 6–12, free for children under 6. Daily 9am–8pm. Bus: 2. Trolley: America Plaza.

This unique museum consists of a trio of fine ships: the full-rigged merchant vessel *Star of India* (1863), whose impressive masts are an integral part of the San Diego cityscape; the gleaming white San Francisco–Oakland steam-powered ferry *Berkeley* (1898), which worked round-the-clock to carry people to safety following the 1906 San Francisco earthquake; and the sleek *Medea* (1904), one of the world's few remaining large steam yachts. You can board and explore each vessel, and from April through October you can watch movies on deck (see chapter 8, "San Diego After Dark").

Museum of Contemporary Art, Downtown (MCA). 1001 Kettner Blvd. (at Broadway). ☎ **619/234-1001.** Admission $2 adults; $1 students, military with ID, and seniors; free for children under 13. Free 1st Tues and Sun of each month. Tues–Sat 10am–5pm, Sun noon–5pm. Parking $2 with validation at America Plaza Complex. Trolley: America Plaza.

MCA Downtown is the second location of the Museum of Contemporary Art, San Diego (the first is in La Jolla). Two large and two smaller galleries present changing exhibitions of nationally and internationally distinguished contemporary artists. Lectures and tours for adults and children are also offered. There's a gift shop and bookstore on the premises.

Villa Montezuma. 1925 K St. (at 20th Ave.). ☎ **619/239-2211.** Admission $3 adults, $5 in combination with Marston House (in Balboa Park), free for children under 13. Sat–Sun noon–4:30pm. Bus: 3, 3A, 4, 5, 16, or 105 to Market and Imperial sts. By car, follow K St.

This stunning mansion just east of downtown was built in 1887 for internationally acclaimed musician and author Jesse Shepard. Lush with Victoriana, it features more stained glass than most churches have; windows depict Mozart, Beethoven, Sappho, Rubens, St. Cecilia (patron saint of musicians), and other notables. The striking ceilings are of Lincrusta Walton—pressed canvas coated with linseed oil, a forerunner of linoleum, which never looked this good. Shepard lived here with his life companion, Lawrence Tonner, for only 2 years and died in obscurity in Los Angeles in 1927. The San Diego Historical Society painstakingly restored the house, which is on the National Register of Historic Places, and furnished it with period pieces. Unfortunately, the neighborhood is not as fashionable as the building, but it's safe to park your car in the daytime. If you love Victorian houses, don't miss this one for its quirkiness.

William Heath Davis House Museum. 410 Island Ave. (at Fourth Ave.). ☎ **619/233-4692.** www.gqhf.com. Admission $2. Mon–Fri 10am–2pm, Sat 10am–4pm, Sun noon–4pm. Call ahead to verify hours. Bus: 1, 3, or 3A. Trolley: Gaslamp Quarter/Convention Center W.

Shipped by boat to San Diego in 1850 from Portland, Maine, this is the oldest structure in the Gaslamp Quarter. It is a well-preserved example of a prefabricated "saltbox" family home, and has remained structurally unchanged for over 120 years. A museum, on the first and second floors, is open to the public, as is the small park adjacent to the house. The house is also home to the Gaslamp Quarter Historical Foundation, which sponsors walking tours of the quarter every Saturday at 11am for $5 (see "Organized Tours," in section 7).

OLD TOWN

The birthplace of San Diego—indeed, of California—Old Town takes you back to the Mexican California, which existed here until the mid-1800s.

Free walking tours leave daily at 10:30am and 2pm from **Seeley Stables Visitor Center** (☎ 619/220-5422), at the head of the pedestrian walkway that is the continuation of San Diego Avenue.

Admission to all museums, open daily from 10am to 5pm, is free. Seven of the park's 20 structures are original; the rest are reconstructed. All museums are free, although donations are welcome.

They're accepted at the Park Headquarters; La Casa de Estudillo, which depicts the living conditions of a wealthy family in 1872; and Seeley Stables, named after A. L. Seeley, who ran the stagecoach and mail service in these parts from 1867 to 1871. The stables have two floors of wagons, carriages, stagecoaches, and other memorabilia, including washboards, slot machines, and hand-worked saddles, as well as a 17-minute slide show.

On weekdays during the school year, Old Town buzzes with fourth graders on field trips to the Park.

Heritage Park. 2455 Heritage Park Row (corner of Juan and Harney sts.). ☎ **619/694-3049.** Free admission. Daily 9:30am–3pm. Bus: 4 or 5/105.

This 7.8-acre county park contains seven original 19th-century houses moved here from other places and given new uses. Among them are a bed-and-breakfast, a doll shop, and a gift shop. The most recent addition is the small synagogue, placed near the park's entrance in 1989. A glorious coral tree crowns the top of the hill.

Junípero Serra Museum. 2727 Presidio Dr., Presidio Park. ☎ **619/297-3258.** Admission $5 adults, $4 seniors and students, $2 children 6–17, free for children under 6. Fri–Sun 10am–4:30pm. Take Interstate 8 to the Taylor St. exit. Turn right on Taylor, then left on Presidio Dr.

Perched on a hill above Old Town, the stately mission-style build-ing overlooks the hillside where California began. Here, in 1769, the first mission and first non-native settlement on the west coast of the United States and Canada were founded. The museum's exhibits introduce visitors to California's origins and to the Native Ameri-can, Spanish, and Mexican people who first called this place home. On display are their belongings, from cannons to cookware; a Span-ish furniture collection; and one of the first paintings brought to California, which survived being damaged in an Indian attack. The mission remained San Diego's only settlement until the 1820s, when families began to move down the hill into what is now Old Town. You can also watch an ongoing archaeological dig uncovering more of the items used by early settlers. From the 70-foot tower, visitors can compare the spectacular view with historic photos to see how this land has changed over time.

The museum is in Presidio Park, called the "Plymouth Rock of the Pacific." The large cross in the park was made of floor tile from the Presidio ruins. Sculptor Arthur Putnam made the statues of Father Serra, founder of the missions in California. Climb up to **Inspiration Point,** as many have done for marriage ceremonies, for a sweeping view of the area.

Mission Basilica San Diego de Alcala. 10818 San Diego Mission Rd., Mission Valley. ☎ **619/281-8449.** Admission $2 adults, $1 seniors and students, 50¢ children under 13. Free Sun and for daily services. Daily 9am–5pm; mass daily 7am and 5:30pm. Take I-8 to Mission Gorge Rd. to Twain Ave. Bus: 6, 16, 25, 43, or 81.

Established in 1769, this was the first link in a chain of 21 missions founded by Spanish missionary Junípero Serra. In 1774, the mission was moved to its present site for agricultural reasons, and to separate Native American converts from the fortress that included the original building. A few bricks belonging to the original mission can be seen in Presidio Park in Old Town. Mass is said daily in this active Catholic parish. Other missions in the San Diego area include Mission San Luis Rey de Francia in Oceanside, Mission San Antonia de Pala near Mount Palomar, and Mission Santa Ysabel near Julian.

Whaley House. 2482 San Diego Ave. ☎ **619/298-2482.** Admission $4 adults, $3 seniors over 60, $2 children 5–18, free for children under 5. June–Sept daily 10am–5pm, Oct–May Wed–Mon 10am–5pm. Closed on major holidays.

In 1856, this striking two-story brick house (the first one in these parts) one block from Old Town State Historic Park was built for Thomas Whaley and his family. Whaley was a New Yorker who arrived via San Francisco, where he had been lured by the gold rush. The house is one of only two authenticated haunted houses in California, and 10,000 schoolchildren visit each year to see for themselves. Apparently, four spirits haunt the house, and other paranormal phenomena have taken place. Exhibits include a life mask of Abraham Lincoln, one of only six made; the spinet piano used in the movie *Gone With the Wind;* and the concert piano that accompanied Swedish soprano Jenny Lind on her final U.S. tour in 1852. Director June Reading will make you feel at home, in spite of the ghosts.

MISSION BAY & THE BEACHES

This is a great area for walking, jogging, in-line skating, biking, and boating. See the appropriate headings in "Outdoor Pursuits," below.

Giant Dipper Roller Coaster. 3190 Mission Blvd. ☎ **619/488-1549.** Ride on the Giant Dipper $3. MC, V. Sun–Thurs 11am–10pm, Fri–Sat 11am–11pm. Take I-5 to the Sea World exit, and follow W. Mission Bay Park to Belmont Park.

A local landmark for 70 years, the Giant Dipper is one of two surviving fixtures from the original Belmont Amusement Park (the other is the Plunge swimming pool). After sitting dormant for 15 years, the vintage wooden roller coaster, with more than 2,600 feet of track and 13 hills, underwent extensive restoration and reopened in 1991. If you're in the neighborhood (especially with older kids), it's worth a stop. You must be 50 inches tall to ride the roller coaster. You can also ride on the Giant Dipper's neighbor, the Liberty Carousel ($1).

LA JOLLA

The area's most scenic spot—star of postcards for over 100 years—is **La Jolla Cove** and **Ellen Browning Scripps Park** on the cliff above it. Both are on Coast Boulevard. The park is a boat-free zone, with protected undersea flora and fauna that draws many scuba divers and other visitors. Swimming, sunning, picnicking, barbecuing, reading, and strolling along the oceanfront walkway are all ongoing activities. The unique 6,000-acre **San Diego–La Jolla Underwater Park,** established in 1970, stretches from La Jolla Cove to the northern end of Torrey Pines State Reserve. It can be reached from La Jolla Cove or La Jolla Shores.

For a scenic drive, follow La Jolla Boulevard to Nautilus Street and turn east to get to **Mount Soledad,** which offers a 360° view of the area. The cross on top, erected in 1954, is 43 feet high and 12 feet wide.

Highlights in town include **Mary Star of the Sea,** 7727 Girard (at Kline), a beautiful Roman Catholic church; and the **La Valencia Hotel,** 1132 Prospect St., a fine example of Spanish Colonial structure. The **La Jolla Woman's Club,** 7791 Draper Ave.; the adjacent **Museum of Contemporary Art, San Diego;** the **La Jolla Recreation Center;** and **The Bishop's School** are all examples of village buildings designed by architect Irving Gill.

At La Jolla's north end, you'll find the 1,200-acre, 15,000-student **University of California, San Diego** (UCSD), which was established in 1960. The campus features the Stuart Collection of public sculpture and the Birch Aquarium at Scripps Institution of Oceanography (see individual listings, below). Louis Kahn designed the **Salk Institute for Biological Studies,** 10010 North Torrey Pines Rd.

Insider's Tip

While droves of folks stroll the sidewalks adjacent to the San Diego–La Jolla Underwater Park and La Jolla Cove, only a few know about Coast Walk. It starts near the **La Jolla Cave & Shell Shop,** 1325 Coast Blvd. (☎ **858/454-6080**), and affords a wonderful view of the beach and beyond.

Museum of Contemporary Art, San Diego. 700 Prospect St. ☎ **858/ 454-3541.** Fax 858/454-6985. www.mcasandiego.org. Admission $4 adults, $2 students and seniors, free for children under 12; free 1st Tues and Sun of each month. Tues, Thurs–Sat 10am–5pm, Wed 10am–8pm, Sun noon–5pm. Take the Ardath Rd. exit off I-5 north or the La Jolla Village Dr. west exit off I-5 south. Take Torrey Pines Rd. to Prospect Place and turn right. Prospect Place becomes Prospect St.

Focusing primarily on work produced since 1950, the museum is known internationally for its permanent collection and thought-provoking exhibitions. The MCA's collection of contemporary art comprises more than 3,000 works of painting, sculpture, drawings, prints, photography, video, and multimedia works. The holdings include every major art movement of the past half-century, with a strong representation by California artists. You'll see particularly noteworthy examples of minimalism, light and space work, conceptualism, installation, and site-specific art—the outside sculptures were designed specifically for this site. The museum is perched on a cliff overlooking the Pacific Ocean, and the views from the galleries are gorgeous. The original building on the site was the residence of the legendary Ellen Browning Scripps, designed by Irving Gill in 1916. It became an art museum in 1941, and the original Gill building facade was recently uncovered and restored.

✪ **Birch Aquarium at Scripps.** 2300 Expedition Way. ☎ **858/534-FISH.** Fax 858/534-7114. Admission $7.50 adults, $6.50 seniors, $4 children 3–17, free for children under 3. Parking $3. AE, MC, V. Daily 9am–5pm. Take I-5 to La Jolla Village Dr. exit, go west 1 mile, and turn left at Expedition Way. Bus: 34.

The Birch Aquarium is operated by Scripps Institution of Oceanography, at the University of California, San Diego. This beautiful facility is both an aquarium and a museum. The aquarium is to the right of the entrance, the museum to the left. To make the most of the self-guided experience, be sure to pick up a visitor guide from the information booth just inside the entrance, and take time to read the text on each of the exhibits. The aquarium affords close-up views of the Pacific Northwest, the California coast, Mexico's Sea of Cortez, and the tropical seas, all presented in 33 marine-life tanks. The giant kelp forest is particularly impressive (keep an eye out for a tiger shark or an eel swimming through). Be sure to notice my favorite sea creatures: the fanciful white anemones and the ethereal moon jellies (which look like parachutes). The rooftop demonstration tide pool not only shows visitors marine coastal life but offers an amazing view of Scripps Pier, La Jolla Shores Beach, the village of La Jolla, and the ocean. Free tide-pool talks are offered on weekends, which is also when the aquarium is most crowded.

The museum section has numerous interpretive exhibits on current and historic research at the Scripps Institution, which was established in 1903 and became part of the university system in 1912. You'll learn what fog is and why salt melts snow; the number of supermarket products with ingredients that come from the sea (toothpaste, ice cream, and matches, to name a few) might surprise you; and you can feel what an earthquake is like and experience a 12-minute simulated submarine ride. The bookstore is well stocked with textbooks, science books, educational toys, gifts, and T-shirts.

A series of **"Seaside Explorations,"** such as the La Jolla Coast Walk, Tidepooling Adventures, and Running with Grunion, are offered. Call ☎ **858/543-6691** for information and prices.

CORONADO

It's hard to miss one of Coronado's most famous landmarks: the **Coronado Bay Bridge.** Completed in 1969, this five-lane bridge spans 2 miles across the bay, linking San Diego and Coronado. When it opened, it put the commuter ferries out of business, although in 1986 passenger ferry service restarted. Crossing the bridge by car or bus is a thrill because you can see Mexico, the San Diego skyline, Coronado, the naval station, and San Diego Bay. The bridge's middle section floats, so that if it's destroyed in wartime, naval ships will still have access to the harbor and sea beyond. From San Diego to Coronado, vehicles with solo occupants pay a $1 toll; there's no charge if two or more people are in the car or if you're traveling from Coronado to San Diego. Bus 901 from downtown will also take you over the bridge.

Coronado Historical Museum. 1126 Loma Ave. ☎ **619/435-7242.** Free admission. Wed–Sat 10am–4pm, Sun noon–4pm. Follow Orange Ave. to Loma Ave. and turn right; it's on the left side beside Chez Loma restaurant.

In the Thomson House (ca. 1898), this little museum goes back to the Coronado of yesteryear. It holds photographs of the Hotel Del in its infancy; the old ferries; and Tent City, a seaside campground for middle-income vacationers from 1900 to 1939. Other memorabilia include army uniforms, old postcards, and even recorded music. You'll learn about the island's military aviation history during World Wars I and II.

FARTHER AFIELD

LEGOLAND. 1 Lego Drive, Carlsbad. ☎ **877/534-6526** or 760/438-5346. www.legolandca.com. Admission $32 adults, $25 seniors and children 3–16, free for children under 3. Daily 10am–dusk, extended summer and holiday hours; call for complete schedule. From I-5, take the Canon exit east, which leads to the entrance.

The ultimate monument to the world's most famous plastic building blocks, LEGOLAND (newly opened in 1999) is the third such theme park; the branches in Denmark and Britain have proven enormously successful. Attractions include "hands-on" interactive displays; a life-size menagerie of tigers, giraffes, and other animals; scale models of international landmarks (the Eiffel Tower, Sydney Opera House, and so on)—all constructed of real LEGO bricks! "MiniLand" is a 1:20 scale representation of American achievement, from a New England Pilgrim village to Mount Rushmore. There's a gravity coaster ride (don't worry, they used steel) through a LEGO castle, and a DUPLO building area to keep smaller children occupied.

5 Free of Charge & Full of Fun

It's easy to get charged up on vacation—$10 here, $5 there, and pretty soon your credit-card balance looks like the national debt. To keep that from happening, we offer this list of free San Diego activities.

DOWNTOWN & BEYOND

It doesn't cost a penny to stroll around the Gaslamp Quarter, which is full of restaurants, shops, and historic buildings, or along the Embarcadero (waterfront), and around the shops at Seaport Village or Horton Plaza. And don't forget: Walkabout International offers free guided walking tours. **Centre City Development Corporation's Downtown Information Center** (☎ **619/235-2222**) offers free trolley tours of the downtown area on the first and third Saturdays of the month from 10am to noon (see "Trolley Tours" in section 7).

If you'd rather drive around, ask for the map of the **52-mile San Diego Scenic Drive** when you're at the International Visitor Information Center.

The downtown branch of the Museum of Contemporary Art, San Diego, is free on the first Tuesday and Sunday of each month. Another fun activity is the **Sunset Cinema,** discussed in "Lights, Camera...Movies!" in chapter 8. And you can fish free of charge from any municipal pier. The **Children's Park,** across the street from the Children's Museum of San Diego, is free, as are all parks in San Diego.

BALBOA PARK

The **San Diego Zoo** is free to all on the first Monday of October (Founders Day), and children under 12 enter free every day during October.

All the **museums** in Balboa Park are open to the public without charge 1 day a month. Here's a list of the free days:

> **1st Tuesday of each month:** Natural History Museum, Reuben H. Fleet Science Center, Model Railroad Museum.
> **2nd Tuesday:** Museum of Photographic Arts, Hall of Champions, Museum of San Diego History.
> **3rd Tuesday:** Museum of Art, Museum of Man, Mingei International Museum of World Folk Art, Japanese Friendship Garden.
> **4th Tuesday:** San Diego Aerospace Museum, San Diego Automotive Museum.

These Balboa Park attractions are always free: The Botanical Building and Lily Pond, House of Pacific Relations International Cottages, and Timken Museum of Art.

Free 1-hour Sunday concerts and free Summer Festival concerts are given at the Spreckels Organ Pavilion.

OLD TOWN & BEYOND

Explore **Heritage Park, Presidio Park,** or **Old Town State Historic Park.** There's free entertainment (mariachis and folk dancers) at the **Bazaar del Mundo,** 2754 Calhoun (☎ **619/296-3161**), on Saturday and Sunday. **Mission Trails Regional Park,** which offers hiking trails and an interpretive center, is at the east end of Highway 52.

MISSION BAY, PACIFIC BEACH & BEYOND

Walk along the beach or around the bay—it's free, fun, and good for you. (See "Hiking/Walking" in "Outdoor Pursuits," in section 8.)

LA JOLLA

Enjoy free outdoor **concerts** at Scripps Park on Sundays from 2 to 4pm, mid-June through mid-September (☎ **858/525-3160**).

Anytime is a good time to walk around the La Jolla Cove, Ellen Browning Scripps Park, and Torrey Pines State Reserve, or watch the fur-seal colony at Seal Rock or the Children's Pool. If you're a diver, check out the 6,000-acre San Diego–La Jolla Underwater Park, which stretches from La Jolla Cove to the northern end of Torrey Pines State Reserve.

If you like arts and crafts, you'll love the **La Jolla Arts Festival,** held the last weekend in September. It's also fun to meander around the campus of the University of California, San Diego (UCSD) and view the Stuart Collection of Outdoor Sculpture. The La Jolla branch of the Museum of Contemporary Art, San Diego, is free on the first Tuesday and Sunday of each month.

For the best vista, follow the "Scenic Drive" signs to Mount Soledad and a 360° view of the area.

CORONADO

Drive across the Coronado Bay Bridge (free for two or more people in a car) and take a self-guided tour of the Hotel del Coronado's grounds and photo gallery. Take a walk on the beach and continue to the Coronado Historical Museum.

6   Especially for Kids

If you didn't know better, you would think that San Diego was designed by parents planning a long summer vacation. Activities abound for toddlers to teens. Dozens of public parks, 70 miles of beaches, and myriad museums are just part of what awaits kids and families. For up-to-the-minute information about activities for children, pick up a free copy of the monthly *San Diego Family Press;* its calendar of events is geared toward family activities and kids' interests. The **International Visitor Information Center,** at First Avenue and F Street (☎ **619/236-1212**), is always a great resource.

THE TOP ATTRACTIONS

- **Balboa Park** *(see p. 117)* has street entertainers and clowns that always rate high with kids. They can usually be found around El Prado on weekends. The Natural History Museum and the Reuben H. Fleet Science Center, with its hands-on exhibits and IMAX/OMNIMAX theater, draw kids like magnets.
- **The San Diego Zoo** *(see p. 108)* appeals to children of all ages, and the double-decker bus tours bring all the animals into easy view of even the smallest visitors.
- **Sea World** *(see p. 112),* on Mission Bay, entertains everyone with killer whales, pettable dolphins, and plenty of penguins— the park's penguin exhibit is home to more penguins than are in all other zoos combined. Try out the new family adventure

land, "Shamu's Happy Harbor," where everyone is encouraged to explore, crawl, climb, jump, and get wet in more than 20 interactive areas; or brave a raging river in Shipwreck Rapids.

- **Wild Animal Park** *(see p. 111)* brings geography classes to life when kids find themselves gliding through the wilds of Africa and Asia in a monorail.

OTHER ATTRACTIONS

- **Children's Museum of San Diego** *(see p. 124)* provides a wonderful interactive and imagination-probing experience.
- **Birch Aquarium at Scripps** *(see p. 130)*, in La Jolla, is an aquarium that lets kids explore the realms of the deep and learn about life in the sea.
- **LEGOLAND** *(see p. 132)*, in Carlsbad, is a brand-new theme park primarily for children; kids can see impressive models built entirely with LEGO blocks. There are also rides, refreshments, and LEGO and DUPLO building contests.

7 Organized Tours

It's almost impossible to get a handle on the diversity of San Diego in a short visit, but one way to maximize your time is to take an organized tour that introduces you to the city. Many are creative, not as touristy as you might fear, and allow you a great deal of versatility in planning your day.

Centre City Development Corporation's Downtown Information Center (☎ **619/235-2222**) offers free downtown residential walking tours for five or more people Saturdays from 1pm to 3pm. The tours require reservations and start at 225 Broadway, Suite 160. Go inside to see models of the Gaslamp Quarter and the downtown area. The office is open Monday through Saturday from 9am to 5pm.

BAY EXCURSIONS

Bahia Belle. 998 W. Mission Bay Dr. ☎ **619/539-7779.** www.sternwheelers.com. Tickets $6 adults, $3 children under 12. June and Sept Wed–Sat 6:30pm–12:30am; July–Aug Wed–Sun 6:30pm–12:30am; Oct 1–Nov 30 and Jan 1–May 31 Fri–Sat 7:30pm–12:30am. Children accompanied by an adult allowed until 9:30pm; after 9:30pm, 21 or over only (with valid ID).

Cruise Mission Bay and dance under the moonlight aboard this festive stern-wheeler. It picks up passengers at the dock of the Bahia Hotel, 998 W. Mission Bay Dr., on the half hour from 7:30pm (6:30 in summer) to 12:30am, and at the Catamaran Resort Hotels,

3999 Mission Blvd., on the hour from 8pm (7pm in summer) to midnight.

Hornblower Cruises & Events. 1066 N. Harbor Dr. ☎ **619/234-8687** for info, or 619/686-8715 for tickets. www.hornblower.com. Tickets start at $49 for dinner cruise, $33.50 for brunch cruise; half price for children. Harbor tours $12–$17.

This company offers 1- and 2-hour narrated tours of San Diego Bay. Nightly dinner cruises with music and dancing run from 7 to 9pm, Sunday brunch cruises from 11am to 1pm. Whale-watching trips are offered in the winter.

❍ **Gondola di Venezia.** 1010 Santa Clara Place, Mission Bay. ☎ **619/221-2999.** Tickets $72 per couple; $17 for each additional passenger. Located east of Mission Blvd.

This unique business operates from centrally located Santa Clara Point near the Catamaran Hotel, plying the calm waters of scenic Mission Bay in gondolas crafted according to centuries-old designs from Venice. It features all the trimmings, right down to the striped-shirt–clad gondolier with ribbons waving from his (or her) straw hat. Mediterranean music plays while you and up to three friends recline with snuggly blankets, and the company will even provide antipasto appetizers and chilled wine glasses and ice for the beverage of your choice (BYOB). A 1-hour cruise for two is $72, and expanded packages are available. Hours of operation are noon to midnight daily, year-round. Reservations are necessary.

San Diego Harbor Excursion. 1050 N. Harbor Dr. (foot of Broadway). ☎ **800/442-7847** or 619/234-4111. Tickets $12 for 1 hr., $17 for 2 hrs.; half price for children.

The company offers daily 1- and 2-hour narrated tours of the bay, plus dinner cruises. In the winter, it runs whale-watching excursions. The narrators have been with the company for at least 5 years. Times and frequency vary seasonally.

BUS TOURS

Note: Both of these bus companies pick up passengers at most area hotels.

San Diego Mini Tours (☎ 619/477-8687) offers city sightseeing tours, including a "Grand Tour" that covers San Diego, Tijuana, and a 1-hour harbor cruise. It also runs trips to the San Diego Zoo, Sea World, Disneyland, Universal Studios, Tijuana, Rosarito Beach, and Ensenada. Prices range from $26 to $62 for adults, $14 to $44 for children under 12, and include admissions. Multiple tours can be combined for discounted rates.

Gray Line San Diego (☎ 800/331-5077 or 619/491-0011; www.graylinesandiego.com) offers city sightseeing, including tours of Cabrillo National Monument, Sea World, and La Jolla. Other trips go farther afield, to the Wild Animal Park, wine country, and Tijuana and Ensenada, Mexico. Prices range from $24 to $56 for adults and $10 to $35 for children.

TROLLEY TOURS

San Diego's most comprehensive, and most popular, tour is the narrated **Old Town Trolley** (☎ 619/298-TOUR). The 30-mile route has more than a dozen stops. You can get off at any of them, explore at leisure, and reboard when you please (a bus-cum-trolley passes each stop every half hour). Stops include the Embarcadero, downtown area, Horton Plaza, Gaslamp Quarter, Coronado, San Diego Zoo, Balboa Park, Heritage Park, and Presidio Park. The tour costs $20 for adults, $8 for children 6 to 12, and is free for children under 5, for one complete loop, no matter how many times you hop on or off the trolley. One loop takes 90 minutes; once you've finished the circuit, you can't go around again. It's a good idea to start early in the day. Old Town Trolley Tours offers tours to Naval Air Station North Island on Friday morning.

Centre City Development Corporation's Downtown Information Center (☎ 619/235-2222) offers free trolley tours of the downtown area on the first and third Saturdays of the month from 10am to noon.

WHALE WATCHING

As it is everywhere along the coast, whale watching is an eagerly anticipated wintertime activity in San Diego. If you've ever been lucky enough to spot one of these gentle behemoths swimming gracefully and purposefully through the ocean, you'll understand the thrill. When they pass the San Diego shores, California gray whales are more than three-quarters of the way from Alaska to their breeding grounds at the southern tip of Baja—or just beginning the trip home to their rich Alaskan feeding grounds (with calves in tow). Mid-December to mid-March is the best time to see the migration, and there are several ways to view the spectacular parade.

The easiest is to grab a pair of binoculars and head to a good landbound vantage point. **Cabrillo National Monument,** on Point Loma peninsula, offers a glassed-in observatory and educational whale exhibits. Each January the rangers conduct a special "Watch Weekend" featuring presentations by whale experts, programs for children, and entertainment. The monument is open daily 10am to

5pm, and admission is $5 per car; call ☎ **619/557-5450** for more information.

In La Jolla, the **Birch Aquarium at Scripps Institution of Oceanography** celebrates the gray whale season with "WhaleFest" throughout January and February. A variety of educational activities and whale exhibits are planned, and the aquarium's outdoor plaza offers an excellent vantage point for spotting the mammals from shore. Aquarium admission is $7.50 for adults, $6.50 for seniors, and $4 for kids 3 to 17. Daily hours are 9am–5pm; call ☎ **858/534-3474** for further information.

If you want to get a closer look, head out to sea on one of the excursions that locate and follow gray whales, taking care not to disturb their journey. **Classic Sailing Adventures** (☎ **800/659-0141** or 619/224-0800) offers two trips per day (8:30am and 1pm); each lasts 4 hours and carries a maximum of six passengers. Sailing is less distracting to the whales, but more expensive; tickets are $50 per person, including beverages and snacks.

Companies that offer traditional, engine-driven expeditions include **Hornblower Cruises & Events** and **San Diego Harbor Excursion** (see "Bay Excursions," above). Excursions are generally 3 hours, and fares run around $19 for adults, with discounts for kids.

The **San Diego Natural History Museum** begins offering naturalist-led half-day whale-watching trips in January aboard the 88-passenger *Pacific Queen*. Your guide will discuss whale behavior and biology, as well as sea birds, harbor seals, sea lions, and other coastal life. Passengers must be 12 years or older, and fares are $49 to $66 for non-museum members. For an excursion schedule and preregistration, call ☎ **619/232-3821,** ext. 203.

WALKING TOURS

Walkabout International, 835 Fifth Ave., Room 407 (☎ **619/231-7463**), sponsors more than 100 free walking tours every month. They're led by volunteers in the San Diego area. A lively guide known as Downtown Sam, who retired from the Air Force in 1972, leads downtown tours, which are particularly popular with retired San Diegans eager for exercise and camaraderie. He's easy to spot, in walking shorts and a cap with a button proclaiming "No thanks, I'd rather walk." Sam's Saturday-morning tours draw 20 to 40 people, and they end with a stop for coffee or a meal. Sam also leads a 1½-hour downtown theme tour at 11am on Tuesday, focusing on bookstores, shopping, pubs, thrift shops, bank lobbies—you name it.

On Saturday from 1 to 3pm, the **Centre City Development Corporation,** 225 Broadway, Suite 160 (☎ **619/235-2222**), offers free walking tours that focus on downtown-area development. Reservations are required.

Coronado Touring, 1110 Isabella Ave., Coronado (☎ **619/435-5993** or 619/435-5444), provides upbeat, informative 90-minute walking tours of Coronado, including the Hotel del Coronado. Enthusiastic guides Nancy Cobb and Gerry MacCartee have been doing this since 1980, so they know their subject well. Tours leave at 11am on Tuesday, Thursday, and Saturday from the Glorietta Bay Inn, 1630 Glorietta Blvd. (near Orange Avenue). The price is $7.

At the **Cabrillo National Monument** on the tip of Point Loma, rangers often lead free walking tours (see "More Attractions," in section 4). **The Gaslamp Quarter Association** offers tours of the quarter on Saturday at 11am for a $5 donation. Tours leave from William Heath Davis House, 410 Island Ave. (☎ **619/233-5227**).

Docents at **Torrey Pines State Reserve** in La Jolla lead guided nature walks on weekends (see "Hiking/Walking" under "Outdoor Pursuits," below).

You can explore La Jolla by taking walking and shopping tours conducted by **La Jolla Walking Tours** (☎ **858/453-8219**). These leave from the Colonial Inn, 910 Prospect St., on Friday and Saturday at 10am and cost $9.

Volunteers from the **Natural History Museum** (☎ **619/232-3821,** ext. 203) lead nature walks throughout San Diego County.

8 Outdoor Pursuits

See section 2 of this chapter for a complete rundown of San Diego's beaches.

BIKING

Most major thoroughfares offer bike lanes. To receive a great map of San Diego County's bike lanes and routes, call **Ride Link Bicycle Information** (☎ **619/231-BIKE** or 619/237-POOL). You might also want to talk to the **City of San Diego Bicycle Coordinator** (☎ **619/533-3110**) or the **San Diego Bicycle Coalition** (☎ **619/685-7742**). For more practical information on biking on city streets, turn to "Getting Around: By Bicycle" in chapter 3. Always remember to wear a helmet; it's the law.

The Mission Bay and Coronado areas, in particular, are good for leisurely bike rides. The boardwalk in Pacific Beach and Mission

Beach can get very crowded, especially on weekends. Coronado has a 16-mile round-trip bike trail that starts at the Ferry Landing Marketplace and follows a well-marked route around Coronado to Imperial Beach.

RENTALS, ORGANIZED BIKE TOURS & OTHER TWO-WHEEL ADVENTURES   Downtown, call **Bike Tours San Diego,** 509 Fifth Ave. (☎ **619/238-2444**), which offers free delivery. In Mission Bay there's **Hamel's Action Sports Center,** 704 Ventura Place, off Mission Boulevard at Ocean Front Walk (☎ **619/488-8889**), and **Hilton San Diego Resort,** 1775 E. Mission Bay Dr. (☎ **619/276-4010**). In La Jolla, try **La Jolla Sports and Photo,** 2199 Avenida de la Playa (☎ **858/459-1114**). In Coronado, check out **Bikes and Beyond,** 1201 First St. at the Ferry Landing Marketplace (☎ **619/435-7180**), which also offers surrey and skate rentals. Expect to pay $5 to $6 for bicycles, $15 to $25 hours for surreys (pedal-powered carriages).

Adventure Bike Tours, 333 W. Harbor Dr., in the San Diego Marriott Marina (☎ **619/234-1500,** ext. 6514), conducts bicycle tours from San Diego to Coronado. The cost of about $40 includes ferry fare and equipment. The company offers a guided tour around the bay (the Bayside Glide) for $22 per person and rent bikes for $8 an hour, $18 for half a day, or $25 for a full day. In-line skates are also for hire.

BOATING

Club Nautico, a concession at the San Diego Marriott Marina, 333 W. Harbor Dr. (☎ **619/233-9311**), provides guests and non-guests with an exhilarating way to see the bay. It rents 20- to 27-foot offshore powerboats by the hour, half day, or full day. Rentals start at $89 an hour. The company allows boats to be taken into the ocean, and also offers diving, water-skiing, and fishing packages.

Seaforth Boat Rental, 1641 Quivira Rd., Mission Bay (☎ **619/223-1681;** www.seaforth-boat-rental.com/seaforth), has a wide variety of boats for bay and ocean. It rents 15- to 135-horsepower powerboats for $45 to $90 an hour, 14- to 30-foot sailboats for $20 to $45 an hour, and ski boats and personal watercraft for $65 an hour. Half- and full-day rates are available. Canoes, pedal boats, and rowboats are available for those who prefer a slower pace.

Mission Bay Sportcenter, 1010 Santa Clara Place (☎ **619/488-1004**), rents sailboats, catamarans, sailboards, kayaks, personal watercraft, and motorboats. Prices range from $12 to $72 an hour, with discounts for 4-hour and full-day rentals. Instruction is available.

San Diego Yacht & Breakfast Club, 1880 Harbor Island Dr. (☎ 619/298-6623), rents kayaks for $20 an hour, 3-horsepower dinghies for $15 an hour, Windriders for $40 an hour, and Waverunners for $65 an hour. Half- and full-day rentals are available. **The San Diego Sailing Club,** at the same address and phone number, rents yachts and offers sailing lessons.

Coronado Boat Rental, 1715 Strand Way, Coronado (☎ 619/437-1514), rents powerboats with 90- and 110-horsepower motors for $55 to $90 an hour, with half- and full-day rates; and 14- to 30-foot sailboats for $25 to $45 an hour. It also rents personal watercraft, ski boats, canoes, pedal boats, fishing skiffs, and charter boats.

FISHING

For information on fishing, call the **City Fish Line** (☎ 619/465-3474). Anglers of any age can fish free of charge without a license off any municipal pier in California. Public fishing piers are on Shelter Island (where there's a statue dedicated to anglers), Ocean Beach, and Imperial Beach.

Fishing charters depart from Harbor and Shelter islands, Point Loma, the Imperial Beach pier, and Quivira Basin in Mission Bay (near the Hyatt Islandia Hotel). Participants over the age of 16 need a California fishing license.

For sportfishing, you can go out on a large boat for about $25 for half a day or $35 to $85 for three-quarters to a full day. To charter a boat for up to six people, the rates run about $550 for half a day and $850 for an entire day, more in summer. Call around and compare prices. Summer and fall are excellent times for excursions. Locally, the waters around Point Loma are filled with bass, bonito, and barracuda; the Coronado Islands, which belong to Mexico but are only about 18 miles from San Diego, are popular for abalone, yellowtail, yellowfin, and big-eyed tuna. Some outfitters will take you farther into Baja California waters. The following outfitters offer short or extended outings with daily departures: **H & M Landing,** 2803 Emerson (☎ 619/222-1144); **Islandia Sportfishing,** 1551 W. Mission Bay Rd. (☎ 619/222-1164); **Lee Palm Sportfishers** (☎ 619/224-3857); **Point Loma Sportfishing,** 1403 Scott St. (☎ 619/223-1627); and **Seaforth Boat Rentals,** 1641 Quivira Rd. (☎ 619/233-1681).

For freshwater fishing, San Diego's lakes and rivers are home to bass, channel and bullhead catfish, bluegill, trout, crappie, and sunfish. Most lakes have rental facilities for boats, tackle, and bait, and they also provide picnic and (usually) camping areas.

For more information on fishing in California, contact the **California Department of Fish and Game** (☎ 619/467-4201).

GOLF

With nearly 80 courses, 50 of them open to the public, San Diego County offers golf enthusiasts innumerable opportunities to play their game. Courses are diverse—some have vistas of the Pacific, others views of country hillsides or desert landscapes.

M & M Tee Times (☎ 800/867-7397 or 858/456-8366; www. torreypines.com) can arrange tee times for you at most golf courses. And where else but San Diego can you practice your golf swing in the middle of the central business district? **Metro Golf Harborside,** 801 W. Ash St. at Pacific Highway (☎ 619/239-GOLF), is open from 7am to 10pm Monday to Friday, 8am to 10pm on Saturday, and 9am to 9pm on Sunday. It offers 80 tees, a putting and chipping area, night lighting, a pro shop, and golf instruction. Club rental is available at $1 each; a large bucket of balls costs $6, a small bucket costs $3.

✪ **Balboa Park Municipal Golf Course.** 2600 Golf Course Dr. (off Pershing Dr. or 26th St. in southeast corner of the park), San Diego. ☎ **619/570-1234** (automated tee times) or 619/239-1660 (pro shop).

Everybody has a humble municipal course like this at home, with a bare-bones 1940s clubhouse where old guys hold down lunch counter stools for hours after the game—and players take a few more mulligans than they would elsewhere. Surrounded by the beauty of Balboa Park, this 18-hole course features mature, full trees; fairways sprinkled with eucalyptus leaves; and distractingly nice views of the San Diego skyline. It's so convenient and affordable that it's the perfect choice for visitors who want to work some golf into their vacation rather than the other way around. The course even rents clubs. Non-resident greens fees are $30 weekdays, $35 weekends; cart rental is $20, pull carts $5. Reservations are suggested at least a week in advance.

Coronado Municipal Golf Course. 2000 Visalia Row, Coronado. ☎ **619/435-3121.**

This is the first sight that welcomes you as you cross the Coronado Bay Bridge (the course is to the left). It is an 18-hole, par-72 course overlooking Glorietta Bay, and there's a coffee shop, pro shop, and driving range. Two-day prior reservations are strongly recommended; call anytime after 7am. Greens fees are $20 to walk and

$32 to ride for 18 holes; $10 to walk and $17 to ride after 4pm. Club rental is $15, and pull-cart rental is $4.

Four Seasons Resort Aviara Golf Club. 7447 Batiquitos Dr., Carlsbad. ☎ **760/603-6900.** From I-5 northbound, take the Aviara Pkwy. exit east to Batiquitos Dr. Turn right and continue 2 miles to the clubhouse.

Uniquely landscaped to incorporate natural elements compatible with the protected Batiquitos Lagoon nearby, Aviara doesn't infringe on the wetlands bird habitat. The course is 7,007 yards from the championship tees, laid out over rolling hillsides with plenty of bunker and water challenges. Casual duffers may be frustrated here. Greens fees are $175 (including mandatory cart), and there are practice areas for putting, chipping, sand play, and driving. The pro shop is fully equipped, as is the clubhouse. Golf packages are available for guests of the Four Seasons.

Morgan Run. 5690 Cancha de Golf, Rancho Santa Fe. ☎ **858/756-3255.** Take I-5 north to Via De la Valle exit east. After about 5 miles, signs will direct you to turn right on Cancha de Golf.

Formerly Whispering Palms, these three 9-hole courses (one par 35; two par 36) are part of a resort, but you don't have to stay there to play. Course architect Jay Morrish redesigned one of the courses in 1995. There's also a driving range. Greens fees are $65 during the week and $80 on weekends, including a cart.

Riverwalk Golf Club. 1150 Fashion Valley Rd., Mission Valley. ☎ **619/698-GOLF.** Take I-8 to Hotel Circle south, turn on Fashion Valley Rd.

Designed by Ted Robinson and Ted Robinson, Jr., these links meander along the Mission Valley floor. Replacing the private Stardust Golf Club, the course reopened in 1998, sporting a slick, upscale new clubhouse, four lakes with waterfalls (in play on 13 of the 27 holes), open, undulating fairways, and one peculiar feature—trolley tracks! The bright red trolley speeds through now and then, but doesn't prove too distracting. Non-resident greens fees, including cart, are $75 Monday through Thursday, $85 Friday and Sunday, and $95 Saturday (fees for residents are $30 less).

Singing Hills. 3007 Dehesa Rd., El Cajon. ☎ **800/457-5568** or 619/442-3425. Take Calif. 94 to the Willow Glen exit. Turn right and continue to the entrance.

The only resort in Southern California offering 54 holes of golf (two championship courses and a par-54 executive course), Singing Hills has taken advantage of the area's natural terrain. Mountains, natural rock outcroppings, and aged oaks and sycamores add character to individual holes. In 1997, this course made the *Golf for Women* magazine Top Fairways list as one of the courses that "best meet women golfers' needs." Singing Hills is the home of the 19-year-old School of Golf for Women. The golf courses are part of the Singing Hills Resort, but non-guests are welcome. Greens fees are $35 Monday through Thursday, $37 Friday, and $42 Saturday and Sunday for the two par-72 courses, and $14 on the shorter course. Cart rental costs $20. The resort offers a variety of good-value packages.

✪ **Torrey Pines Golf Course.** 11480 Torrey Pines Rd., La Jolla. ☎ **858/552-1784** for information, 858/570-1234 to book a tee time, 858/452-3226 for the pro shop.

Two gorgeous 18-hole championship courses are on the coast between La Jolla and Del Mar, only 15 minutes from downtown San Diego. Home of the Buick Invitational Tournament, these municipal courses are very popular. Both overlook the ocean; the north course is more picturesque, the south course more challenging.

Tee times are taken by computer, starting at 5am, up to 7 days in advance by telephone only. Confirmation numbers are issued, and you must have the number and photo identification with you when you check in with the starter 15 minutes ahead of time. If you're late, your time may be forfeited.

Insider's tip: Single golfers stand a good chance of getting on the course if they just turn up and wait for a threesome. The locals also sometimes circumvent the reservation system by spending the night in a camper in the parking lot. The starter lets these diehards on before the reservations made by the computer go into effect at 7:30am.

Golf professionals are available for lessons, and the pro shop rents clubs. Greens fees for out-of-towners are $48 during the week and $52 Saturday, Sunday, and holidays for 18 holes; $26 for 9 holes. After 4pm April through October and after 3pm November through March, the 18-hole fee is only $26. Cart rental is $28. San Diego city and county residents pay much less.

HIKING/WALKING

San Diego's mild climate makes it a great place to walk or hike most of the year, and the options are diverse. Walking along the water is particularly popular. The best **beaches** for walking are La Jolla Shores, Mission Beach, and Coronado, but pretty much any shore   .

is a good choice. You can also walk around Mission Bay on a series of connected footpaths. If a four-legged friend is your walking companion, head for Dog Beach in Ocean Beach or Fiesta Island in Mission Bay—two of the few areas where dogs can legally go unleashed. Coast Walk in La Jolla offers supreme surf-line views (see "La Jolla" under "More Attractions," in section 4).

The **Sierra Club** sponsors regular hikes in the San Diego area, and non-members are welcome to participate. There's always a Wednesday mountain hike, usually in the Cuyamaca Mountains, sometimes in the Lagunas; there are evening and day hikes as well. Most are free. For a recorded message about upcoming hikes, call ☎ **619/299-1744,** or call the office (☎ **619/299-1743**) weekdays from noon to 5pm or Saturday from 10am to 4pm.

Torrey Pines State Reserve in La Jolla (☎ **858/755-2063**) offers hiking trails with wonderful ocean views and a chance to see the rare torrey pine. To reach it, use North Torrey Pines Road. Trail access is free; parking costs $4 per car, $3 for seniors. Guided nature walks are available on weekends.

The **Bayside Trail** near Cabrillo National Monument also affords great views. Drive to the monument and follow signs to the trail.

Mission Trails Regional Park, 8 miles northeast of downtown, offers a glimpse of what San Diego looked like before development. Located between Highway 52 and I-8 and east of I-15, rugged hills, valleys, and open areas provide a quick escape from the urban bustle. A visitor and interpretive center (☎ **619/668-3275**) is open daily from 9am to 5pm. Access is by way of Mission Gorge Road.

Marian Bear Memorial Park, a.k.a. San Clemente Canyon (☎ **619/581-9952** for park ranger), is a 10-mile, round-trip trail that runs directly underneath Highway 52. Most of the trail is flat, hard-packed dirt, but some areas are rocky. There are benches and places to sit and have a quiet picnic. From Highway 52 west, take the Genesee South exit; at the light, make a U-turn and an immediate right into the parking lot. From Highway 52 east, exit at Genesee and make a right at the light, then an immediate right into the parking lot.

Lake Miramar Reservoir has a 5-mile, paved, looped trail with a wonderful view of the lake and mountains. Take I-15 north and exit on Mira Mesa Boulevard. Turn right on Scripps Ranch Boulevard, then left on Scripps Lake Drive, and make a left at the Lake Miramar sign. Parking is free, but the lot closes at 6:30pm.

Volunteers from the **Natural History Museum** (☎ 619/232-3821, ext. 203) lead nature walks throughout San Diego County.

JOGGING/RUNNING

An invigorating route downtown is along the wide sidewalks of the Embarcadero, stretching around the bay. One of my favorite places to jog is the sidewalk that follows the east side of Mission Bay. Start at the Visitor Information Center and head south past the Hilton to Fiesta Island. A good spot for a short run is La Jolla Shores Beach, where there's hard-packed sand even when it isn't low tide. The beach at Coronado is also a good place for jogging, as is the shore at Pacific Beach and Mission Beach—just watch your tide chart to make sure you won't be there at high tide.

Safety note: Avoid secluded areas of Balboa Park, even in broad daylight.

SCUBA DIVING & SNORKELING

San Diego Divers Supply, 4004 Sports Arena Blvd. (☎ 619/224-3439) and 5701 La Jolla Blvd. (☎ 858/459-2691), will set you up with scuba and snorkeling equipment. The **San Diego–La Jolla Underwater Park,** especially the La Jolla Cove, is the best spot for scuba diving and snorkeling. For more information, see "San Diego's Beaches," earlier in this chapter. The Underwater Pumpkin Carving Contest, held at Halloween, is a fun local event. For information, call ☎ 858/565-6054.

SKATING

Gliding around San Diego, especially the Mission Bay area, on in-line skates is the quintessential Southern California experience. In Mission Beach, rent a pair of regular or in-line skates from **Skates Plus,** 3830 Mission Blvd. (☎ 619/488-PLUS), or **Hamel's Action Sports Center,** 704 Ventura Place, off Mission Boulevard at Ocean Front Walk (☎ 619/488-8889). In Pacific Beach, try **Pacific Beach Sun and Sea,** 4539 Ocean Blvd. (☎ 619/483-6613). In Coronado, go to **Mike's Bikes,** 1343 Orange Ave. (☎ 619/435-7744), or **Bikes and Beyond,** 1201 First St. and at the Ferry Landing (☎ 619/435-7180). Be sure to ask for protective gear.

If you'd rather ice-skate, try the **Ice Capades Chalet** at University Towne Center, La Jolla Village Drive at Genesee Street (☎ 858/452-9110).

SURFING

With its miles of beaches, San Diego is a popular surf destination. Some of the best spots include Windansea, La Jolla Shores, Pacific Beach, Mission Beach, Ocean Beach, and Imperial Beach. In North County, you might consider Carlsbad State Beach and Oceanside.

If you didn't bring your own board, they are available for rent at stands at many popular beaches. Many local surf shops also rent equipment; they include **La Jolla Surf Systems,** 2132 Avenida de la Playa, La Jolla Shores (☎ 858/456-2777), and **Emerald Surf & Sport,** 1118 Orange Ave., Coronado (☎ 619/435-6677).

For surfing lessons, with all equipment provided, check with **Kahuna Bob's Surf School** (☎ 760/721-7700) or **San Diego Surfing Academy** (☎ 800-477-SURF; www.surfSDSA.com).

TENNIS

There are 1,200 public and private tennis courts in San Diego. Public courts include the **La Jolla Tennis Club,** 7632 Draper, at Prospect (☎ 858/454-4434), which is free and open daily from dawn until the lights go off at 9pm. At the **Balboa Tennis Club,** 2221 Morley Field Dr., in Balboa Park (☎ 619/295-9278), court use is free, but reservations are required. The courts are open Monday through Friday from 10am to 8pm, Saturday and Sunday 8am to 6pm. The brand-new **Barnes Tennis Center,** 4490 W. Point Loma Blvd., near Ocean Beach and Sea World (☎ 619/221-9000; www.tennissandiego.com) has 20 lighted hard courts and four clay courts; they're open every day from 8am to 9pm. Court rental is $5 to $10 an hour, instruction an additional $12 to $14 per hour.

9 Spectator Sports

BASEBALL

The **San Diego Padres,** led to the National League championship in 1998 by stars Tony Gwynn and Trevor Hoffman, play from April through October at **Qualcomm Stadium,** 9449 Friars Rd., in Mission Valley (☎ 619/283-4494 for schedules and information; 619/29-PADRES for tickets). The **Padres Express** bus (☎ 619/233-3004 for information) costs $5 round-trip and picks up fans at several locations throughout the city, beginning 2 hours before the game. The bus operates only for home games on Friday, Saturday, and Sunday. Tickets are readily available.

BOATING

San Diego has probably played host to the America's Cup for the last time, but several other boating events of interest are held here. They include the **America's Schooner Cup,** held every March or April (☎ **619/223-3138**), and the **Annual San Diego Crew Classic,** held on Mission Bay every April (☎ **619/488-0700**). The Crew Classic rowing competition draws teams from throughout the United States and Canada. The **Wooden Boat Festival** is held on Shelter Island every May (☎ **619/574-8020**). Approximately 90 boats participate in the festival, which features nautical displays, food, music, and crafts.

FOOTBALL

The **San Diego Chargers** play at **Qualcomm Stadium,** "The Q," 9449 Friars Rd., Mission Valley (☎ **619/280-2111**). The season runs from August through December. The Chargers Express bus (☎ **619/233-3004** for information) costs $5 round-trip and picks up passengers at several locations throughout the city, beginning 2 hours before the game. The bus operates for all home games.

The collegiate **Holiday Bowl,** held at Qualcomm Stadium every December, pits the Western Athletic Conference champion against a team from the Big 10. For information, call ☎ **619/283-5808.**

GOLF

San Diego is the site of some of the country's most important golf tournaments, including the **Buick Invitational,** held in February at Torrey Pines Golf Course in La Jolla (☎ **800/888-BUICK** or 858/281-4653). The **HGH Pro-Am Golf Classic** takes place at Carlton Oaks Country Club in September (☎ **619/448-8500**).

HORSE RACING

Live Thoroughbred racing takes place at the **Del Mar Race Track** (☎ **858/755-1141** for information; ☎ **619/792-4242** for the ticket office; www.dmtc.com) from late July through mid-September. Post time for the nine-race program is 2pm (except the first four Fridays of the meet, when it's 4pm); there is no racing on Tuesdays. Admission to the clubhouse is $6; to the grandstand, $3. Bing Crosby and Pat O'Brien founded the track in 1937, and it has entertained stars such as Lucille Ball and Desi Arnaz, Dorothy Lamour, Red Skelton, Paulette Goddard, Jimmy Durante, and Ava Gardner. Del Mar's 1993 season marked the opening of a new $80-million grandstand, built in the Spanish mission style of the original structure. The new grandstand features more seats, better race viewing, and a centrally located scenic paddock. The $1-million Pacific Classic, featuring the top horses in the country, is held the second weekend in August.

HORSE SHOWS

The **Del Mar National Horse Show** takes place at the Del Mar Fairgrounds from late April to mid-May. Olympic-caliber and national championship riders participate. For information, call ☎ **858/792-4288** or 858/755-1161.

ICE HOCKEY

The **San Diego Gulls** of the West Coast Hockey League skate at the San Diego Sports Arena from late October into March. For schedules, tickets, and information, call ☎ **619/224-4625** or 619/224-4171.

SOCCER

The **San Diego Sockers,** popular members of the Continental Indoor Soccer League, play from June through September at the San Diego Sports Arena, 3500 Sports Arena Blvd. (☎ **619/224-GOAL**). Admission is $5 to $12.50.

TENNIS

San Diego plays host to some major tennis tournaments, including the **Toshiba Tennis Classic,** held at the La Costa Resort and Spa in Carlsbad. The tournament is usually held between late July and early August. For tickets, call ☎ **619/438-LOVE;** for information, ☎ **619/436-3551.**

7

Shopping

*W*hether you're looking for a souvenir, a gift, or a quick replacement for an item inadvertently left at home, you'll find no shortage of stores in San Diego. This is, after all, Southern California, where looking good is a high priority and shopping is a way of life.

1 The Shopping Scene

All-American San Diego has embraced the suburban shopping mall with vigor. At several massive complexes in Mission Valley, many residents do the bulk of their shopping; every possible need is represented. The city has even adapted the mall concept, with typically California examples like whimsical Horton Plaza and historic Old Town Plaza.

Local neighborhoods, on the other hand, offer specialty shopping that meets the needs—and mirrors the personality—of that part of town. For example, trendy Hillcrest is the place to go for cutting-edge boutiques, while conservative La Jolla offers many upscale traditional shops, especially jewelers. And don't forget that Mexico is only half an hour away; *tiendas* (stores) in Tijuana, Rosarito Beach, and Ensenada stock colorful crafts perfectly suited to the California lifestyle. San Diegans head across the border *en masse* each weekend in search of bargains.

Shops tend to stay open late, particularly in malls like Horton Plaza and Fashion Valley, tourist destinations like Bazaar del Mundo and Seaport Village, and areas like the Gaslamp Quarter and Hillcrest that see a lot of evening foot traffic. Places like these keep the welcome mat out until 9pm on weeknights and 6pm on Saturdays and Sundays. Individual stores elsewhere generally close by 5 or 6pm.

Sales tax in San Diego is 7.75%, and savvy out-of-state shoppers have larger items shipped directly home at the point of purchase, avoiding the tax.

2 Shopping Neighborhoods

DOWNTOWN & THE GASLAMP QUARTER

Space is at a premium in the constantly improving Gaslamp Quarter, and rents are rising. While a few intrepid shops—mostly women's boutiques and vintage clothing shops—are scattered among the area's multitudinous eateries, shopping is primarily concentrated in the destination malls listed below.

Horton Plaza. 324 Horton Plaza. ☎ **619/238-1596.** www.hortonplaza.com. Bus: 2, 7, 9, 29, 34, or 35. Trolley: City Center.

The Disneyland of shopping malls, Horton Plaza is in the heart of San Diego; in fact, it is the heart of the revitalized city center, bounded by Broadway, First and Fourth avenues, and G Street. Covering $7^1/_2$ city blocks, the multilevel shopping center has 140 specialty shops, including art galleries, clothing and shoe stores, several fun shops for kids, and bookstores. There's a 14-screen cinema, three major department stores, and a variety of restaurants and short-order eateries. It's almost as much an attraction as Sea World or the San Diego Zoo, transcending its genre with a conglomeration of rambling paths, bridges, towers, piazzas, sculptures, fountains, and live greenery. Performers provide background entertainment throughout the year. Supposedly inspired by European shopping streets and districts like Athens' Plaka and London's Portobello Road, Horton Plaza opened in 1985 to rave reviews and has steadily grown in popularity.

Parking is free with validation for the first 3 hours (4 hours at the movie theater and the Lyceum Theatre), $1 per half-hour thereafter. The parking levels are confusing, and temporarily losing your car is part of the Horton Plaza experience. Open Monday through Friday from 10am to 9pm, Saturday 10am to 6pm, Sunday 11am to 6pm, with extended summer and holiday hours.

Seaport Village. 849 W. Harbor Dr. (at Kettner Blvd.). ☎ **619/235-4014,** or 619/235-4013 for events information. Bus: 7. Trolley: Seaport Village.

This 14-acre ersatz village snuggled alongside San Diego Bay was built to resemble a small Cape Cod community, but the 75 shops are very much the Southern California cutesy variety. Favorites include the **Tile Shop;** the **Seasick Giraffe** for resort wear; and the **Upstart Crow bookshop and coffeehouse,** with the Crow's Nest children's bookstore inside. Be sure to see the 1890 carousel imported from Coney Island, New York. Open September to May, daily from 10am to 9pm; June to August, daily 10am to 10pm.

HILLCREST/UPTOWN

Compact Hillcrest is an ideal shopping destination. You can browse the unique and often wacky shops, and check out the area's vintage-clothing stores, memorabilia shops, chain stores, bakeries, and cafes. Start at the neighborhood's hub, the intersection of University and Fifth avenues. Street parking is available; most meters run 2 hours and devour quarters at a rate of one every 15 minutes, so be armed with plenty of change. You can also park in a lot—rates vary, but you'll come out ahead if you're planning to stroll for several hours.

If you're looking for postcards or provocative gifts, step into wacky **Babette Schwartz,** 421 University Ave. (☎ **619/220-7048**), a pop-culture emporium named for a local drag queen. You'll find books, clothing, and accessories that follow current kitsch trends. A couple of doors away, **Cathedral,** 435 University Ave. (☎ **619/ 296-4046**), is dark and heady, filled with candles of all scents and shapes, plus unusual holders.

Around the corner, **Circa a.d.,** 3867 Fourth Ave. (☎ **619/ 293-3328**), is a floral design shop with splendid gift items; at holi-day time it has the most extravagant Christmas ornaments in the area. Head gear from straw hats to knit caps to classy fedoras fills the **Village Hat Shop,** 3821 Fourth Ave. (☎ **619/683-5533;** www.villagehatshop.com), whose best feature may be its minimuseum of stylishly displayed vintage hats.

Lovers of rare and used books will want to poke around the used bookstores on Fifth Avenue between University and Robinson avenues. This block is also home to **Off the Record,** 3865 Fifth Ave. (☎ **619/298-4755**), a new and used music store known for an alternative bent and the city's best vinyl selection. For a comprehen-sive choice of brand-new CDs and tapes, you're better off at **Block-buster Music,** 3965 Fifth Ave. (☎ **619/683-3293**), where you can preview any disc before committing to the purchase.

San Diego's self-proclaimed **Antique Row** is north of Balboa Park, along Park Boulevard (beginning at University Avenue in Hillcrest) and Adams Avenue (extending to around 40th Street in Normal Heights). Antique and collectible stores, vintage-clothing boutiques, coffeehouses and pubs, funky restaurants, and dusty used book and record stores line this L-shaped district, providing many hours of happy browsing and treasure hunting. For more information and an area brochure with a map, contact the **Adams Avenue Business Association** (☎ 619/282-7329; www.GoThere.com/AdamsAve).

Lovers of vintage clothing—both female and male—won't want to miss **Wear It Again Sam,** 3922 Park Blvd., at University Avenue (☎ **619/299-0185**). It's a classy step back in time, with only the most pristine examples of styles from the '20s to the '50s. It has occupied this off-the-beaten-path corner of Hillcrest for 15-plus years, and I'm always surprised by how reasonably priced it is.

OLD TOWN & MISSION VALLEY

Old Town Historic Park is a restoration of some of San Diego's historic sites and adobe structures, a number of which now house shops that cater to tourists. Many have a "general store" theme, and carry gourmet treats and inexpensive Mexican crafts alongside the obligatory T-shirts, baseball caps, snow domes, and other souvenirs. A reconstruction of San Diego's first tobacco shop carries cigars and smoking paraphernalia; more shops are concentrated in colorful Bazaar del Mundo (see below).

Mission Valley is ground zero of San Diego's suburban mall explosion. There are several sprawling shopping centers here, all discussed in detail below (see "Malls," under Shopping A to Z in section 3).

Bazaar del Mundo. 2754 Calhoun St., Old Town State Historic Park. ☎ **619/ 296-3161.** Bus: 4 or 5/105.

Take a stroll down Mexico way and points south through the arched passageways of this colorful corner of Old Town. Always festive, its central courtyard vibrates with folkloric music, mariachis, and a splashing fountain. Shops feature one-of-a-kind folk art, home furnishings, clothing, and textiles from Mexico and South America. You'll also find a top-notch bookstore, **Libros,** with a large kids' selection. Don't miss the **Design Center** and the **Guatemala Store.** You won't find any bargains here—it's clearly tourist central—but there isn't a more colorful place to browse in San Diego. Open daily from 10am to 9pm.

MISSION BAY & THE BEACHES

The beach communities offer laid-back shopping in typical California fashion, with plenty of surf shops, recreational gear, casual garb, and youth-oriented music stores.

If you're in need of a new bikini, the best selection is at **Pilar's,** 3745 Mission Blvd., Pacific Beach (☎ **619/488-3056**), where choices range from chic designer suits to hot trends like suits inspired by surf- and skate-wear. There's a smaller selection of one-piece suits, too. It's open daily.

Some of the area's best **antiquing** can be found in Ocean Beach, along a single block of **Newport Avenue,** the town's main drag. The selection is high quality enough to make it interesting, without pricey, centuries-old European antiques. Most of the stores are mall-style, featuring multiple dealers under one roof. Highlights include **Newport Avenue Antiques,** 4836 Newport Ave. (☎ 619/224-1994), which offers the most diversity. Its wares range from Native American crafts to Victorian furniture and delicate accessories, from Mighty Mouse collectibles to carved Asian furniture. **O.B. Emporium,** 4847 Newport Ave. (☎ 619/523-1262), has a more elegant setting and glass display cases filled with superb collectible pottery and china. Names like Rockwood, McCoy, and Royal Copenhagen abound, and there's a fine selection of quality majolica and Japanese tea sets. The **Newport Ave. Antique Center,** 4864 Newport Ave. (☎ 619/222-8686), is the largest store, and has a small espresso bar. One corner is a haven for collectors of 1940s and '50s kitchenware (Fire King, Bauer, melamine); there's also a fine selection of vintage linens. Most antique stores in Ocean Beach are open daily from 10am to 6pm.

LA JOLLA

It's clear from the look of La Jolla's village that shopping is a major pastime in this upscale community. Women's clothing boutiques tend to be conservative and costly, like those lining Girard and Prospect streets (**Ann Taylor, Armani Exchange, Polo Ralph Lauren, Talbots,** and **Sigi's Boutique**).

Recommended stores include **Island Hoppers,** 7844 Girard Ave. (☎ 858/459-6055), for colorful Hawaiian-print clothing from makers like Tommy Bahama; the venerable **Ascot Shop,** 7750 Girard Ave. (☎ 858/454-4222), for conservative men's apparel and accessories; **La Jolla Shoe Gallery,** 7852 Girard Ave. (☎ 858/551-9985), for an outstanding selection of Clark's, Birkenstock, Mephisto, Josef Siebel, and other shoes built for walking; and the surprisingly affordable **Clothes Minded,** 7880 Girard Ave. (☎ 858/454-3700), a ladies' casual boutique where everything is just $15.

Even if you're not in the market for furnishings and accessories, La Jolla's many home-decor boutiques make for great window shopping, as do its ubiquitous jewelers: Swiss watches, tennis bracelets, precious gems, and pearl necklaces sparkle in windows along every street.

No visit to La Jolla is complete without seeing **John Cole's Bookshop,** a local icon discussed in section 3 under "Books."

Another unique shopping experience awaits at the **La Jolla Cave and Shell Shop,** 1325 Coast Blvd., just off Prospect Street (☎ 858/454-6080). This cliff-top treasure chest sells dozens of varieties of individual loose shells. It also carries jewelry, wind chimes, decorative hangings, nightlights, and sculptures crafted from common varieties like tiny cowrie shells. But the main attraction is **Sunny Jim Cave,** reached by a steep and narrow staircase through the rock; it lets out on a wood-plank observation deck from which you can gaze out at the sea. It's a cool treat, particularly on a hot summer day, and costs only $1.50 per person (75¢ for kids). Hold the handrail and your little ones' hands tightly.

CORONADO

This rather insular, conservative navy community doesn't have a great many shopping opportunities; the best of the lot lines Orange Avenue at the western end of the island. You'll find some scattered housewares and home-decor boutiques, several small women's boutiques, and the gift shops at Coronado's major resorts.

Also check out **Kensington Coffee Company** for coffee-related paraphernalia. Coronado also has an excellent independent bookshop, **Bay Books,** 1029 Orange Ave. (☎ 619/435-0700). It carries a nice selection in many categories, plus volumes of local historical interest, and books on tape available for rent. **La Provençale,** 1122 Orange Ave. (☎ 619/437-8881) is a little shop stocked with textiles, pottery, and gourmet items from the French countryside.

The Ferry Landing Marketplace. 1201 First St. (at B Ave.), Coronado. ☎ **619/435-8895.** Fax 619/522-6150. Take I-5 to Coronado Bay Bridge, to B Ave., and turn right. Bus: 901. Ferry: From Broadway Pier.

The entrance is impressive—turreted red rooftops with jaunty blue flags that draw closer as the ferry pulls in. As you stroll up the pier, you'll find yourself in the midst of shops filled with gifts, imported and designer fashions, jewelry, and crafts. You can get a quick bite to eat or have a leisurely dinner with a view, wander along landscaped walkways, or laze on a beach or grassy bank. Open daily from 10am to 9pm.

3 Shopping A to Z

Large stores and shops in malls tend to stay open until about 9pm weekdays, 6pm weekends. Smaller businesses usually close at 5 or 6pm or may keep odd hours. When in doubt, call ahead.

ANTIQUES

See also "Hillcrest/Uptown" and "Mission Bay & the Beaches," om section 2.

The Cracker Factory Antiques Shopping Center. 448 W. Market St. (at Columbia St.). ☎ **619/233-1669.** Bus: 7. Trolley: Seaport Village.

Prepare to spend some time here, exploring three floors of individually owned and operated shops filled with antiques and collectibles. It's across the street from the Hyatt Regency San Diego, a block north of Seaport Village.

Unicorn Antique Mall. 704 J St. (at Seventh Ave.). ☎ **619/232-1696.**

Antiques and collectibles fill three floors of this 30,000-square-foot building. You'll see a wide selection of American oak and European furniture. Free off-street parking is available.

ART

The San Diego area stages numerous arts-and-crafts fairs, such as the **La Jolla Arts Festival,** which is held every September (☎ **858/ 454-5718**).

The Artists Gallery. 7420 Girard Ave., La Jolla. ☎ **858/459-5844.**

This gallery features 20 regional artists in a variety of media, including paintings, sculpture, and three-dimensional paper wall sculptures.

Brushworks. 2400 Kettner Blvd. #212 (south of Laurel St.), Little Italy. ☎ **619/232-7329.**

Brushworks presents changing exhibits of contemporary work, often of a whimsical nature. Call ahead for an appointment.

David Zapf Gallery. 2400 Kettner Blvd. (south of Laurel St.), Little Italy. ☎ **619/232-5004.**

David Zapf specializes in the works of San Diego–area artists. Contact the gallery for a copy of the *Arts Down Town* guide.

Debra Owen Gallery. 354 11th Ave., Downtown. ☎ **619/231-3030.** Fax 619/237-1808.

This gallery specializes in art from Mexico and California.

International Gallery. 643 G St., Gaslamp Quarter. ☎ **619/235-8255.**

Here you'll find authentic African and Melanesian primitive art, including ritual masks and sculpture, as well as contemporary American crafts in ceramics, glass, jewelry, and wood.

Many Hands. 302 Island Ave., Suite 101, Gaslamp Quarter. ☎ **619/557-8303.**

This cooperative gallery, in existence since 1972, has 35 members who engage in a variety of crafts, including toys, jewelry, posters, pottery, baskets, and wearable art.

Pratt Gallery. 2400 Kettner Blvd. ☎ **619/236-0211.**

Pratt displays original paintings, including landscapes and cityscapes by Southern California artists. It's located between Downtown and Hillcrest/Uptown.

SOMA and Quint. 7661 Girard Ave., La Jolla. SOMA ☎ **858/551-5821;** Quint ☎ **858/454-3409.**

These galleries, in the space once occupied by I. Magnin, specialize in contemporary art.

Taboo Studio. 1615^1/$_2$ W. Lewis St., Mission Hills. ☎ **619/692-0099.**

This impressive shop exhibits and sells the work of jewelry designers from throughout the United States. It's made of silver, gold, and inlaid stones, in one-of-a-kind pieces, limited editions, or custom work. The gallery represents 65 artists.

BOOKS

Barnes & Noble Booksellers. 7610 Hazard Center Dr., Mission Valley. ☎ **619/220-0175.** Daily 9am–11pm.

The San Diego branch of this book discounter sits among Mission Valley's mega-malls. Besides a wide selection of paperback and hardcover titles, it offers a comprehensive periodical rack.

Borders Books & Music. 1072 Camino del Rio N., Mission Valley. ☎ **619/295-2201.** Mon–Thurs 9am–11pm, Fri–Sat 9am–midnight, Sun 9am–10pm.

This full-service book and CD store in Mission Valley's main shopping region offers discounts on many titles. Borders also stocks a stylish line of greeting cards and encourages browsing; there's an adjoining coffee lounge.

John Cole's Book Shop. 780 Prospect St., La Jolla. ☎ **858/454-4766.** Fax 858/454-8377. Mon–Sat 9:30am–5:30pm.

Cole's, a favorite of many locals, is in a turn-of-the-century wisteria-covered cottage, the former guest house of philanthropist Ellen Browning Scripps. John and Barbara Cole founded the shop in 1946 and moved it into the cottage 20 years later. Barbara and her children continue to run it today. Visitors will find cookbooks in the old kitchen, paperbacks in a former classroom, and CDs and harmonicas in Zach's music corner. The children's section bulges with a diverse selection, and there are plenty of books about La Jolla and San Diego. Sitting and reading in the patio garden is acceptable, and even encouraged.

Obelisk Bookstore. 1029 University Ave., Hillcrest. ☎ **619/297-4171.** Fax 619/297-5803. Mon–Sat 10am–11pm, Sun noon–8pm.

This bookstore, which caters to gay men and lesbians, is where Greg Louganis signed copies of his book *Breaking the Surface.*

Traveler's Depot. 1655 Garnet Ave., Pacific Beach. ☎ **619/483-1421.** Fax 619/483-2743. Mon–Fri 10am–6pm (until 8pm in summer), Sat 10am–5pm, Sun noon–5pm.

This bookstore offers an extensive selection of travel books and maps, plus a great array of travel gear and accessories, with discounts on backpacks and luggage. The well-traveled owners, Ward and Lisl Hampton, are happy to give advice about restaurants in a given city while pointing you to the right shelf for the appropriate book or map.

Warwick's Books. 7812 Girard Ave., La Jolla. ☎ **858/454-0347.** Mon–Sat 9am–6pm, Sun 11am–5pm.

This popular family-run bookstore is a browser's delight, with more than 40,000 titles, a large travel section, gifts, cards, and stationery. The well-read Warwick family has been in the book and stationery business for almost 100 years, and the current owners are the third generation involved with the store.

DEPARTMENT STORES

Macy's. Horton Plaza. ☎ **619/231-4747.** Fax 619/645-3295. Mon–Fri 10am–9pm, Sat 10am–8pm, Sun 11am–7pm. Bus: 2, 7, 9, 29, 34, or 35.

There are several branches of this comprehensive store, which carries clothing for women, men, and children, as well as housewares, electronics, and luggage. Macy's also has stores in Fashion Valley (clothing only), Mission Valley (housewares only), University Towne Center, and North County Fair.

✪ **Nordstrom.** Horton Plaza. ☎ **619/239-1700.** Mon–Fri 10am–9:30pm, Sat 10am–7pm, Sun 11am–6pm. Bus: 2, 7, 9, 29, 34, or 35.

An all-time San Diego favorite, Nordstrom is best known for its outstanding customer service and fine selection of shoes. It features a variety of stylish fashions and accessories for women, men, and children. Tailoring is done on the premises. There's a full-service restaurant on the top floor, where coffee and tea cost only 25¢. Nordstrom also has stores in Fashion Valley, University Towne Center, and North County Fair.

FARMERS' MARKETS

San Diegans love their open-air markets. Throughout the county there are no fewer than two dozen regularly scheduled street fests stocked with the freshest fruits and vegetables from Southern California farms, augmented by crafts, fresh-cooked ethnic foods, flower stands, and other surprises. San Diego County produces over $1 billion worth of fruits, flowers, and other crops each year. Avocados, known locally as "green gold," are the most profitable crop and have been grown here for more than 100 years. Citrus fruit follows close behind, and flowers are the area's third most important crop; ranunculus bulbs from here are sent all over the world, as are the famous Ecke poinsettias.

Here's a schedule of farmers' markets in the area:

In **Hillcrest,** the market runs Sundays from 9am to noon at the corner of Normal Street and Lincoln Avenue, several blocks north of Balboa Park. The atmosphere is festive, and exotic culinary delights reflect the eclectic neighborhood. For more information, call the **Hillcrest Association** (☎ 619/299-3330).

In **Ocean Beach,** there's a fun-filled market Wednesday evenings between 4 and 8pm (until 7pm in fall and winter) in the 4900 block of Newport Avenue. In addition to fresh-cut flowers, produce, and exotic fruits and foods laid out for sampling, the market features llama rides and other entertainment. For more information, call the **Ocean Beach Business Improvement District** (☎ 619/224-4906).

Head to **Pacific Beach** on Saturday from 8am to noon, when Mission Boulevard between Reed Avenue and Pacific Beach Drive is transformed into a bustling marketplace.

In **Coronado,** every Tuesday afternoon the Ferry Landing Marketplace (corner of First and B streets) hosts a produce and crafts market from 2:30 to 6pm.

FLEA MARKETS

Kobey's Swap Meet. Sports Arena Parking Lot (west end), 3500 Sports Arena Blvd. ☎ **619/226-0650** for information. Admission Thurs–Fri 50¢, Sat–Sun $1; children under 12 free. Take I-8 to Sports Arena Blvd. turnoff or I-5 to Rosecrans St. and turn right on Sports Arena Blvd.

Since 1980, this gigantic open-air market has been a bargain-hunter's dream-come-true. Approximately 3,000 vendors fill row after row with new and used clothing, jewelry, electronics, hardware, appliances, furniture, collectibles, crafts, antiques, auto accessories, toys, and books. There's produce, too, along with food stalls and rest rooms. Open Thursday through Sunday from 7am to 3pm.

Insider's Tip: Skip weekdays. Saturday and Sunday are when the good stuff is out—and it goes quickly, so arrive early.

MALLS

See "Downtown & the Gaslamp Quarter" in section 2 for details on **Horton Plaza.**

Fashion Valley Center. 352 Fashion Valley Rd. ☎ **619/297-3381.** Mon–Fri 10am–9pm, Sat 10am–6pm, Sun 11am–6pm. Hwy. 163 to Friars Rd. W. Bus: 6, 16, 25, 43, or 81.

The Mission Valley–Hotel Circle area, northeast of downtown along I-8, contains San Diego's major shopping centers. Fashion Valley is the most attractive and most upscale, with anchor stores like **Neiman Marcus, Nordstrom** (which keeps longer hours), **Saks Fifth Avenue,** and **Macy's,** plus 140 specialty shops and a quadriplex movie theater. Particularly interesting specialty shops include **Williams Sonoma, Smith & Hawken,** and **Bang & Olufsen.**

Mission Valley Center. 1640 Camino del Rio N. ☎ **619/296-6375.** Mon–Fri 10am–9pm, Sat 10am–6pm, Sun 11am–6pm. I-8 to Mission Center Rd. Bus: 6, 16, 25, 43, or 81.

This old-fashioned outdoor mall predates sleek Fashion Valley, and has found a niche with budget-minded stores like **Loehmann's, Nordstrom Rack, Michael's** (arts and crafts), and **Montgomery Ward.** There's a 20-screen movie theater and about 150 other stores and places to eat.

San Diego Factory Outlet Center. 4498 Camino de la Plaza, San Ysidro. ☎ **619/690-2999.** Mon–Fri 10am–8pm, Sat 10am–7pm, Sun 10am–6pm. I-5 or I-805 south to Camino de la Plaza exit (last exit in U.S.). Turn right and continue 1 block; center is on right. Trolley: Southbound to last stop (San Ysidro). Walk back (north) 1 block and turn left on Camino de la Plaza; it's a $1/2$-mile walk or a short taxi ride.

This strip of 35 factory outlets saves you money because you buy directly from the manufacturers. Some familiar names include **Mikasa, Levi's, Calvin Klein, Guess?, Maidenform, Van Heusen, Bass, Nike, Carter's, Osh Kosh B'Gosh, Ray-Ban,** and **Jockey.**

University Towne Center (UTC). 4545 La Jolla Village Dr. ☎ **858/546-8858.** Fax 858/552-9065. Mon–Fri 10am–9pm, Sat 10am–7pm, Sun

11am–6pm. I-5 to La Jolla Village Dr. and go east, or I-805 to La Jolla Village Dr. and go west. Bus: 50 express, 34, or 34A.

This outdoor shopping complex has a landscaped plaza and 160 stores, including some big ones like **Nordstrom, Sears,** and **Macy's.** It is also home to a year-round ice-skating rink, the popular Hops Bistro and Brewery, and a six-screen cinema.

TRAVEL ACCESSORIES

Along with the stores listed below, try **Eddie Bauer** in Horton Plaza (☎ **619/233-0814**) or **Traveler's Depot** (see "Books," above) for travel gear.

John's Fifth Avenue Luggage. 3833 Fourth Ave. ☎ **619/298-0993** or 619/298-0995. Mon–Fri 9am–5:30pm, Sat 9am–4pm.

This San Diego institution carries just about everything you can imagine in the way of luggage, travel accessories, business cases, pens, and gifts. The on-premises luggage-repair center is an authorized airline repair facility. There is also a store in Fashion Valley.

Le Travel Store. 745 Fourth Ave. (between F and G sts.). ☎ **619/544-0005.** Fax 619/544-0312. www.letravelstore.com. Mon–Sat 10am–10pm, Sun 11am–7pm. Bus: 2, 7, 9, 29, 34, or 35. Trolley: Gaslamp.

In business since 1976, Le Travel Store has a good selection of soft-sided luggage, travel books, language tapes, maps, and lots of travel accessories. The cafe serves beverages and snacks. The long hours and central location make this spot extra handy.

The Map Centre. 2611 University Ave. (3 blocks east of Texas St.). ☎ **619/291-3830.** Fax 619/291-3840. E-mail: GBROWN9922@aol.com. Tues–Fri 10am–5:30pm, Sat 10am–5pm.

This shop may be tiny, but it has the whole world covered—in maps, that is. If you plan to spend some serious time in San Diego, buy the *Thomas Guide;* it's $16.95, but indispensable. The Map Centre is easily recognizable by its bright yellow awning.

8

San Diego After Dark

San Diego's rich and varied cultural scene includes classical and contemporary plays at more than a dozen theaters throughout the year; performances by the San Diego Opera; and rock and pop concerts. Among the numerous movie houses and multiscreen complexes are several that feature foreign and avant-garde films. Not all of the city streets pulsate with nightlife, but there are growing areas of late-night activity.

Half-price tickets to theater, music, and dance events are available at the **Times Arts Tix** booth, in Horton Plaza Park, at Broadway and Third Avenue. Park in the Horton Plaza parking garage and have your parking validated, or pause at the curb nearby. The kiosk is open Tuesday through Thursday from 11am to 6pm, Friday and Saturday from 10am to 6pm. Half-price tickets are available only the day of the show except for Sunday performances, for which half-price tickets are sold on Saturday. Only cash is accepted. For a daily listing of half-price offerings, call ☎ **619/497-5000.** Full-price advance tickets are also sold; the kiosk doubles as a Ticketmaster outlet, selling tickets to concerts throughout California.

For a rundown of the latest performances, gallery openings, and other events, check the listings in "Night and Day," the Thursday entertainment section of the *San Diego Union-Tribune* (www.uniontrib.com), or the *Reader* (www.sdreader.com), San Diego's free alternative newspaper, published weekly on Thursday. For what's happening at the gay clubs, get the weekly *San Diego Gay and Lesbian Times. What's Playing?* is a performing arts guide produced every 2 months by the **San Diego Performing Arts League.** You can pick one up at the Times Art Tix booth or write to 701 B St., Suite 225, San Diego, CA 92101-8101 (☎ **619/238-0700;** www.sandiego-online.com/sdpal).

1 The Performing Arts

These listings focus on the best-known of San Diego's many talented theater companies. Don't hesitate to try a less prominent venue if the show appeals to you.

The **San Diego Repertory Theatre** mounts plays and musicals at the Lyceum Theatre, 79 Broadway Circle, in Horton Plaza (☎ 619/544-1000; www.SanDiegoRep.com). The theaters—the 550-seat Lyceum Stage and the 250-seat Lyceum Space—present dance and musical programs, as well as other events. Situated at the entrance to Horton Plaza, the two-level subterranean theaters are tucked behind a tile obelisk. Ticket prices are $21 to $32.

Founded in 1948, the **San Diego Junior Theatre,** at Balboa Park's Casa del Prado Theatre (☎ 619/239-8355; fax 619/239-5048; www.juniortheatre.com), is one of the country's oldest continuously producing children's theaters. It provides training and performance opportunities for children and young adults. Students make up the cast and technical crew of six main-stage shows each year.

In Coronado, **Lamb's Players Theatre,** 1142 Orange Ave. (☎ 619/437-0600; www.lambsplayers.org), is a professional repertory company whose season runs from February through December. Shows take place in the 340-seat theater in Coronado's historic Spreckels Building, where no seat is more than seven rows from the stage. Tickets cost $18 to $34. Highlights in 1999 included *My Fair Lady* and the Dorothy L. Sayers mystery *Busman's Honeymoon.*

MAJOR THEATER COMPANIES

La Jolla Playhouse. 2910 La Jolla Village Dr. (at Torrey Pines Rd.). ☎ **858/550-1010.** Fax 858/550-1025. www.lajollaplayhouse.com. Tickets $19–$49. Bus: 30, 34, or 34A.

Winner of the 1993 Tony Award for outstanding American regional theater, the playhouse stages six productions each year. Its 500-seat Mandell Weiss Theater and 400-seat Mandell Weiss Forum are on the University of California, San Diego campus. Performances are held May through November. Playhouse audiences cheered *The Who's Tommy* and Matthew Broderick in *How to Succeed in Business Without Really Trying* before they went on to Broadway. Other recent highlights were the first West Coast production of the Tony Award–winning musical *Rent,* and the American premiere of the musical *Jane Eyre.*

Gregory Peck, Dorothy McGuire, and Mel Ferrer founded the original La Jolla Playhouse in 1947; it closed in 1964. This stellar reincarnation emerged in 1983. The box office is open Monday from 11am to 6pm, Tuesday through Sunday 10am to 8pm. For each show, one Saturday matinee is a "pay what you can" performance. Reduced-price "public rush" tickets are available 10 minutes before curtain, subject to availability.

Old Globe Theatre. Balboa Park. ☎ **619/239-2255,** or 619/23-GLOBE (24-hr. hot line). Fax 619/231-5879. www.oldglobe.org. Tickets $23–$39. Senior and student discounts. Bus: 7 or 25. Free parking.

This Tony Award–winning theater sits near the entrance to Balboa Park, just behind the Museum of Man. It has produced world premieres of such Broadway hits as *Into the Woods,* plus the revival of *Damn Yankees,* and has booked such notable performers as Marsha Mason, Cliff Robertson, Jon Voight, and Christopher Walken. The 581-seat Old Globe, fashioned after Shakespeare's, is part of the Simon Edison Centre for the Performing Arts. The complex, which includes the 245-seat Cassius Carter Centre Stage and the 620-seat open-air Lowell Davies Festival Theatre, mounts a dozen plays a year on the three stages between January and October. Tours are offered Saturday and Sunday at 11am and cost $3 for adults, $1 for students, seniors, and military. The box office is open Tuesday through Sunday from noon to 8:30pm.

OPERA

San Diego Opera, Civic Theatre. 202 C St. ☎ **619/570-1100** (box office) or 619/232-7636. Fax 619/231-6915. www.sdopera.com. Tickets $31 to $112. Standing room, student and senior discounts available. Bus: 2, 7, 9, 29, 34, or 35. Trolley: Civic Center.

Founded in 1964, the company showcases internationally renowned performers in operas and occasional special recitals. The season runs January through May. The 1999 season included Verdi's *Falstaff* and *A Masked Ball, Così fan tutte* by Mozart, Humperdinck's *Hansel and Gretel,* the English-language *Of Mice and Men,* and the anthological *Great Richard Wagner Concert.*

The box office is outside Golden Hall, adjacent to the Civic Theatre. It's open Monday through Friday from 10am to 5:30pm; hours vary on weekends on the day of performance. Performances are Tuesday, Wednesday, and Saturday at 7pm, Friday at 8pm, and Sunday at 2pm.

DANCE

San Diego–based dance companies include the **California Ballet** (☎ 619/560-5676), a traditional ballet company, plus other minor companies. San Diego's **International Dance Festival,** held annually in January, spotlights the city's ethnic dance groups and emerging artists. Most performances are at the **Lyceum Theatre,** 2 Broadway Circle, in Horton Plaza (☎ **619/235-8025** or 619/231-3586), and there are free performances in public areas. Dance companies generally perform in San Diego from September through June. For specific information or a monthly calendar of events, call the **San Diego Area Dance Alliance Calendar** (☎ 619/239-9255).

2 The Club & Music Scene

ROCK, POP, FOLK, JAZZ & BLUES

Belly Up Tavern. 143 S. Cedros Ave., Solana Beach. ☎ **760/481-9022.** www.bellyup.com.

This club in Solana Beach, a 20-minute drive from downtown, has played host to critically acclaimed and international artists of all genres. The eclectic mix ranges from John Mayall to Ladysmith Black Mombazo to Golden Smog to Lucinda Williams. A funky setting in recycled Quonset huts underscores the venue's uniqueness. Look into advance tickets, if possible.

The Casbah. 2501 Kettner Blvd., near the airport. ☎ **619/232-4355.** www.casbahmusic.com. Ticket prices vary.

Although it's kind of a dive, the Casbah has a rep for booking breakthrough alternative and rock bands. Past headliners have included Alanis Morissette, Jon Spencer Blues Explosion, and Royal Crown Revue, plus local acts Rocket from the Crypt, the Rugburns, and many more. Look into advance tickets, if possible.

Croce's Nightclubs. 802 Fifth Ave. (at F St.). ☎ **619/233-4355.** www.croces.com. Cover $5–$10.

You'll hear traditional jazz every night in Croce's Jazz Bar, and rhythm and blues at Croce's Top Hat. Both adjoin the Croce's restaurants in the heart of the Gaslamp Quarter (see chapter 5, "Dining"). The clubs are named for the late Jim Croce and owned by his widow, Ingrid. Their son, A. J., an accomplished musician, often performs. The cover charge is waived if you eat at one of the restaurants.

4th & B. 345 B St., downtown. ☎ **619/231-4343.**

It's impossible to peg this venue, except to say that it's comfortable and bookings are always of quality. Past performers include artists

A Note on Smoking

In January 1998, California enacted controversial legislation that banned smoking in all restaurants and bars. While opponents immediately began lobbying to repeal the law, it's a good idea to check before you light up in clubs, lounges, or other nightspots.

as various as Bryan Adams, Joan Baez, B.B. King, and local-girl-made-good Jewel, and regular appearances by the San Diego Chamber Orchestra. Look into advance tickets, if possible.

SOMA Live. 5305 Metro St., Mission Bay. ☎ **619/296-SOMA.**

This concert venue in a warehouse-like building has booked Courtney Love, Social Distortion, Faith No More, and Fugazi, plus many other cutting-edge alternative bands. Because it's one of San Diego's few all-ages serious venues, expect the audience to include people 15 to 50. Look into advance tickets, if possible.

LARGER LIVE VENUES

San Diego has become a popular destination for many major recording artists. In fact, there is a concert just about every week. The *Reader* is the best source of concert information; check the Web site (www.sdreader.com) for an advance look. Tickets typically go on sale at least 6 weeks before the event. Depending on the popularity of a particular artist or group, last-minute seats are often available through the box office or **Ticketmaster** (☎ **619/220-8497**). You can also go through an agency like **Advance Tickets** (☎ **619/581-1080**) and pay a higher price for prime tickets at the last minute.

Main concert venues include the **San Diego Sports Arena** (☎ **619/225-9813;** www.sandiegoarena.com), on Point Loma, west of Old Town. The 15,000- to 18,000-seat indoor venue doesn't have the best acoustics, but a majority of concerts are held here because of the seating capacity and availability of paid parking. **Qualcomm Stadium** (☎ **619/641-3131**), in Mission Valley, is a 71,000-seat outdoor stadium. It has acceptable acoustics and is used only for concerts by major bands like the Who and the Rolling Stones. **SDSU Open Air Amphitheater** (☎ **619/594-6947**), on the San Diego State campus, northeast of downtown along I-8, is a 4,000-seat outdoor amphitheater. It has great acoustics—if you can't get a ticket, you can stand outside and hear the entire show. **Embarcadero Marina Park,** on San Diego Bay adjacent to downtown, is a 4,400-seat outdoor setting with great acoustics.

Humphrey's, 2241 Shelter Island Dr. (☎ **619/523-1010;** www.humphreysconcerts.com), is a 900-seat outdoor venue on the water. It has great acoustics, and its seasonal line-up covers the spectrum of entertainment—rock and jazz to comedy, blues, folk and international music. Concerts are held from mid-May through October only. Parking is $5.

COMEDY CLUBS

The Comedy Store. 916 Pearl St., La Jolla. ☎ **858/454-9176.** Cover $6–$10.

This southern branch of L.A.'s venerable Sunset Strip institution can be relied upon for lots of laughs. Amateur night is Monday. Shows start Sunday and Thursday at 8:30pm, Tuesday and Wednesday at 8, and Friday and Saturday at 8 and 10:30pm.

Tidbits. 3838 Fifth Ave., Hillcrest. ☎ **619/543-0300.**

A huge cabaret with outstanding drag revues, Tidbits is a class act equally patronized by Hillcrest gays and adventuresome straights. It's campy and hilarious, as is the karaoke action that often takes over between shows. Performances begin around 8 to 10pm.

DANCE CLUBS & DISCOS

The following clubs impose cover charges that vary with the night of the week and the entertainment.

Olé Madrid. 751 Fifth Ave., Gaslamp Quarter. ☎ **619/557-0146.**

Loud and energetic, this dance club features a changing line-up of celebrated DJs spinning house, funk, techno, and hip-hop. The adjoining restaurant has terrific *tapas* and sangria.

Sevilla. 555 Fourth Ave., Gaslamp Quarter. ☎ **619/233-5979.**

Most nights of the week you can salsa and meringue to Brazilian dance music; sometimes the club features Spanish-language rock. Sevilla also has a *tapas* bar.

Supper Club A-Go-Go. 322 Fifth Ave., Gaslamp Quarter. ☎ **619/235-4646.**

Postmodern swingers head to this stylish club for the 1940s ambiance; you can dance up a sweat, or just sip a martini and watch the pros.

3 The Bar & Coffeehouse Scene

BARS & COCKTAIL LOUNGES

The Bitter End. 770 Fifth Ave., Gaslamp Quarter. ☎ **619/338-9300.**

With three floors, the Bitter End manages to be sophisticated martini bar, after-hours dance club, and relaxing cocktail lounge all in one.

Cannibal Bar. In the Catamaran Hotel, 3999 Mission Blvd. ☎ **619/539-8650.**

With a tropical theme to match the adjoining hotel, this large, lively club features Polynesian cocktails, music videos, and live bands on occasion.

Club 66. 901 Fifth Ave., Gaslamp Quarter. ☎ **619/234-4166.**

Holding court underneath popular Dakota's restaurant and the Gaslamp Plaza Suites hotel above that, this dance bar sports a Route 66 theme complete with filling-station memorabilia. Relax with a drink, or dance to disco and Top 40.

Mr. A's Restaurant. 2550 Fifth Ave. (at Laurel St.). ☎ **619/239-1377.**

Perched atop an uptown high-rise, this anachronistic Continental restaurant excels at genteel cocktails with a view. Skip the genteel dining room, which appeals to an older, conservative clientele. The bar is much more comfortable, looking out on a panorama of Balboa Park, the harbor, and planes landing at Lindbergh Field.

Ould Sod. 3373 Adams Ave., Normal Heights. ☎ **619/284-6594.**

Irish through and through, this little gem sits in a quiet neighborhood of antique shops northeast of Hillcrest. Occasionally the tavern hosts low-key folk or world-music performances.

Pacific Shqres. 4927 Newport Ave., Ocean Beach. ☎ **619/223-7549.**

Straight from the 1940s, this undersea-themed neighborhood hangout with a vintage seashell bar has rock-bottom prices and an unpretentious air.

Palace Bar. In the Horton Grand Hotel, 311 Island Ave., downtown. ☎ **619/544-1886.**

A class act inside the frilly Victorian Horton Grand, this cocktail lounge is close to the Gaslamp Quarter action, but nowhere near as frenetic.

Top O' The Cove. 1216 Prospect Ave., La Jolla. ☎ **858/454-7779.**

At this intimate piano bar in one of La Jolla's most scenic restaurants, the vibe is mellow and relaxing. On nice evenings, the music—mainly standards and show tunes—is piped into the outdoor patio.

Turf Supper Club. 1116 25th Ave., Golden Hills. ☎ **619/234-6363.**

Hidden in one of San Diego's old, obscure, and newly hip neighborhoods (about 10 minutes east of downtown), this retro steakhouse's gimmick is "grill your own" dinners. The decor and piano bar are pure '50s, and wildly popular with the cocktail crowd.

COFFEEHOUSES WITH PERFORMANCES

Java Joe's. 4994 Newport Ave., Ocean Beach. ☎ **619/523-0356.**

A popular hangout for OB locals, this friendly coffeehouse has entertainment most nights—from acoustic folk acts to open mike to occasional poetry readings.

Twiggs Tea and Coffee Co. 4590 Park Blvd. (south of Adams Ave.), University Heights. ☎ **619/296-0616.**

Tucked away in a peaceful neighborhood, this popular coffeehouse has adjoining room for poetry readings. It often books performances by artists like Cindy Lee Berryhill.

4 The Gay & Lesbian Nightlife Scene

Also check out **Tidbits** cabaret (see "Comedy Clubs," in section 2).

Bourbon Street. 4612 Park Blvd., University Heights. ☎ **619/291-0173.**

With an elegant piano bar and outdoor patio meant to evoke jazzy New Orleans, this relaxing spot draws mainly smartly dressed, dignified men.

The Brass Rail. 3796 Fifth Ave., Hillcrest. ☎ **619/298-2233.**

San Diego's oldest (since the '60s) gay bar, this Hillcrest institution is loud and proud, with energetic dancing every night, go-go boys, bright lights, and a come-as-you-are attitude.

Club Bombay. 3175 India St. (at Spruce St.). ☎ **619/296-6789.**

Mellower than the Flame, this casual lesbian gathering place north of Little Italy has a small dance floor, occasional live entertainment, and popular Sunday barbecues.

Club Montage. 2028 Hancock St. ☎ **619/294-9590.** Fax 619/294-9592. www.clubmontage.com.

This state-of-the-art dance club has all the bells and whistles: laser-and-light show, 12-screen video bar, pool tables, and arcade games.

The Flame. 3780 Park Blvd. ☎ **619/295-4163.** Cover Sun–Fri $2, Sat $3. Bus: 7 or 7B.

The city's top lesbian hangout has a large dance floor and two bars. It's packed on Saturdays. A mixed crowd attends Friday's drag show, and gender reversal takes place for Tuesday's "Boys Night Out."

Kickers. 308 University Ave. (at Third Ave.), Hillcrest. ☎ **619/491-0400.**

This country-western dance hall next to Hamburger Mary's restaurant attracts an equally male-female crowd for two-stepping and line-dancing. There are free lessons on weekdays.

Rich's. 1051 University Ave. (between 10th and 11th aves.). ☎ **619/295-2195,** or 619/497-4588 for upcoming events.

High-energy and popular with the see-and-be-seen set, Rich's has nightly revues, plenty of dancing to house music, and a small video bar. Thursday is Club Hedonism, with compelling tribal rhythms.

5 Lights, Camera . . . Movies!

Many multiscreen complexes around the city show first-run films. More avant-garde and artistic current releases play at **Hillcrest Cinema,** 3965 Fifth Ave., Hillcrest, which offers 3 hours' free parking (☎ **619/299-2100**); the **Ken Cinema,** 4061 Adams Ave., Kensington near Hillcrest (☎ **619/283-5909**); and the **Cove,** 7730 Girard Ave., La Jolla (☎ **858/459-5404**). The irrepressible *Rocky Horror Picture Show* is resurrected every Friday and Saturday at midnight at the Ken. The **OMNIMAX** theater at the Reuben H. Fleet Science Center (☎ **619/238-1233**), in Balboa Park, features movies and three-dimensional laser shows projected onto the 76-foot tilted dome screen.

Unique movie venues include **Movies Before the Mast (☎ 619/234-9153),** aboard the *Star of India* at the Maritime Museum. Movies of the nautical genre (such as *Black Beard the Pirate, Captain Blood,* and *Hook*) are shown on a special "screensail" from April through October. At the **Sunset Cinema Film Festival (☎ 858/454-7373)** in August, you can view classic and current films free of charge from a blanket or chair on the beach. Films are projected onto screens mounted on floating barges from San Diego to Imperial Beach. The Plunge (☎ **619/488-3110**), an indoor swimming pool in Mission Beach, shows **Dive-In Movies.** Viewers float on rafts in 91° water and watch water-related movies projected onto the wall. *Jaws* is a perennial favorite.

6 Only in San Diego

San Diego's top three attractions—the San Diego Zoo, Wild Animal Park, and Sea World—keep extended summer hours. Sea World caps its **Summer Nights** off at 9pm with a free **fireworks** display. You can catch them from Sea World or anywhere around Mission Bay.

Free concerts are offered on Sunday at 2pm year-round at the Spreckels Organ Pavilion in Balboa Park. In the summer, concerts are also held on Monday nights from 8 to 9:30pm as part of **Twilight in the Park (☎ 619/235-1105). Starlight Theater** presents

Broadway musicals in the Starlight Bowl in Balboa Park in July and August (☎ **619/544-STAR** [7827]). This venue is in the flight path to Lindbergh Field, and when planes pass overhead, singers stop in midnote and wait for the roar to cease. The **Festival Stage** (☎ **619/ 239-2255**) in Balboa Park is a popular outdoor summer theater venue.

Another Balboa Park event, **Christmas on the Prado,** has been a San Diego tradition since 1977. The weekend of evening events is held the first Friday and Saturday in December. The park's museums and walkways are decked out in holiday finery, and the museums are free and open late, from 5 to 9pm. There is entertainment galore, from bell choruses to Renaissance and baroque music to barbershop quartets. Crafts (including unusual Christmas ornaments), ethnic nibbles, hot cider, and sweets are for sale. A Christmas tree and nativity scene are displayed at the Spreckels Organ Pavilion.

Index

See also separate Accommodations and Restaurants indexes, below.

GENERAL INDEX

Accommodations, 34–72. *See also* Accommodations Index
  best, 3–4
  hotel tax, 32, 35
  money-saving tips, 34–35
  reservation services, 35
Activities, 113–17, 139–47. *See also specific activities*
Aerospace Museum, San Diego, 118, 133
Airfares, 15
Airlines, 14–15, 16
Airport, San Diego International, 14–15, 16
  accommodations near, 71–72
Airport shuttles, 16, 18
American Express, 29
America's Schooner Cup, 148
Amtrak, 13, 18, 27
Animal parks
  San Diego Zoo, 18, 108, 110, 111, 133, 134
  Sea World, 3, 112–13, 134–35
  Wild Animal Park, 111–12, 135
Annual San Diego Crew Classic, 148
Annual San Diego Lesbian and Gay Pride Parade, Rally, and Festival, 10, 13

Antique Row, 152–53
Antiques, 152–53, 154, 156
Aquariums
  Birch Aquarium at Scripps, 130–31, 135, 138
  Sea World, 3, 112–13, 134–35
Area codes, 29
Arriving in San Diego, 14–15, 16, 18
Art, Museum of (Balboa Park), 118, 120, 133
Art, Museum of Contemporary, Downtown, 125
Art, Museum of Contemporary, San Diego (La Jolla), 129, 130, 134
Art, Timken Museum of, 124, 133
Art galleries, 156–57
Arts Festival, La Jolla, 134, 156
Automotive Museum, San Diego, 121, 133
Auto show, 11
Aviara Golf Club, 143

Baby-sitters, 29
Bahia Belle, 28, 135–36
Baja fish tacos, 5, 106–7
Balboa Park, 3, 117–24, 134
  Christmas on the Prado, 12, 171

free activities, 133, 170–71
free organ recitals, 2, 9,
   124, 133, 170
gardens
   Botanical Building,
      121–22, 133
   Japanese Friendship
      Garden, 122, 133
   Lily Pond, 121–22, 133
golf, 142
money-saving tips, 118
museums, 118, 120–24
   free days, 133
   Fleet Science Center,
      120, 133, 134, 170
   Hall of Champions,
      122, 133
   House of Pacific
      Relations International
      Cottages, 122, 133
   International Aerospace
      Hall of Fame, 118
   Marston House
      Museum, 122–23
   Mingei International
      Museum, 121, 133
   Model Railroad
      Museum, 123, 133
   Museum of Art, 118,
      120, 133
   Museum of Man,
      120–21, 133
   Museum of
      Photographic Arts,
      120, 133
   Museum of San Diego
      History, 123, 133
   Natural History
      Museum, 120, 133,
      134, 139, 146
   San Diego Aerospace
      Museum, 118, 133
   San Diego Automotive
      Museum, 121, 133
   Timken Museum of Art,
      124, 133
   Old Globe Theatre, 164
   Passport to, 118
   safety tips, 32, 146
   Spreckels Organ Pavilion, 2,
      9, 123–24, 133, 170–71
   tennis, 147
   transportation in, 118
   Visitors Center, 6, 118
Balboa Park Municipal Golf
   Course, 142
Balboa Tennis Club, 147
Ballet, 164
Ballooning, 9
Barnes & Noble, 157
Barnes Tennis Center, 147
Bars, 167–68
   gay and lesbian, 169–70
Baseball, 147
Batiquitos Lagoon, 143
Bayside Trail, 145
Bazaar del Mundo, 133, 153
   restaurants, 91
Beaches, 113–17
   best place to stay on, 4
   nudist: Black's Beach, 117
   sandcastle competition, 10,
      114
   softball tournament, 9–10
   sunset-watching, 2
   tide pools, 124, 130–31
   walking on, 144–45
   Black's Beach, 117
   Boneyards Beach, 117
   Bonita Cove, 114
   Carlsbad State Beach, 147
   Children's Pool, 116, 133
   Coronado Beach, 114, 144
   Del Mar Beach, 117

Ellen Browning Scripps
Park, 3, 116–17, 129, 133
Imperial Beach, 10, 114,
147
La Jolla, 116–17
La Jolla Cove, 11, 116–17,
129, 133, 146
La Jolla Shores Beach, 117,
129, 144, 146, 147
Mariner's Point, 114
Mission Bay Park, 116
Mission Beach, 116, 144
Mission Point, 114
Moonlight Beach, 117
Ocean Beach Park, 114,
147
Pacific Beach, 114, 116
Swami's Beach, 117
Tourmaline Surfing Park,
116
Windansea Beach, 116, 147
Belly Up Tavern, 165
Belmont Amusement Park,
128–29, 170
Berkeley, 125
Biking, 2, 28–29, 139–40
Birch Aquarium at Scripps,
130–31, 135, 138
Bird watching, 110, 143
Bishop's School, 129
Bitter End, 167
Black's Beach, 117
Blues, 165
Boating, 140–41. *See also*
Houseboating; Sailing
special events, 148
Boat tours and cruises, 28,
135–36, 138. *See also* Ferry
Boneyards Beach, 117
Bonita Cove, 114
Bookstores, 152, 155, 157–58
Borders Books & Music, 157

Botanical Building (Balboa
Park), 121–22, 133
Bridge, Coronado Bay, 2, 15,
66, 131, 134
Broadway Pier, ferry, 2, 27–28
Brushworks, 156
Buick Invitational, 8, 144, 148
Buses, 24–26
to/from airport, 16, 18
for disabled travelers, 12
tours, 136–37
Business hours, 29–30

Cabrillo National Monument,
124, 137–38, 139
Cabs, 16, 27
Cafes, 2, 169. *See also*
Restaurants Index
Calendar of Events, 8–12
California Ballet, 164
Camera repair, 30
Campgrounds, 57–58
Cannibal Bar, 167–68
Canoeing, 140–41
Carlsbad
golf, 143
LEGOLAND, 132, 135
tennis tournament, 149
Carlsbad Ranch, 8
Carlsbad State Beach, 147
Carlsbad Village Faire, 11
Carlton Oaks Country Club,
148
Car rentals, 21–23
insurance, 22–23
money-saving tips, 21–22
package deals, 23
Car show, 11
Car travel, 21–24
driving rules, 24
52-mile San Diego Scenic
Drive, 132

parking, 24, 74
to San Diego, 15
Casbah, The, 165
Centre City Development
Corporation, 132, 135, 137,
139
Chargers, 148
Cheese Shop, 5, 107
Children
accommodations, best, 3
sights and activities, 134–35
travel tips, 13–14
Children's Museum of San
Diego, 124–35, 135
Children's Park, 132–33
Children's Pool, 116, 133
Children's Zoo (San Diego
Zoo), 110
Christmas on the Prado, 12,
171
Cinco de Mayo, 9
City layout, 18–19
Civic Theatre, 164
Club 66, 168
Coast Walk, 129, 131, 145
restaurants, 98
Cocktail lounges, 167–68
Comedy clubs, 167
Concerts, free, 133, 170–71
Balboa Park, 2, 9, 124, 133,
170
Concours d'Elegance, 11
Consolidators, 15
Contemporary Art, Museum
of, Downtown, 125
Contemporary Art, Museum
of, San Diego (La Jolla), 129,
130, 134
Coronado, 20–21, 66, 131
accommodations, 66–71
beach, 114, 144, 146
biking, 139–40

boating, 141
farmers' markets, 159
ferry, 2, 27–28
fishing, 141
free activities, 134
golf, 142–43
guided walking tours, 139
main streets, 19
restaurants, 101–5
shopping, 155
sightseeing, 131
Visitors Bureau, 6
Coronado, Hotel del, 3, 21,
68–69, 101
Coronado Bay Bridge, 2, 15,
66, 131, 134
Coronado Beach, 114, 144, 146
Coronado Historical Museum,
131, 134
Coronado Islands, 141
Coronado Municipal Golf
Course, 142–43
Coronado Shuttle, 25
Coupons, 6, 111
Cracker Factory Antiques
Shopping Center, 156
Croce's Restaurants &
Nightclubs, 2, 78, 165
Cruises, 28, 135–36, 138
Cuyamaca Mountains, 145

Dance clubs, 167
gay and lesbian, 169–70
Dance companies, 164–65
Dance Festival, International,
164
David Zapf Gallery, 156
Davis House Museum, 126, 139
Day Trippers, 26
Debra Owen Gallery, 156
Del Mar Beach, 117
Del Mar Fair, 9

Del Mar Fairgrounds, 9, 149
Del Mar National Horse Show, 9, 149
Del Mar Race Track, 10, 148–49
Dentists, 30
Department stores, 158–59
Dining. *See* Restaurants; Restaurants Index
Dinner theater, 168
Dinosaurs, 120
Disabled travelers, 4, 12
Discos, 167
    gay and lesbian, 169–70
Discount coupons, 6, 111
Dive-In Movies, 170
Doctors, 30
"Dog Beach," 114, 145
Dolphin Interaction Program, at Sea World, 113
Downtown San Diego, 19. *See also* Gaslamp Quarter; Horton Plaza; Little Italy
    accommodations, 35–45
    art galleries, 156–57
    bars, 168
    free activities, 132–33
    guided walking tours, 135, 138–39
    main streets, 18
    music venues, 165–66
    restaurants, 77–83
    shopping, 151–52
    sightseeing, 124–26
Driving rules, 24
Dr. Seuss (Theodor Geisel), 11–12
Drugstores, 31

El Cajon, golf, 143–44
Ellen Browning Scripps Park, 3, 116–17, 129, 133

Embarcadero, 3, 19, 132
    parking, 24
    restaurants, 77, 79
Embarcadero Marina Park, 3, 166
Emergencies, 30
Escondido: Wild Animal Park, 111–12, 135
Eyeglass repair, 30

Factory outlet, 160
Families. *See* Children
Farmers' markets, 159
Fashion Valley Center, 160
Ferry, 2, 27–28
Ferry Landing Marketplace, 140, 155, 159
    restaurants, 103, 104
Festivals, 8–12
Fiesta Island, 10, 145, 146
Film Festival, Sunset Cinema, 10, 170
Firehouse Museum, 125
Fishing, 141–42
Fish market, 107
Fish tacos, 5, 106–7
Flea market, 159–60
Fleet Science Center, 120, 133, 134, 170
Folk Art, Mingei International Museum of World, 121, 133
Folk music, 165
Food. *See also* Seafood
    shopping for, 5, 107
        farmers' markets, 159
Football, 148
Ford Building, 118
Four Seasons Resort Aviara Golf Club, 143
Free activities, 132–34
Free concerts, 133, 170–71
    Balboa Park, 2, 9, 124, 133, 170

Gardens, in Balboa Park
   Botanical Building, 121–22,
      133
   Japanese Friendship
      Garden, 122, 133
   Lily Pond, 121–22, 133
Gaslamp Quarter, 1–2, 19, 132
   art galleries, 156–57
   bars, 167, 168
   dance clubs, 167
   guided walking tours, 135,
      138–39
   restaurants, 77–83
   safety tips, 32
   shopping, 151–52
   sightseeing, 126
   Street Scene, 10–11
   Web site, 7
Gay and lesbian travelers, 12–13
   bookstores, 158
   nightlife, 169–70
   Pride Parade, Rally, and
      Festival, 10, 13
Geisel, Theodor (Dr. Seuss),
   11–12
Giant Dipper Roller Coaster,
   128–29
Gill, Irving, 62, 122–23, 129,
   130
Girard Gourmet, 5, 107
Golden Hills, 168
Golf, 142–44
   tournaments, 148
      Buick Invitational, 8,
         144, 148
Gondola di Venezia, 136
Gone With the Wind (movie),
   128
Gray Line San Diego, 137
Greyhound, 13
G Street Pier, 79
Guided tours. See Tours

Hall of Champions, 122, 133
Harbor. See San Diego Harbor
Hard Rock Cafe, 81
Heritage Park, 127, 133
HGH Pro-Am Golf Classic,
   148
Hiking, 144–46
Hillcrest Cinema, 170
Hillcrest/Uptown, 19–20.
   See also Balboa Park
   accommodations, 45–48
   comedy club, 167
   farmers' markets, 159
   gay nightlife, 20, 169–70
   main streets, 18–19
   restaurants, 83–89
   shopping, 152–53
Hockey, 149
Holiday Bowl, 148
Hornblower Invader Cruises,
   28, 136
Horse racing, 10, 148–49
Horse Show, Del Mar
   National, 9, 149
Horton Plaza, 19, 132, 151, 160
   information center, 6, 18
   parking, 24
   restaurants, 81
Horton Plaza Park, 162
Hospitals, 30
Hot-air ballooning, 9
Hotel Circle, 48–50, 51
Hotel del Coronado, 3, 21,
   68–69, 101
Hotels. See Accommodations;
   Accommodations Index
Hot lines, 31
Houseboating, 4, 40–41, 141
House of Pacific Relations
   International Cottages, 122,
   133
Humphrey's, 166

Ice hockey, 149
Ice skating, 146
IMAX theater, 120, 134, 170
Imperial Beach, 10, 114, 147
Imperial Beach Pier, 141
Indian Fair, 121
Information sources, 6–7, 18
Inspiration Point, 127
International Aerospace Hall of
    Fame, 118
International Dance Festival,
    164
International Gallery, 156
International Visitor
    Information Center, 6, 18,
    134

Japanese Friendship Garden,
    122, 133
Jazz music, 2, 165
Jogging, 146
John Cole's Bookshop, 155,
    157–58
Junípero Serra Museum, 127

Kayaking, 2, 140–41
Kensington, 20
Kensington Coffee Company,
    104–5, 155
Kite Festival, Ocean Beach, 8
Kobey's Swap Meet, 159–60
Krasne, Karen, 5, 87

La Costa Resort and Spa, 149
La Jolla, 20, 58–59, 129
    accommodations, 58–66
    art galleries, 156
    bars, 168
    beaches, 116–17
    biking, 140
    comedy club, 167
    free activities, 133–34

    golf, 144
    guided walking tours, 139
    hiking, 139, 145
    main streets, 19
    restaurants, 95–101
    shopping, 154–55
    sights and activities, 129–31
    surfing, 147
    tennis, 147
    theater, 163
    Web site, 7
La Jolla Arts Festival, 134, 156
La Jolla Cave and Shell Shop,
    129, 155
La Jolla Cove, 11, 116–17,
    129, 133, 146
La Jolla Playhouse, 163
La Jolla Recreation Center,
    129
La Jolla Rough-Water Swim,
    11
La Jolla Shores Beach, 117,
    129, 144, 146, 147
La Jolla Tennis Club, 147
La Jolla Underwater Park,
    116–17, 129, 134, 146
La Jolla Woman's Club, 129
Lake Miramar Reservoir, 145
Lamb's Players Theatre, 163
Layout, 18–19
LEGOLAND, 132, 135
Lily Pond, 121–22, 133
Lindbergh Field. See San Diego
    International Airport
Liquor laws, 31
Little Italy, 19, 156
    accommodations, 3–4, 45
    nightlife, 169
    restaurants, 82
Live music. See Concerts, free;
    Music
Lyceum Theatre, 163, 164

Macy's, 158
Magazines, 7, 31
Malls, shopping, 160
Many Hands, 157
Map Centre, 161
Marian Bear Memorial Park, 145
Marina Cortez, 40–41
Mariner's Point, 114
Maritime Museum, 125, 170
Markets
    farmers, 159
    fish, 107
    flea, 159–60
Marston House Museum, 122–23
Mary Star of the Sea, 129
MCA Downtown, 125
MCA La Jolla, 129, 130, 134
Medea, 125
Mingei International Museum of World Folk Art, 121, 133
Miramar, Lake, 145
Mission Basilica San Diego de Alcala, 128
Mission Bay, 20, 128–29, 133
    accommodations, 51–58
    biking, 2, 139–40
    boating, 140–41
    cruises, 28, 135–36, 138
    fishing, 141
    jogging, 146
    kayaking, 2, 140–41
    music venues, 166
    restaurants, 92–95
    Sea World, 3, 112–13, 134–35
    shopping, 153–54
    skating, 2, 146
Mission Bay Park, 116
Mission Beach, 20
    beaches, 2, 116, 144

Dive-In Movies, 170
    restaurants, 95
Mission Point, 114
Mission Trails Regional Park, 133, 145
Mission Valley, 20
    accommodations, 48–51
    shopping, 153
Mission Valley Center, 160
Model Railroad Museum, 123, 133
Montezuma, Villa, 126
Moonlight Beach, 117
Morgan Run (Rancho Santa Fe), 143
Mount Soledad, 129, 134
Movies, 170
    Dive-In Movies, 170
    Movies Before the Mast, 3, 170
    Sunset Cinema Film Festival, 10, 170
Museum of Art, 118, 120, 133
Museum of Contemporary Art, Downtown, 125
Museum of Contemporary Art, San Diego (La Jolla), 129, 130, 134
Museum of Man, 120–21, 133
Museum of Photographic Arts, 120, 133
Museum of San Diego History, 123, 133
Music, 165–66
    current schedule, 166
    free concerts, 133, 170–71
        Balboa Park, 2, 9, 124, 133, 170
    opera, 162, 164
    tickets, 166
    venues, 166

Natural History Museum
(Balboa Park), 120, 133, 134,
139, 146
Neighborhoods, 19–21. *See also
specific neighborhoods*
Newport Avenue, antiquing, 154
Newspapers, 7, 18, 31
Nightlife, 162–71. *See also*
Bars; Dance clubs; Dance
companies; Movies; Music;
Theater
current schedule, 18, 33, 162
tickets, 33, 162
Nordstrom, 158–59
Normal Heights, 152, 168
North Park, 20, 95

Obelisk Bookstore, 158
Ocean Beach, 20
bars, 168
beaches, 114, 147
coffeehouses, 169
farmers' markets, 159
restaurants, 92–93
Ocean Beach Kite Festival, 8
Ocean Beach Park, 114, 147
Ocean Beach Pier, 114, 141
Ocean Beach Recreational
Center, 8
Ocean Front Walk, 114, 116, 146
Oceanside, 117, 147
Old Ferry Landing, 2, 27–28
Old Globe Theatre, 164
Old Town, 20, 126–28. *See
also* Bazaar del Mundo
accommodations, 48–51
Cinco de Mayo, 9
free activities, 133
restaurants, 89–92
shopping, 153
sightseeing, 127–28
visitor center, 126
Old Town Trolley, 27, 137

OMNIMAX theater, 120, 134,
170
Opera, 162, 164
Organized tours. *See* Tours
Organ recitals, in Balboa Park,
2, 9, 124, 133, 170
Ould Sod, 168
Outlet center, 160

Pacific Beach, 20, 133
beaches, 114, 116
farmers' markets, 159
main streets, 19
restaurants, 93–94, 95
sunset-watching, 2
Pacific Coast Highway,
beaches, 117
Pacific Queen, 138
Pacific Shores, 168
Packing tips, 14
Padres, 147
Parking, 24, 74
Parks. *See also* Balboa Park;
Beaches
Cabrillo National
Monument, 124, 137–38,
139
Children's Park, 132–33
Heritage Park, 127, 133
Marian Bear Memorial
Park, 145
Mission Trails Regional
Park, 133, 145
Presidio Park, 127, 133
Torrey Pines State Reserve,
117, 133, 134, 139, 145
Passport to Balboa Park, 118
Performing arts, 162–65. *See
also* Dance companies; Music;
Theater
current schedule, 18, 162
tickets, 33, 162
Pets, traveling with, 4

Pharmacies, 31
Photographic Arts, Museum of, 120, 133
Photographic supplies, 30
Picnicking, 3, 5, 107. *See also* Farmers' markets; Parks
Piers
    Broadway Pier, ferry from, 2, 27–28
    fishing from, 132, 141
    G Street Pier, 79
    Imperial Beach Pier, 141
    Ocean Beach Pier, 114, 141
Pizza, wood-fired, 105–6
Planet Hollywood, 81
Plunge, The, 128, 170
Point Loma, 124, 141, 147
Police, 31, 32
Post office, 31
Pratt Gallery, 157
Presidio Park, 127, 133
Puck, Wolfgang, 105, 106
Pump House Gang (Wolfe), 116
Pumpkin Carving Contest, Underwater, 11, 146

Qualcomm Stadium, 147, 148, 166
Quivira Basin, 141

Railroad Museum, Model, 123, 133
Rainfall, average monthly, 8
Rancho Santa Fe, golf, 143
Reader, 7, 18, 31, 162, 166
Recreational activities, 113–17, 139–47. *See also specific activities*
Reservation services, 35
Restaurants, 73–107. *See also* Restaurants Index

Baja fish tacos, 5, 106–7
    best, 4–5
    by cuisine, 74–77
    dinner theater, 168
    pizza, wood-fired, 105–6
    theme, 81
Rest rooms, 32
Reuben H. Fleet Science Center, 120, 133, 134, 170
Riverwalk Golf Club, 143
Rock music, 165
Rocky Horror Picture Show (movie), 170
Roller Coaster, Giant Dipper, 128–29
Rowing competition, 148
Running, 146

Safety, 32
Sailboarding, 140–41
Sailing, 138, 140–41
Sales tax, 32, 150
Salk Institute for Biological Studies, 20, 129, 134
San Clemente Canyon, 145
San Diego (magazine), 7, 31
San Diego Aerospace Museum, 118, 133
San Diego Automotive Museum, 121, 133
San Diego Chargers, 148
San Diego de Alcala Mission Basilica, 128
San Diego Factory Outlet Center, 160
San Diego Gulls, 149
San Diego Harbor
    cruises, 28, 135–36, 138
    ferry, 2, 27–28
San Diego Harbor Excursion, 28, 136
San Diego History, Museum of, 123, 133

San Diego International
Airport, 14–15, 16
accommodations near,
71–72
San Diego Junior Theatre, 163
San Diego-La Jolla Underwater
Park, 116–17, 129, 134, 146
San Diego Mini Tours, 136
San Diego Natural History
Museum, 138
*San Diego Official Visitors
Guide,* 6
San Diego Opera, 162, 164
San Diego Padres, 147
San Diego Repertory Theatre,
163
San Diego Sockers, 149
San Diego Sports Arena, 149,
166
flea market, 159–60
San Diego Trolley, 2, 26–27
Bike-N-Ride, 29
San Diego Union-Tribune, 18,
31, 162
San Diego Zoo, 18, 108, 110,
134
free day, 133
money-saving tips, 111
Santa Fe Station, 18, 26, 27
San Ysidro, 160
Science Center, Reuben H.
Fleet, 120, 133, 134, 170
Scripps Institution of
Oceanography, Birch
Aquarium at, 130–31, 135,
138
Scripps Park, 3, 116–17, 129,
133
Scuba diving, 146
San Diego-La Jolla
Underwater Park,
116–17, 129, 134, 146

SDSU Open Air Amphitheater,
166
Seafood, 73, 107
Baja fish tacos, 5, 106–7
restaurants index, 77
Seal Rock, 133
Seaport Village, 132, 151–52
Seasons, 7–8
Sea World, 3, 112–13, 134–35
Summer Nights, 170
Senior citizen travelers, 13
Serra, Junípero, 128
Museum, 127
Shamu, at Sea World, 113,
134–35
Shopping, 150–61
hours, 29–30, 150
Sierra Club, 145
Sightseeing, 108–35
Singing Hills (El Cajon),
143–44
Skating, 2, 146
Skinner, Lake, 9
Smoking, 32, 74, 165
Snorkeling, 146
San Diego-La Jolla
Underwater Park,
116–17, 129, 134, 146
Soccer, 149
Softball tournament, 9–10
Solana Beach, 27, 165
SOMA and Quint, 157
SOMA Live, 166
Some Like It Hot (movie), 68
Special events, 8–12
Sports, 139–47. *See also specific
sports*
museum: Hall of
Champions, 122, 133
spectator, 147–49
Sports Arena. *See* San Diego
Sports Arena

Spreckels Organ Pavilion, 2, 9, 123–24, 133, 170–71
Starlight Theater, 170–71
Star of India, 125, 170
Street Scene, Gaslamp Quarter, 10–11
Sunny Jim Cave, 155
Sunset Cinema, 132
    Film Festival, 10, 170
Super Savings Coupon Book, 6, 111
Surfing, 116, 147
    reports, 33
Swami's Beach, 117
Swap meet, 159–60

Taboo Studio, 157
Tapas, 167
Taxes, 32, 150
Taxis, 16, 27
    water, 28
Telephone numbers, useful, 33
Television, 32
Temecula Valley Balloon & Wine Festival, 9
Temperatures, average monthly, 8
Tennis, 147
    tournaments, 149
Theater, 163–64
Theme restaurants, 81
Thomson House, 131
Thoroughbred Racing Season, 10, 148–49
Tickets, 162, 166
    half-price, 33, 162
Tidbits, 167
Tide pools, 124, 130–31
Tijuana, Mexico, trolley, 2, 26–27, 29
Times Arts Tix, 162
Time zone, 32

Timken Museum of Art, 124, 133
Toilets, 32
Top Gun (movie), 82
Top O' the Cove, 97–98, 168
Torrey Pines Golf Course, 8, 11, 144, 148
Torrey Pines State Reserve, 117, 133, 134, 139, 145
Toshiba Tennis Classic, 149
Tourist information, 6–7, 18
Tourmaline Surfing Park, 116
Tours, 135–39. *See also* Trolleys
    by bike, 140
    by boat, 28, 135–36, 138
    by bus, 136–37
    guided walking, 135, 138–39
Train travel, 18, 27
Transit Store, 24–25, 29
Transportation, 21–29
    to/from airport, 16, 18
    Day Trippers pass, 26
    for disabled travelers, 12
    senior citizen discounts, 13
    transit information, 32
Travel accessories, 158, 161
Traveler's Aid, 31
Traveler's Depot, 158, 161
Traveling to San Diego, 14–15, 16, 18
Travel Web sites, 15
Trolleys, 26–27, 137
    for disabled travelers, 12
    Old Town Trolley, 27, 137
    San Diego Trolley, 2, 26–27, 29
Turf Supper Club, 168
12-step programs, 31
Twilight in the Park, 9, 170–71

Underwater Park, San Diego-
  La Jolla, 116–17, 129, 134,
  146
Underwater Pumpkin Carving
  Contest, 11, 146
Unicorn Antique Mall, 156
University Heights, 19, 169
University of California, San
  Diego, 129
University Towne Center,
  160–61
Uptown. *See* Hillcrest/Uptown
U. S. Open Sandcastle
  Competition, 10, 114

Villa Montezuma, 126
Vintage clothing, 153
Visitor information, 6–7, 18

Walkabout International, 13,
  132, 138
Walking, 3, 133–34, 144–46
Walking tours, guided, 135,
  138–39
Warwick's Books, 158
Waterfront. *See* Embarcadero
Water taxis, 28
Weather, 7–8
  updates, 33
Web sites, 6–7, 15
Whale watching, 8, 124,
  137–38
Whaley House, 128
Whispering Palms, 143
Wild Animal Park, 111–12,
  135
Wildflowers, 8
William Heath Davis House
  Museum, 126, 139
Windansea Beach, 116, 147
Wine festival, 9
Wolfe, Tom, 116

Wooden Boat Festival, 148
World Championship Over-
  the-Line Tournament, 9–10

Zoos
  San Diego Zoo, 18, 108,
    110, 133, 134
  Wild Animal Park, 111–12,
    135

ACCOMMODATIONS
Balboa Park Inn, 45–46
Beach Cottages, 55–56
Bed & Breakfast Inn at La
  Jolla, 62
Best Western Bayside Inn, 42
Best Western Blue Sea Lodge,
  54–55
Best Western Inn by the Sea,
  64–65
Best Western Seven Seas, 51
Campland on the Bay, 57
Catamaran Resort Hotel,
  51–52
Clarion Hotel Bay View San
  Diego, 42–43
Colonial Inn, 59
Comfort Inn-Downtown, 44
Comfort Inn & Suites, 48–49
Coronado Inn, 71
Coronado Island Marriott
  Resort, 66–68
Cottage, The, 46–47
Crone's Cobblestone Cottage
  Bed & Breakfast, 47
Crystal Pier Hotel, 55
Days Inn Suites, 44
El Cordova Hotel, 70–71
Elsbree House, 58
Embassy Suites, 35–36
Empress Hotel of La Jolla,
  62–63

Four Seasons Resort, 143
Gaslamp Plaza Suites, 43–44
Glorietta Bay Inn, 68
Hacienda Hotel, 49
Hanalei Hotel, 49–50
Heritage Park Bed & Breakfast Inn, 50
Hilton San Diego Resort, 3, 52, 54, 140
Holiday Inn on the Bay, 39–40
Horton Grand, 40
Hotel del Coronado, 3, 68–69, 134
Hyatt Regency La Jolla, 58, 96
Hyatt Regency San Diego, 4, 36, 38
Keating House, 44–45
La Jolla Beach & Tennis Club, 4, 63–64
La Jolla Cove Travelodge, 65–66
La Pensione Hotel, 3–4, 45
La Valencia Hotel, 59–60, 129
Loews Coronado Bay Resort, 11–12, 69–70, 101
Marriott Residence Inn, 58
Mission Valley Center Travelodge, 51
Ocean Park Inn, 56
Pacific Shores Inn, 56–57
Pacific Terrace Inn, 54
Park Manor Suites, 47–48
Prospect Park Inn, 65
Ramada Inn, 51
San Diego Marriott Marina, 38
San Diego Yacht & Breakfast Company, 4, 40–41, 141
Scripps Inn, 64
Sea Lodge, 60, 62
Sheraton San Diego Hotel and Marina, 72
Sommerset Suites Hotel, 3, 46

Surfer Motor Lodge, 57
Travelodge Hotel-Harbor Island, 72
U. S. Grant Hotel, 4, 41–42
Vacation Inn, 50–51
Vagabond Inn, 51
Village Inn, 71
Westgate Hotel, 39

RESTAURANTS

Anthony's Star of the Sea Room, 77–78
Azzura Point, 101
Bay Beach Cafe, 104
Berta's Latin American Restaurant, 90
Boudin Sourdough Bakery and Cafe, 107
Bread & Cie. Bakery and Cafe, 86, 107
Brigantine Seafood Grill, 89, 101
Brockton Villa, 4, 99
Cafe Japengo, 96
Café Lulu, 81–82
Cafe Pacifica, 89–90
California Cuisine, 83–84
Casa de Bandini, 90–91
Casa de Pico, 91
Celadon, 84–85
Chameleon Cafe & Lizard Lounge, 102
Chart House, 101–2
Chez Loma, 102–3
Corvette Diner, 86–87
Cottage, The, 100
Croce's Restaurant, 2, 78
Dakota Grill and Spirits, 79–80
D'Lish, 100–101, 105
Extraordinary Desserts, 5, 87
Filippi's Pizza Grotto, 4–5, 82
Fio's, 5, 78–79

Firehouse Beach Cafe, 95
Fish Market, 5, 79
Garden House Coffee & Tea, 91
George's at the Cove, 96–97
George's Ocean Terrace and
  Cafe/Bar, 99
Green Flash, 93–94
Hard Rock Cafe, 81
Hob Nob Hill, 85
Kansas City Barbecue, 82
Karl Strauss Downtown
  Brewery & Grill, 80
Kensington Coffee Company,
  104–5, 155
Laurel, 84
Liaison, 85
Mandarin House, 87–88
Marrakesh, 97
Miguel's Cocina, 101
Mission, The, 95
Mixx, 86
Mr. A's Restaurant, 168
Newbreak Coffee Co., 88
Old Spaghetti Factory, 83
Old Town Mexican Cafe,
  91–92

Osteria Panevino, 80–81
Palenque, 5, 94
Panda Inn, 81
Peohe's, 103
Pizza Nova, 106
Planet Hollywood, 81
Point Loma Seafoods, 107
Primavera Pastry Caffé, 105
Primavera Ristorante, 103
Prince of Wales Grill, 101
Princess Pub & Grille, 83
Qwiig's, 93
Rhinoceros Cafe & Grill, 104,
  107
Rubio's Baja Grill, 5, 106–7
Sammy's California Woodfired
  Pizza, 105
Spice & Rice Thai Kitchen,
  99–100
Sushi Ota, 94–95
Thee Bungalow, 92–93
Top of the Market, 5, 79
Top O' the Cove, 97–98, 168
Trattoria Acqua, 98
Vegetarian Zone, 88–89
Wolfgang Puck Cafe, 106